A CARTESIAN INTRODUCTION TO PHILOSOPHY

A CARTESIAN INTRODUCTION TO PHILOSOPHY

Fred Feldman
University of Massachusetts

McGRAW-HILL BOOK COMPANY
New York   St. Louis   San Francisco   Auckland   Bogotá
Hamburg   Johannesburg   London   Madrid   Mexico   Montreal   New Delhi
Panama   Paris   São Paulo   Singapore   Sydney   Tokyo   Toronto

This book was set in Times Roman by Publication Services.
The editor was Emily G. Barrosse;
the production supervisor was Marietta Breitwieser;
the cover was designed by John Hite.
Project supervision was done by Publication Services.
Halliday Lithograph Corporation was printer and binder.

A CARTESIAN INTRODUCTION TO PHILOSOPHY

1 2 3 4 5 6 7 8 9 0 HALHAL 8 9 8 7 6 5

ISBN 0-07-020383-0

Library of Congress Cataloging in Publication Data

Feldman, Fred, date
    A Cartesian introduction to philosophy

    Includes index.
    1. Philosophy—Introductions.   2. Descartes, René,
1596–1650.   Meditationes de prima philosophia.
3. First philosophy.   I. Title.
BD21.F38   1986   100   85-11035
ISBN 0-07-020383-0

CONTENTS

PREFACE

When I first started teaching Introduction to Philosophy several years ago, I tried to do things in the traditional way. I made use of one of the well-known anthologies, and I tried to cover the normal range of topics. Thus, there was a unit on freedom and determinism, and a unit on the existence of God, and a unit on skepticism, and a unit on ethics. For each unit, the students were expected to read several items. Some of the items were longish selections from classic texts, and others were more modern journal articles. In my lectures, I tried to explain the issues, I tried to show how each philosopher's position fitted into the general scheme of things, and I tried to analyze and evaluate the main arguments from the readings.

As time went by, I began to realize that something was wrong. I noticed that many of the students were simply memorizing the material I presented in class, and ignoring the reading assignments. I also noticed that class discussions were dominated by a very small number of especially bright and talkative students. I also noticed that there was rarely anything original or creative in the examination papers they submitted. It seemed to me that my students were not really enjoying philosophy, and that they were not learning the things I hoped they would learn.

I discussed these problems with several of my students, with my teaching assistants, and with some of my colleagues. Finally, I came to some conclusions about what was wrong. One problem had to do with the reading assignments. They were simply too hard and too complicated for beginners to understand. It wasn't that the students lacked the intelligence one needs in order to read philosophy. Plenty of them were quite smart. The problem was, rather, that they were being asked to read selections that presuppose an understanding of some very subtle philosophical issues, and that are written in archaic, technical terminology. In many cases, the students were being asked to wade through forty or fifty pages of excruciatingly complex material just so they could see one interesting argument in its original setting. It was no wonder they didn't like to do the readings.

When I looked over my lectures notes, I discovered that it wasn't just a problem with the readings. How could I have thought that students with no previous training in philosophy would be able to understand what I was talking about? How could I have thought that they might be able to follow the intricacies of the arguments I was analyzing and criticizing? How could I have deceived myself into thinking that they might care about such inaccessible and technical stuff?

Another problem had to do with the structure of the course. We discussed four separate topics. For each topic, the students were asked to read a bunch of selections, illustrating various opposing positions on the topic. I found that my students were getting the impression that philosophy is just a collection of incompatible views on a variety of unrelated questions. Nothing I had done in the course would have given the students any conception of the beauty and coherence of a well-articulated philosophical work.

I decided that it would be necessary to overhaul the course. I settled on the idea of focusing the entire course on one classic text. The text to be selected would have to satisfy several important criteria. First, it would have to be sufficiently clear so that, with a little help from me, even a beginner would be able to understand the main issues. Second, the issues discussed in it would have to be ones that could capture the interest of students who had never studied philosophy before. Third, the issues would have to be reasonably diverse. It would be too risky to spend a whole semester on a book that discussed no topic other than, for example, the analysis of the concept of knowledge.

I promptly settled on Descartes' *Meditations*. It deals with central issues in epistemology, philosophical theology, and philosophical anthropology. It also raises puzzles in ontology, the philosophy of mind, and related fields. In addition to this, it is relatively simple and clear. Surely no one could reasonably maintain that Descartes is a dull writer, or that the topics he discusses are of interest only to professionals.

I had to face certain objections. For one, some people felt that there was something fishy about a full-credit, semester-long course in which the students were required to read a grand total of only 56 pages. Others objected to the fact that my students were not getting the mandatory three weeks on ethics. Still others felt that it would be inappropriate to teach introduction to philosophy without requiring the students to read snippets from Plato, Aristotle, Kant, Hume, and other "greats."

After reflecting on these objections, I decided that the benefits I hoped to gain from the revised course far outweighed all of these costs. Indeed, I think some of the objections are without merit. Why must students in Introduction to Philosophy struggle with three weeks of ethics? After all, we have a course in introductory ethics that's supposed to introduce them to that topic. Furthermore, why should they be forced to learn tiny tidbits from each of a large number of philosophical greats? Wouldn't it be better to learn a whole lot of really interesting things about one philosophical great? I have always found it difficult to read philosophy quickly. To my way of thinking, we ask too much of our students if we ask them to understand several hundred pages of intricate philosophy in a month's time. The *Meditations*, together with a collection of handouts, seemed to me to be sufficient reading.

In any case, I forged ahead and developed my course. The present book is a sort of record of some of the things I tried to do there. I have attempted to present a clear and sympathetic account of some of the main arguments and doctrines of the *Meditations*. I have also attempted to present a fairly substantial amount of closely related material on skepticism, the existence of God, and the nature of persons. My hope is that students who use this book will gain some appreciation for the unity and coherence of Descartes' thought, as well as for the subtlety of his arguments. I also hope that they will come to a reasonably clear understanding of one way of doing philosophy. Most of all, I hope they will come to enjoy the approach to philosophy that's illustrated here, will learn something of value from it, and will be motivated to continue.

I have benefited in this project from the encouragement, suggestions, and criticisms of many friends, colleagues, and students. The graduate students who served as teaching assistants for my Introduction to Philosophy course have been especially helpful. Among those who deserve thanks are Larry Hohm, Mark Aronszajn, Carol Gabriel, David Austin, Richard Brown, Blake Barley, Donna Benedetti, and Bill Hills. I'm sure there are others who have also made useful suggestions, and I hope they will forgive me for failing to mention them here.

Throughout the time I have been working on this book, David Benfield has given me many useful suggestions and lots of encouragement. Many of his suggestions have guided me in the writing of the book, and his careful critical comments have surely helped me to avoid some embarrassing blunders. I thank him for his generous help.

William Robinson and Eric Russert Kraemer read a draft of the book, and gave me detailed and valuable suggestions for improvement. Each of them also deserves thanks. Jaegwon Kim gave me a number of useful suggestions concerning some material in Chapter 9. For this and other help, I thank him.

Finally, I must express my gratitude to Lois, Lindsay, and Elizabeth. They put up with my grumpiness when things weren't going so well, they asked provocative questions that forced me to think things out more carefully, and they helped to provide the sort of environment I needed in order to write.

I dedicate this book to my teacher, colleague, and friend, Herbert Heidelberger.

Fred Feldman

A CARTESIAN INTRODUCTION TO PHILOSOPHY

PRELIMINARIES

WHAT IS PHILOSOPHY?

Philosophy is one of the strangest of academic disciplines. It differs from most other disciplines in several interesting respects. I want to begin by pointing out three interesting respects in which I think philosophy is strange.

Suppose you are browsing in a bookstore, and you see a book entitled *Modern European History.* Even before you open that book, you will have a pretty good idea of what's to be found inside. You will know that the book contains accounts of some of the more important political, military, social, and intellectual developments that took place in Europe during the past few hundred years or so. Of course, you may not know exactly how these events are described, and you may know almost nothing of the events themselves. Nevertheless, there is a sense in which it is correct to say that you know what the book is about, even before you read it.

A similar thing would happen if you were to pick up a book entitled *Elements of Nursing* or *Fundamentals of Wildlife Management.* While you would probably be ignorant of the details (and perhaps that's why you need to read the book) you would have a fairly accurate conception of the subject matter of the book. You would know that the book about nursing would contain accounts of the main jobs that nurses have to perform, and it would contain descriptions of the equipment and procedures with which nurses must be familiar. A similar point holds in the case of the book about wildlife management. Even before you open the book, you know that it contains accounts of the problems faced by a wildlife manager, and it probably also contains descriptions of various successful and unsuccessful methods for dealing with those problems. Perhaps it would be fair to put the point in this way: with most academic disciplines, even though beginners may be ignorant of the

1

answers to the questions in those disciplines, at least they know what the main questions are.

In this respect, philosophy is not like these other disciplines. Quite frequently, people who have not studied philosophy in any formal way find that they simply have no conception of philosophy at all. Even intelligent and reasonably well-educated people may simply "draw a blank" when they are asked about the nature of philosophy. My own personal experience bears this out. Often at a social gathering, a stranger will ask me what I do. I say that I teach philosophy. The stranger will then mumble something about how interesting that must be, and will say that he had once intended to take a course in that. Then, after a few moments of awkward silence, he will wander off looking for a fresh drink. I'm convinced that this sort of reaction is to be explained (at least in some cases) by the fact that my answer has meant just about nothing to the stranger. He doesn't want to admit his ignorance, but he doesn't know what to say next.

So the first respect in which philosophy is odd has to do with the extent to which outsiders understand what it's about. People who have not studied philosophy often have no clear conception of the subject matter of philosophy. Most other disciplines are not like this. Outsiders generally have a fairly good idea of the subject matters of those disciplines.

A second interesting fact about philosophy has to do with the extent to which the field has been misconceived by outsiders. Some people think it has something to do with "taking things philosophically." They think that philosophers are people who have learned to accept the bumps and bruises of life with a calm, resigned, fatalistic attitude. The study of philosophy, as they conceive of it, should have a straightforward payoff. The more we know about it, the greater will be our capacity to deal with misfortune.

It must be admitted that there is some historical basis for this misconception. Quite a few ancient philosophers apparently claimed that the study of philosophy would be beneficial in this way. Furthermore, there are certain Oriental schools of thought that clearly do advocate fatalism and calm resignation, and some of these are called "philosophies." However, the modern Western academic discipline of philosophy does not answer to this conception. Very little of what goes on in the classroom, and just about none of what goes on in professional journals and books, is directed toward the end of making us more "philosophical," in this sense.

Sometimes, when a person is asked to explain his philosophy, he will respond by stating some grand, general principles that have guided him in his career. For example, a professional football coach might say that his philosophy is this: "Winning isn't just the main thing. Winning is the only thing." Another coach might say that he has a different philosophy: "It isn't whether you win or lose. It's how you play the game."

No matter what activity or occupation we choose, we can find someone who will expound a philosophy of that activity. I have heard fishermen debating various philosophies of fishing; and I have heard gardeners debating various philosophies of gardening. If you watch certain television shows, you will have the opportunity of hearing motion picture directors and other show business celebrities discussing

their philosophies, too. You might even say that a maxim such as "There's no substitute for cubic inches" is the philosophy that for many years guided certain American automobile manufacturers.

If academic philosophy had something to do with this sort of "philosophy of _____," then it would be hard to see how there could be any such academic field as philosophy. What would philosophers do? Surely it would be absurd to suppose that the academic philosopher would be an expert in all fields of human activity. In any case, it doesn't matter. Academic philosophy, as it is currently practiced, has virtually nothing to do with the philosophy of gardening or the philosophy of fishing. If you want to discover some grand general principles that can guide your investment policy, or your selection of roommates, philosophy is not the place to look.

So the second odd thing about philosophy is this: quite frequently, when an outsider does have a conception of philosophy, it turns out that his conception is very seriously distorted. People who have not studied philosophy in any rigorous way, but who have merely drifted into some notion of what it is about, quite often have drifted into a mistaken notion. I think that the extent to which this happens in the case of philosophy is greater than the extent to which it happens in other academic disciplines.

The third odd thing about philosophy has to do with the fact that philosophy is "reflective." By this, I mean to indicate that one of the things that philosophers think about is the question, "what is philosophy?" The question about the nature of philosophy is itself a question in philosophy. Quite a few major figures in philosophy gained their professional fame by defending views about what philosophy is or how it ought to be pursued. Some, in fact, gained their greatest fame (or notoriety) by claiming either that philosophy is dead or that it never existed in the first place. Such debates are said to be in "metaphilosophy," which is generally considered to be the philosophical study of philosophy.

Of course, historians have reflected on the nature of history, and mathematicians have reflected on the nature of mathematics. For every academic discipline, we can raise the question concerning its nature and proper practice. However, when we raise these questions, we leave the sphere of the discipline in question. The question, "what is history?" is not a question _in_ history—it is a question in the philosophy of history. Similarly, the question, "what is the nature of law?" is not a question in law—it is a question in the philosophy of law. So I am not saying that there is no question about the nature of any other discipline. I'm saying that, for each other discipline, the question about its nature is not a question in it. It is a question in the philosophy of that discipline. When a historian begins to reflect on the nature of his field of study, he leaves history proper, and enters "metahistory," and begins to tackle philosophical questions.

So, in my view, there are at least three interesting respects in which philosophy differs from most other academic disciplines. First, so many outsiders have no conception of philosophy. Second, so many outsiders have distorted conceptions of philosophy. Finally, philosophy is reflective. The question about the nature of philosophy is itself a question in philosophy.

SOME CONCEPTIONS OF PHILOSOPHY

The question about the nature of philosophy is itself a philosophical question. Furthermore, it is a *disputed* question. Different philosophers answer the question in different ways. Let's consider some of the most popular answers.

Philosophy as the Love of Wisdom

Some philosophers adopt what I call the "Etymological Approach." They note that the word "philosophy" is derived from two Greek words, "philos" and "sophia," which are generally translated as "lover" and "wisdom." Thus, it is frequently said that philosophy is the love of wisdom, and a philosopher is a person who loves wisdom. This conception of philosophy is apparently presupposed by the ancient Greek philosopher Plato (ca. 428 B.C.–347 B.C.). In Books V and VI of his *Republic,* Plato discusses the view that philosophers ought to be kings, and he characterizes the true philosopher as a person who loves wisdom.

I suspect that there may have been a time in the distant past when something like this suggestion was true. Perhaps in ancient Greece everyone who loved wisdom was entitled to the Greek equivalent of the name "philosopher," and there may even have been a time when everyone who was properly called a philosopher did in fact love wisdom. But whether or not the etymological approach was true at some time in the past, it is surely not true now. Nowadays, there are millions of people who love wisdom, but who are not philosophers. For example, consider any biblical scholar who pursues his or her research with genuine devotion. Such a person apparently loves wisdom, but for all that he or she is still not a philosopher. For that matter, consider a mathematician or physicist or any other academic who pursues his or her research with the relevant sort of love. In spite of their love of wisdom, these people are properly housed in the department of mathematics or the department of physics. They are not misplaced philosophers.

It might be suggested that I have misunderstood the proposal. It's not that philosophy is supposed to be the love of wisdom. Rather, the idea is that philosophy is the love of wisdom *for its own sake,* and philosophers are people who love wisdom for its own sake. Perhaps academics in other fields pursue wisdom only because it will help them achieve better results in mathematics, physics, history, and the rest. Only philosophers, it might be said, pursue wisdom for its own sake. Philosophers want to be wise, but not because they think wisdom will make them richer or more powerful. They seek wisdom because they think wisdom is good in itself.

This modification makes the proposal even less plausible. For, in the first place, surely it is possible for there to be philosophers who do not love wisdom for its own sake. Maybe they are just in it for the money. This wouldn't make their work any less philosophical, and it wouldn't make them any less philosophers. In the second place, we must recognize that plenty of nonphilosophers do love wisdom for its own sake. A mathematician might love mathematical wisdom just for itself and not for any ulterior purpose. The same holds true of a physicist, a historian, and even for the baseball fan who is proud of knowing the lifetime batting average of every player

in the National League since 1900. Such people may just love to have the knowledge they have, even though it is not particularly useful. So that can't be the mark of the philosopher.

Perhaps someone will say that what's distinctive about philosophers is not just that they love wisdom—plenty of others can make the same claim. What's special in the case of the philosopher is something about the sort of wisdom that he or she loves. This is a deeper and more general sort of wisdom. We can call it "philosophical wisdom." No matter how much some mathematician loves mathematical wisdom, that won't make the mathematician into a philosopher. To be a philosopher, on this proposal, one must love *philosophical* wisdom.

The emptiness of this version of the etymological approach should be clear. We get no insight at all into the nature of philosophy if we are merely told that philosophy is the love of philosophical wisdom. In order to give this suggestion some point, we would have to add some clear account of the nature of "philosophical wisdom." Perhaps it will be said that philosophical wisdom is the sort of wisdom sought in philosophy. Now, however, the proposal is clearly circular. That is, in our effort to explain what philosophy is, we make use of the concept of "philosophical wisdom." Then, when we try to explain this otherwise unexplained term, we make use of the concept of philosophy. But this is the very concept we want to understand! Explanations such as this one, which make essential use of the concept they purport to explain, are said to be circular. It's hard to see how any such explanation could be enlightening.

Philosophy as the Queen of the Sciences

According to another conception, philosophy should be viewed as "Queen of the Sciences." In order to understand this proposal, we must first consider some ideas about the various sciences. We might suppose that for each science, there is a certain body of empirical data concerning particular concrete facts (e.g., the gas in this closed container was heated, and its pressure went up). In addition to this factual data, there are various generalizations (e.g., whenever any gas in any closed container is heated, its pressure goes up). Once we reach a certain level of abstraction, the generalizations may be considered scientific laws. By appeal to them, we can explain and predict the data to be found at the lower level within the science.

Furthermore, for each science, there are certain fundamental concepts. These concepts are used by the scientists within the field, but are not subjected to scrutiny within that field. For example, a biologist might make use of the concepts of *oxygen, water,* and *heat* quite frequently, but biologists are not especially interested in studying these concepts. Chemists and physicists (perhaps not much interested in biology) are better qualified to investigate such concepts.

If each scientist works exclusively within his or her own domain, it may turn out that the highest-level generalizations of one science do not mesh very well with those of other sciences. Furthermore, it may turn out that the fundamental concepts employed by the biologist will be found to conflict with those of the chemist. But if the biologist sticks to biology, and chemist sticks to chemistry, such "interscientific discontinuities" may never be discovered. In order to ensure that this doesn't happen, someone has to master the concepts and generalizations of all the main sciences, and determine whether or not there are conflicts. If such conflicts are discovered, this person has to suggest adjustments that will remove them.

There is a tradition according to which this job is the central job of the philosopher. The maxim here is that philosophy is the queen of the sciences. In a remarkable passage, Henry Sidgwick forcibly expressed this position. He said that the primary job of the philosopher is:

> to coordinate the most important general notions and fundamental principles of the various sciences.[1]

It's easy to understand how a philosophical novice could be pretty frightened if he thought that he was about to embark upon a study of the queen of the sciences. I suspect that there are very few people in the world today who would be able to pursue such a subject. Surely, the typical college student is not quite ready to take it on. Nowadays, the various sciences are so complex and technical that one must study for years before achieving a satisfactory understanding of the fundamental principles of any *one* of them. Obviously, it would take a lifetime to prepare oneself to coordinate them all.

I do not think that it is correct to think of the modern academic discipline of philosophy as the queen of the sciences. The majority of currently practicing philosophers probably would not be able to undertake the sort of project Sidgwick described. At any rate, very few of them try. Furthermore, I think it is important to recognize that there are plenty of interesting problems that clearly do belong to philosophy, but which don't seem to fit very neatly into the framework of the queen of the sciences. For example, there are questions in ethics, aesthetics, and philosophical theology. It is hard to see why we need to solve these problems if our main goal is to "coordinate the most important general notions and fundamental principles of the various sciences."

Of course, there is such a thing as the philosophy of science, and some of the work done there seems to fit the description Sidgwick gave. So I'm not claiming that philosophers never do this sort of thing. Rather, my point is that it is wrong to *identify* philosophy in this way. Philosophy may include this coordination problem, but it contains a lot of other, seemingly unrelated problems, too.

Philosophy as a Method

Some philosophers have maintained that if you study philosophy, you will "learn how to think." They have suggested that a really good philosopher is one who has a whole bunch of important intellectual skills. The philosopher is good at spotting fallacious arguments, drawing subtle distinctions, and discovering previously un-noticed cases that refute seemingly plausible hypotheses. If you submit yourself to the philosopher's course of training, you too will end up with these wonderful

---

[1] Henry Sidgwick, *Philosophy, Its Scope and Relations*, London, 1902.

talents. Then, if you're smart, you will go into law or medicine or science, and make use of the abilities developed in your philosophy course.

Although I doubt that he would endorse this conception of philosophy, the author of a recent textbook summed up this conception of philosophy in a marvelous way:

> Philosophy, that is, is a *method*. It is *learning how* to ask and re-ask questions until meaningful answers begin to appear. It is *learning how* to relate materials. It is *learning where* to go for the most dependable, up-to-date information that might shed light on some problem. It is *learning how* to double check fact-claims in order to verify or falsify them. It is *learning how* to reject fallacious fact-claims—to reject them no matter how prestigious the authority who holds them or how deeply one would personally like to believe them.[2]

This much I think is true: really good philosophers generally are able to spot fallacious arguments, draw subtle distinctions, and ask probing questions. Quite a few of them are also able to use the card catalogue in the library, and they usually can resist the conclusion of a weak argument, even if the person presenting the argument is very famous. So I think that good philosophers have at least some of the talents mentioned above in the passage from Professor Christian.

However, I do not think that we should conclude that "philosophy is a method." For, in the first place, the method described here is common to every form of serious intellectual activity. If you study to become a lawyer, you will surely have to learn to spot bad arguments, and to draw subtle distinctions. Furthermore, you will need to develop the ability to check your fact claims. The same can be said of the detective, the medical diagnostician, and the research chemist. They all have to reason carefully, avoid fallacious arguments, and make nice distinctions. Without these skills, a person is not fit for any sort of sustained, rigorous thought. So we mustn't think that philosophers have somehow cornered the market in clear thinking.

Furthermore, this conception of philosophy leaves out far too much. It suggests that there is no special subject matter for philosophy. It's as if philosophers had a nifty method for answering questions, but were utterly lacking in questions to which to apply the method. To apply the method, you would have to look into some other field of inquiry. Anyone who has studied philosophy for a while knows that this is wrong. There are plenty of philosophical questions. In addition to its method (which it largely shares with other intellectual disciplines) philosophy does have certain traditional subject matters.

Philosophy as Analysis

Some critics of recent British and American philosophy seem to think that philosophers spend all their time analyzing concepts. Some of these critics seem to think that philosophers have more important jobs to do, and so they also think that it's a

---

[2]James L. Christian, *Philosophy: an introduction to the art of wondering,* New York, 1977: Holt, Rinehart and Winston, p. xvii.

pity that so much time is wasted in conceptual analysis. Others apparently believe that if one is going to be a philosopher, then one must analyze concepts—since philosophy just *is* conceptual analysis. A person who takes this view may conclude that it's a pity that so much time is wasted in philosophy.

What's meant by "conceptual analysis"? Perhaps I can explain it by showing how it figures in a certain theory about concept development.

There is an old and rather plausible view according to which each person's mind starts off perfectly empty—a blank slate. Then, as individuals begin to have sensory experiences, they begin to have concepts. If they see a round, yellow, bumpy lemon, they will come to have the concepts of roundness, yellowness, and bumpiness. The same holds true for all the other simple concepts. The only way such concepts can get into the mind in the first place is by sensory experience.

Obviousy, it would be wrong to suppose that *all* concepts come in by way of the senses, since some concepts do not correspond to anything we can sense. For example, consider the concept of an angel, or the concept of a frictionless bearing. No one has ever seen such things, and so the first person to entertain these concepts must have gotten them in some non-sensory way.

We can postulate the existence of some relatively small number of mental operations that can be performed on concepts. For example, consider conjunction. This is the operation of "putting together" two concepts. So, suppose you have the concept of yellowness (which you got by seeing a lemon) and you have the concept of a cube (which you got by seeing a pair of dice). Now you can conjoin these concepts so as to create the compound concept of a yellow cube—even if you have never seen or heard about a yellow cube.

Other mental operations might include abstraction, negation, conditionalization, etc. For present purposes the details are not important. Now we can state an interesting thesis about human concept development: if a person comes to have a certain concept, then either (*a*) he got it directly by sensory experience, or (*b*) he got it as a result of operations performed on other concepts he already had. This view is the empiricist thesis concerning concept development.

If you accept the empiricist thesis, then you are faced with the task of showing, in particular cases, how certain complex concepts could have been constructed out of concepts gained through sensory experience. This can be an extremely challenging project. In many instances, it is very hard to see how a certain concept could have been derived from sense experience at all. The concepts of *cause* and *effect*, of *good* and *evil*, and of *necessity* and *possibility*, for example, are exceedingly difficult to explain in the prescribed way.

Many empiricist philosophers have taken up this challenge, and have tried to show how the problematic concepts might have been constructed. Traditionally, the way in which this is done is by formulating definitions of the words that express the concepts in question. So, for example, if you wanted to analyze the concept of *cause*, you would try to present a satisfactory definition of the word "cause." Your definition might look something like this:

    D1 x causes y = df. x is an event, and y is an event, x occurs before y occurs.

If the definition is a good one, then the expression on the right-hand side of the "=df." sign expresses the same concept as does the expression on the left. Furthermore, every word that occurs on the right-hand side must be legitimate. It must express either a sensory concept, or a compound concept whose construction has already been explained, or one of the specified mental operations. If these conditions can be satisfied, then the definition shows how the concept of *cause* might have been constructed. (Obviously, D1 is not a very plausible proposal. I use it here merely to illustrate the form of an analytical definition.)

It is clear, then, that an empiricist philosopher might have reason to spend some time in conceptual analysis. However, it is unlikely that such a philosopher would pursue such analyses for their own sake. Rather, he or she would attempt to construct the analyses in order to show how the more fundamental empiricist thesis might be true. Analysis, in this case, would just be one of many philosophical projects.

There are other purposes for which a philosopher might want to produce an analysis. For example, he or she might want to draw an important distinction. Perhaps the best way to do this would require definitions of the terms to be distinguished. In all such cases, however, analysis is not the ultimate goal. There is always some further philosophical purpose. The analytical definition is produced, not for its own sake, but because the philosopher thinks it will be useful. Thus, it cannot be correct to say that philosophy just *is* conceptual analysis.

I do not know of anyone who seriously thinks that the central task of philosophy is analysis. Of course, there might be a few philosophers, unknown to me, who do maintain this view. Be that as it may, I do not maintain it, and this book is not written on the assumption that it is true. I think philosophers have other and more interesting challenges to face.

SOME MAIN FIELDS OF PHILOSOPHY

So far, then, I have described a variety of misconceptions of philosophy, but I have not yet said what philosophy is. Perhaps I can make the topic a bit clearer by saying something about the main fields into which philosophy is traditionally divided.

Metaphysics

Metaphysics is sometimes said to be the philosophical study of the "ultimate nature of reality." Although the words are surely sufficiently high-sounding, I suspect that they may carry very little meaning.

The ancient Greek philosopher, Aristotle (384–322 B.C.), was an enormously productive writer. His works (and works subsequently attributed to him) cover a wide range of topics, including many that would now be considered strictly scientific, rather than philosophical. According to a traditional story, several hundred years after Aristotle's death, an editor called Andronicus of Rhodes attempted to organize his writings into a coherent collection. He found a number of essays that didn't fit very well anywhere else, so he put them together, and filed them right after

Aristotle's book on physics. Since the new book was filed after the physics book, it came to be known as Aristotle's *Metaphysics*—"meta" meaning "after," and "physics" meaning "Physics." As a result of this historical accident, the modern field of metaphysics now consists largely of discussions of the topics that were treated by Aristotle in the essays included in that ancient book.

Some of the main questions in metaphysics, then, are these. What are the main sorts of things that exist in the world? Of these things, which are fundamental, and which are somehow constructed out of the others? What is the difference between a substance and its attributes? What is the nature of time and space? What are necessity and possibility? What is causation? What is truth? Unless you have already studies some metaphysics, I suspect that this explanation may be a bit too vague to be useful. If so, I encourage you to be patient. It will eventually become clearer.

Epistemology

Epistemology (or "Theory of Knowledge") is the philosophical study of knowledge. Since ancient times, it has been thought that a person knows something only if (a) he or she believes that thing; (b) it is true; and (c) he or she is justified in holding this belief—perhaps because he or she has adequate evidence in favor of it. In light of this, epistemology also includes the philosophical study of belief, truth, and justification. Furthermore, since so much of our knowledge seems to depend upon sensory experience, epistemology also includes the philosophical study of sense perception.

There is an interesting question about the scope of human knowledge. How much can we know? Are there any areas concerning which people cannot have any knowledge? Those who think that our knowledge is seriously limited in some way (the "skeptics") may try to prove that it is impossible to know certain things that most of us would normally assume can be known. A total skeptic would go so far as to say that it is impossible to know anything. The investigation of all such claims falls into the field of epistemology.

Ethics

Ethics is the philosophical study of such value concepts as *right* and *wrong,* and *good* and *evil.* Broadly conceived, ethics also includes reflection on such questions as these: What is the nature of "the good life"? What are the virtues and vices? What, if any, are the fundamental human rights? Do animals have rights? What is the connection between law and morality?

Two areas of philosophical inquiry that are closely allied with ethics are *social and political philosophy* and *aesthetics.* The former deals with a variety of questions concerning the nature and justification of the state. If you are wondering how social organization might have arisen, and when and why the needs of the society should take precedence over the rights of the individual, then you are raising questions normally studied in social and political philosophy. One of the fundamental questions here is the question how the state ought to be organized. *Aesthetics* is the philosophical study of art. It includes inquiry into the nature of beauty and ugliness, just as ethics includes inquiry into the nature of right and wrong. Furthermore, aesthetics involves inquiry into the nature of the work of art itself. The question "what makes something a work of art?" is a question in aesthetics.

Some philosophers believe that their conclusions in ethics and the allied fields should be put into practice. So, for example, if a philosopher has come to the conclusion that the death penalty is always morally wrong, he or she might actively seek to bring about the repeal of the laws that permit capital punishment.

Logic

We can say that an *argument* is a series of sentences, the last of which (the *conclusion*) is supposed to follow from the others (the *premises*). In some cases, the conclusion really does follow. Any such argument is said to be *valid.*[3]

Logic is the study of the formal features of premises and conclusions in virtue of which certain arguments are valid, and others are invalid. Traditionally, it was assumed that every valid argument could be reformulated as some sort of syllogism. So, for example, consider this argument: "Socrates must be mortal. After all, he is only a man." In order to show why this is valid, we can recast it as a syllogism:

1 All men are mortal.
2 Socrates is a man.
3 Therefore, Socrates is mortal.

Having done this, we can see that the argument must be valid, since it exemplifies one of the valid forms. That form is:

1 All A's are B's.
2 x is an A.
3 Therefore, x is a B.

This sort of syllogistic logic has now given way to much more powerful forms of symbolic logic. These new systems of logic are apparently able to explain the validity of arguments whose forms are not adequately represented in any syllogism.

Philosophical Anthropology

Philosophical anthropology (or "philosophy of persons") is the philosophical study of persons. I think that philosophical anthropology should be viewed as a special branch of metaphysics, but it is sufficiently rich and interesting in its own right so as to be generally treated as a separate field.

The fundamental question here is: "What is the nature of a person?" When we raise this question, we are not looking for an answer to the psychological question about human nature. Rather, we are inquiring into the metaphysics of people. Are

---

[3] For further discussion of arguments and validity, see below, Chapter 2, under "Soundness and Validity."

people just complex and interesting physical objects? Or are they also endowed with a nonphysical component—a mind? If so, what is the connection between the mind and rest of the person?

Philosophical Theology

This too is really just a special branch of metaphysics. In this case, however, it is the philosophical study of the nature and existence of God.

If you set out to do philosophical theology, one of your first projects must be to establish the existence of God—for if there is no God, what would there be for you to investigate? Thus, those who do philosophical theology spend a remarkable amount of time attempting to formulate and evaluate various arguments for and against the existence of God. They also inquire into the nature of God. They raise such questions as these. "What are the main features that God is supposed to have?" "Does God exist in time and space?" "Is it possible for human beings to have knowledge of God?"

Philosophy of...

I suggested above that if you raise a sufficiently abstract question about history, you will enter the realm of the philosophy of history. This would be the philosophical study of history. There are many other "philosophies of": philosophy of education, philosophy of law, philosophy of language, philosophy of mathematics, philosophy of sport, just to mention a few.

Some purists would catalogue each of these under one of the more traditional headings, rather than listing them as if they were on a par with metaphysics and epistemology. Indeed, some purists would undoubtedly dismiss some of these philosophies of, claiming that they are not genuine areas of philosophy at all. However, there are philosophy courses in all of these areas, and books and journals and societies, and it seems to me that they should be counted as fields of philosophy. Purists are free to ignore them, if they like.

History of Philosophy

One final field should be mentioned. That is the History of Philosophy.

Philosophy has a long and honorable history, going back at least to the Golden Age of Greece. Some of the most brilliant and influential thinkers of the last two thousand years have been philosophers. Surely any list of great thinkers would have to include such philosophers as Socrates, Plato, Aristotle, St. Augustine, St. Thomas Aquinas, Descartes, Leibniz, Spinoza, Locke, Berkeley, Hume, Kant, J. S. Mill, Dewey, Russell, G. E. Moore, and Wittgenstein. Their writings have provided enlightenment (and puzzlement) to generations of readers. When a philosopher studies the work of some illustrious predecessor, attempting to elucidate its meaning, and to evaluate its significance, he or she is engaged in the history of philosophy.

Some work that has been done in the history of philosophy looks very much like straightforward metaphysics, or epistemology. The modern writer may pay only the slightest attention to the actual words of the philosopher whose work he or she is interpreting, simply seeking to capture the spirit of the thought of the historical figure. Other work in this area looks more like "intellectual history," rather than philosophy. Here, the modern writer may be primarily interested in discovering the historical facts concerning some philosophical work, rather than in reformulating it or evaluating it. He or she may seek to determine the precise date at which some doctrine was first formulated, or the intellectual influences that operated on some important figure. So long as the intent of the modern writer is clear to all parties concerned, I can see no reason to say that either of these extremes is preferable to the other, or to something between them.

A Minor Problem

I suspect that some readers may feel that they have been shortchanged here. I have attempted to explain what philosophy is by describing some of its main fields. Yet, in many cases, I have described the field by saying that it is the *philosophical* study of something-or-other. For example, I said that epistemology is the *philosophical* study of knowledge, that ethics is the *philosophical* study of morality, and that philosophical anthropology is the *philosophical* study of persons. Surely, there is something circular about my explanation!

I must acknowledge that my explanation is somewhat empty. A person who does not know what philosophy is probably doesn't know what a philosophical study is, either. If you are such a person, I must encourage you to be patient. If you stay with me for a while, you will eventually come to have a somewhat better understanding of metaphysics, epistemology, philosophical theology, and philosophical anthropology. It will take some time and effort, but, at the end, you will be closer to knowing what each of these fields of philosophy is, and so you will be closer to knowing what philosophy itself is.

THE AIM OF THIS BOOK

My purpose in this book is to introduce you to philosophy. I could try to do that simply by stating some of the main problems of philosophy, and then describing some of the main solutions that have been proposed. I fear, however, that if I were to do that, you would come away with the unfortunate notion that philosophy consists of a lot of relatively unconnected puzzles, together with a lot of incompatible and controversial proposed solutions. In any case, I have proceeded in a different way.

The *Meditationes de prima philosophia,* or *Meditations on First Philosophy,* written by René Descartes in 1641, is undoubtedly one of the most important philosophy books ever written. In adddition to this, it is very short, relatively easy to understand, and quite beautifully written. In this work, Descartes presents the elements of a unified and coherent philosophical system. His system includes doctrines in metaphysics, epistemology, philosophical theology, and philosophical anthropology. Throughout the book, Descartes presents interesting, and often persuasive arguments for the views he defends. Although many of Descartes' answers are not universally accepted, and some of his arguments are pretty widely rejected, I think it is clear that he asked the right questions. These are the questions that have dominated Western philosophy since Descartes' time. In virtue of this, Descartes has been called "the founder of modern philosophy."

In light of these facts about Descartes' *Meditations,* I think that no other book provides a better introduction to philosophy than it does. You might think, then, that Descartes has already done the job I mean to do in this book. Perhaps we should just give a copy of the *Meditations* to each new student, and tell him or her to read it.

However, if a person with no previous philosophical training attempts to read the *Meditations,* he or she may very well fail to appreciate some of its virtues. One reason for this is that Descartes makes use of certain technical terms, and it is quite unlikely that an untrained modern reader would know what all of these mean. Another reason is that Descartes sometimes seems to assume that his reader will already be familiar with the views and arguments of certain other philosophers. He presents objections to those views without spending very much time explaining them. The modern reader may simply not know what he's talking about. A final problem must also be acknowledged. Some of Descartes' arguments are extremely intriguing, but at the same time quite baffling. Scholars have wrangled for centuries over their precise significance. Since the experts cannot agree on the proper interpretation of these passages, it is quite unlikely that a novice will know what to make of them.

So modern readers with no previous philosophical training need a sort of guidebook to help them over the rough spots in the *Meditations.* They need a book that explains the meanings of Descartes' technical terms. They need a book that fills them in on the alternatives to the views that Descartes defends. They need a book that presents clear formulations of the most plausible interpretations of the arguments of the *Meditations.* They need an account of the main objections that can be directed against Descartes' doctrines and arguments.

I have attempted, in the present book, to give modern readers the help they need. I have tried to write a book that is a sort of introduction to the finest introduction to philosophy ever written.

THE PLAN OF THIS BOOK

In order to explain the plan of this book, I must first briefly describe the plan of the *Meditations.*

The *Meditations* consists of several parts. There is some preliminary material, including a dedication, a *Preface,* and an outline. Then there is the body of the work, which consists of six chapters, or "meditations." Descartes pretends that the book is the record of his thoughts over a period of six days—one day for each meditation. In the *First Meditation,* Descartes explains his project: he has accepted many false opinions for true, and now he wants to rectify the situation. He wants to get rid of all of his beliefs, and then begin to accept new beliefs only if they are perfectly certain. In order to convince himself that his old beliefs are unworthy of acceptance, he considers a bunch of skeptical arguments. By the end of this *Meditation,* he thinks he has found reason to doubt everything he formerly believed.

In the *Second Meditation,* Descartes finds the first belief that is certain enough to be accepted. It is the belief that he himself exists. His realization of this fact is somehow connected with the fact that he thinks. (Descartes is the philosopher who made the expression "I think, therefore I exist" so famous.) He goes on to consider the reliability of beliefs based upon sense experience. He seems to conclude that they are not very reliable.

In the *Third Meditation,* Descartes explains why he needs to prove that God exists, and that God is no deceiver. If there is no God, or if God is a deceiver, then Descartes cannot be perfectly certain of anything beyond the mere fact that he himself exists. Descartes then proceeds to formulate and defend a fairly complicated argument for the existence of God. By the end of the *Third Meditation,* Descartes thinks he has established that God exists, and that God is no deceiver. Thus, he thinks it will be possible for him to become perfectly certain of all sorts of things.

Before he can proceed, however, he has to answer a certain objection: if God is so wise, powerful, and good, why does he allow Descartes to make mistakes? Why hasn't he made Descartes "epistemically perfect"? In the *Fourth Meditation,* Descartes answers this objection, and presents an important conclusion in epistemology: all his clear and distinct perceptions must be true.

The *Fifth Meditation* contains another argument for the existence of God. This one, generally called "The Ontological Argument," is based on the claim that God has all perfections. Since necessary existence is a perfection, God must exist.

The final *Meditation* is devoted to a discussion of the nature of persons. Descartes presents arguments against the view that he is just a living body. He tries to show that, in addition to the body, a person must have a nonphysical thinking part—a mind (or soul). He also tries to explain how the body and mind are connected. He concludes this *Meditation,* and the book as a whole, by considering the potential scope of human knowledge. He closes on a somewhat pessimistic note, saying that "the life of man is vulnerable to errors regarding particular things, and we must acknowledge the infirmity of our nature."[4]

The plan of the *Meditations* has determined the plan of this book. This book is divided into three main parts. In the first part (Chapters 2, 3, and 4), I focus on epistemology. First, in Chapter 2, I give some needed background, and I try to explain some traditional skeptical arguments. In Chapter 3, I turn to Cartesian epistemology, focusing on the skeptical arguments of the *First Meditation.* Chapter 4 is devoted to the passage in which Descartes discovers his first perfect certainty.

The second main part of this book is about philosophical theology. Chapters 5 and 6 contain accounts of the most important traditional arguments for the existence of God, together with a proposed analysis of the concept of God. In Chapter 7, I turn to Cartesian philosophical theology. I present and evaluate Descartes' arguments for the existence of God, and I try to explain how Descartes deals with the problem of error. Finally, in Chapter 8, I turn to "atheology"—arguments *against* the

---

[4]René Descartes, *Meditations on First Philosophy,* translated from the Latin by Donald A. Cress, Indianapolis, 1979: Hackett Publishing Company, p. 56. In subsequent footnotes, I refer to this book as "Cress."

existence of God—and I consider whether theists can defend themselves against these attacks.

The third part, consisting of Chapters 9 and 10, is devoted to philosophical anthropology—the philosophical study of the nature of persons. Descartes rejected "materialism," which is the view that each person is just a living body. So I attempt to explain the materialist conception of persons, and I present and comment on some of the standard arguments pro and con. In Chapter 10, I give my interpretation of Descartes' own view about people—"Cartesian Dualism." I try to explain how he argued for it, and I point out some of its most serious difficulties.

The final chapter of this book is devoted to summing up, and tying together some loose ends. I try to draw some conclusions about the significance of Descartes' work, and I point out what I take to be his greatest achievements, and his most important failures.

A NOTE ON TEXTS AND PROCEDURES

I have made use of Donald Cress's translation of the *Meditations*.[5] This is readily available and quite inexpensive. Of course, there are several other editions of the *Meditations,* and most of these are perfectly satisfactory. One useful feature of the Cress book, however, is that it contains a nice little account of Descartes' life, and it also contains a very brief, but excellent bibliography of works by and about Descartes.

Descartes wrote many books in addition to the *Meditations*. The standard English translation of his philosophical writings is *The Philosophical Works of Descartes,* edited and translated by Elizabeth Haldane and G. R. T. Ross, Cambridge University Press. This work, in two volumes, was first published in 1911. It was revised in 1931, and has gone through many editions since then. I have made use of a paperback edition published in 1976. In footnotes, I refer to this work as "HR," and I indicate the volume by either a "I" or a "II."

At several places in this book, I will suggest that you get out your copy of the *Meditations* and read certain passages. It seems to me that you cannot properly understand what Descartes says unless you study his own words carefully. Thus, I must emphasize the importance of reading the *Meditations*.

In many places, I have discussed important arguments and views of philosophers other than Descartes. Where it has seemed feasible, I have quoted passages in which these philosophers have presented the arguments and views in question. Thus, for present purposes, it may not be necessary for you to have any books in addition to the *Meditations* and this book. However, most of the passages I have cited can be found in easily accessible, classic philosophical texts. These can be found in just about any college library. Whenever you find something that seems especially interesting, or if you can't believe that anyone could have said what I attribute to some great figure in the history of philosophy, then you must look up the original. I sincerely hope that you will find that I haven't misrepresented anyone's views. In any case, I urge you to look into the classics.

[5]Above, note 4.

KNOWLEDGE, SKEPTICISM, AND THE COGITO

Part One of this book consists of Chapters 2, 3, and 4. Each of these chapters concerns some issue in epistemology. In Chapter 2, I present a traditional account of the nature of knowledge. According to this view, knowledge is justified, true belief. I go on to present several famous old skeptical arguments. Each of these is designed to show that we really don't know quite as much as we might have thought. By appeal to an important Cartesian distinction, I explain one way in which these arguments may (perhaps) be answered.

In Chapter 3, we turn to the first of Descartes' *Meditations*. I attempt to explain the central epistemological problem that Descartes faced. Descartes recognized that some of his beliefs were less than perfectly certain. He wanted to get rid of all of his less than perfectly certain beliefs, and come to have the largest number of perfectly certain beliefs that it would be possible for him to have. In order to get into this exalted epistemic state, Descartes thought he would first have to get rid of *all* of his old beliefs, good and bad alike. To do this, he needed some arguments designed to show that those old beliefs were really less than perfectly certain. In Chapter 3, I present and explain Descartes' arguments. I try to explain the fundamental difference between Descartes' skeptical arguments and the previously discussed traditional skeptical arguments.

In Chapter 4, I discuss one of the most famous passages in Western philosophy. This is the passage in which Descartes seems to claim that since he thinks, he must exist. "Cogito, ergo sum" is Latin for "I think, therefore I exist." The passage, which appears at the beginning of the *Second Meditation* is known as "the Cogito." In this passage, Descartes achieves his first perfect certainty as he starts to regain his old beliefs. That certainty, of course, is "I exist." Descartes evidently thinks that no thinks that no skeptical argument, neither his own nor any traditional one, casts doubt on his own existence. The reasoning behind this claim is a topic to be explored in Chapter 4.

Let's start, then, with a consideration of the concept of knowledge, and some classic skeptical arguments.

KNOWLEDGE AND SKEPTICISM

In the *First Meditation*, Descartes presents several extremely important arguments. These arguments are generally taken to be designed to show that we really don't know many of the things we ordinarily take ourselves to know. These Cartesian "skeptical" arguments will be discussed in some detail in Chapter 3. In this chapter, I provide some essential background concerning the nature of knowledge itself. I also try to prepare the way by explaining some famous non-Cartesian skeptical arguments.

KNOWLEDGE

The first question we have to consider here is one of the oldest and most puzzling of philosophical questions. It can be formulated in a variety of ways. In one form, it is the question: "What is knowledge?"

When the question is formulated in this way, it may be a bit shocking. One hardly knows where to begin to answer it. Shall we say that knowledge is a special sort of feeling? Or should we say that knowledge is a certain idea or concept? Perhaps knowledge is a word that we use to indicate assent, or agreement?

I'm inclined to believe that a large part of the trouble here is caused by the needlessly abstract form of the question. We can ask for pretty much the same information, but in a less troublesome manner, if we bring the question back down to earth. Instead of asking about the nature of knowledge, we can ask for an account of the circumstances in which it would be correct to say that someone knows something.

Three Kinds of Knowledge

However, before we turn to a consideration of some possible answers to this question, it is important that we come to a somewhat clearer understanding of the question. We can distinguish among a variety of ways in which the word "knows" can be used. Here are some examples:

1 She knows the queen.
2 She knows how to swim.
3 She knows that Descartes was a mathematician.

In example (1), the thing she is said to know is a person, the queen. We can say that the "object" of her knowledge, if (1) is true, is some person. Presumably, (1) would be true if she and the queen are old friends, or if she has spent some time interviewing the queen. We could say that (1) means pretty much the same as "She is quite well acquainted with the queen."

The object of the alleged knowledge in (2) is quite different. (2) seems to mean that she has a certain skill, or ability. If (2) is true, then she is able to swim. It should be clear that this sort of knowledge is different from the knowledge involved in sentence (1). When we say that she knows how to swim, we don't mean that she has met "how to swim," or that she is acquainted with "how to swim." It has been suggested that a sentence such as (2) just means that she learned how to swim, and hasn't forgotten.

The third example introduces yet a third sort of knowledge. The object here seems to be a fact—the fact that Descartes was a mathematician. The sort of knowledge involved here seems, at least at first glance, to be different from the sorts of knowledge involved in (1) and (2). When we say that someone knows a fact, we don't just mean that he or she "has met it." Factual knowledge isn't just acquaintance. Some people would say that it doesn't even make sense to suppose that a person could meet a fact, or be introduced to it. So the knowledge involved in (3) is different from that involved in (1). Similarly, there seems to be a difference between "knowing how," as in (2), and "knowing that," as in (3). A person might know that in order to swim, one must move one's arms and legs in such-and-such a manner, and yet, perhaps because he has never had a chance to try it, he might still not know how to swim. Another person might know how to swim, but might be unable to explain how she does it. Perhaps we could say that she does not know that one must move one's arms and legs in such-and-such a manner in order to swim. These cases seem to show that there is a difference between "knowing that" and "knowing how."

Let's focus on factual knowledge, such as that involved in sentence (3). Some other examples might be:

4 He knows that Socrates was a philosopher.
5 She knows that it will rain tomorrow.
6 He knows that there is a chicken in the pot.
7 She knows that every square has four sides.

In each of these examples, the "object" of the alleged knowledge is something indicated by a that-clause. I have already suggested that such things are to be thought of as facts. Some philosophers take facts to be true propositions. Later on,[1] we will have occasion to consider the nature of propositions more carefully. For now, we can simply say that a proposition is a thing that can be expressed by a

---

[1]Chapter 9, under "Ontological Systems."

declarative sentence, or indicated by a that-clause. So, for example, consider the proposition that every square has four sides. This proposition is expressed by the sentence, "every square has four sides," and it is indicated by the that-clause that appears in sentence (7). In any case, some knowledge apparently takes propositions as its object. This sort of knowledge is often called "propositional knowledge," and this is the sort of knowledge that we are most interested in here. Our question, then, is this: what must be the case in order for a person to have this sort of propositional knowledge?

Knowledge and Belief

Many philosophers agree that if a person knows something, he or she must believe it. If you know that it will rain tomorrow, then you believe that it will rain tomorrow. If you know that there is a chicken in the pot, then you believe that there is a chicken in the pot. I think that if you reflect on the question, you will see that it's impossible to know something if you don't believe it. If this is right, then knowledge entails belief. More exactly, we can say that it is necessary that if a person, S, knows some proposition, p, then S believes p.

We can test this thesis about knowledge and belief by trying to imagine a case in which someone *does* know something, but *does not* believe it. If we can conceive of such a case, we will have shown that knowledge does not entail belief—because we will have established that it is possible to know something without believing it. Here's a case that might seem to refute the thesis. Suppose I purchased a lottery ticket. I had no hope of winning—I just bought it to amuse my friends. Now a man has come to my door, has told me that I won the lottery, and is handing me a check for one million dollars. It is clearly a genuine check, and it is clearly made out to me. I am astonished. I exclaim, "I can't believe it! I've won the lottery!"

Shall we say that this is a case in which (*a*) I know that I have won the lottery, and (*b*) I don't believe that I have won the lottery? If so, the example shows that it is possible to know a thing without believing it. My own view is that this is no counterexample to the thesis. As I see it, the exclamation, "I can't believe it!" should not be taken literally. It is just an idiomatic expression that we use to express shock, amazement, and surprise. When, in the example, I say "I can't believe it!" I don't really mean to assert that it is impossible for me to believe that I have won the lottery. I only mean to express my surprise. I never expected that I would win. But now that I see the check made out to me, I do believe that I have won.

In order to clarify the connection between factual knowledge and belief let's consider a case in which someone *does not believe* a certain proposition. Suppose that my wife is genuinely skeptical about the check. She suspects that it might be a hoax. Maybe some friends have made out a phoney check just to fool us. In this case, she really doesn't believe that we have won the lottery. It seems to me, then, that in this case it would also be incorrect to say that she *knows* that we have won. Until she starts to believe that we're winners, she doesn't yet know that we're winners. So I am inclined to believe that if a person, S, knows a proposition, p, then S believes p. Equivalently, we can say that if S doesn't believe p, then S doesn't know p. This principle holds, obviously enough, only for propositional knowledge.

Knowledge and Truth

It should be clear that merely believing a thing is not sufficient to guarantee that you know it. To see this, we can consider a slightly modified version of the lottery example. Suppose my wife's suspicions are justified. My friends in fact are tricking me. The check is a phony, and I have not won the lottery. But suppose I am fooled, and I still believe that I have won. Shall we then say that I know that I have won? It seems clear that this would be wrong. If in fact I have not won, I cannot know that I have won, no matter how convinced I might be. This reveals a second important fact about knowledge. Knowledge entails truth. If S knows p, then p is true. If p isn't true, then no one knows p.

Once again, we can test the principle by attempting to imagine a case that runs counter to it. Can we conceive of a case in which a person has propositional knowledge of something, but in which that thing is false? The following example is sometimes given. In ancient Egypt, all the experts believed that the earth was flat. Suppose some student went to school, and was told on the highest authority that the earth was flat. Suppose this student also read this in the most up-to-date textbooks. Suppose he learned his lesson well, and came to believe that the earth was flat. Surely his teachers, parents, and classmates would all agree then that he had learned his lessons well, and so they would think that he finally knew that the earth was flat. Anyone who denied that the lad had this knowledge would be taken to be a fool. Thus, it might be maintained that the Egyptian youngster knew that the earth was flat, even though, of course, the earth was not flat. So, perhaps knowledge does not entail truth. Maybe we can know things that are not true.

I'm not impressed by the example. No matter how sure the youngster might have been, and no matter how many people might have agreed that he knew the earth was flat, it still seems to me that he didn't know it. He thought he knew it. They all thought he knew it. Everyone would have said that he knew it. But they all would have been wrong. In fact, he didn't know it. He couldn't have known it, since it was false.

It would be good to be able to prove this point, but I am afraid that I cannot do so. I know of no way to prove that knowledge entails truth. The best I can do is to ask you to reflect carefully on your own intuitions about knowledge, and to consider carefully what you would say about the cases we have imagined. I hope you will agree that if a proposition is not true, then no one can know it. (Of course, someone can know that it is false—but that's true!)

Se we have seen that propositional knowledge entails truth and belief. If S knows p, then S believes p, and p is true. Shall we say, then, that knowledge is true belief? That is, shall we say that a person knows a thing if he believes it, and it is true?

Knowledge and Justification

The answer, of course, is "no." A person can believe a true proposition without knowing it. Truth and belief are not "sufficient" for knowledge. We can see this by considering another lottery example. Suppose I think that today is my lucky day. I go out and buy a lottery ticket. I'm sure I'm going to win. I can "feel it in my bones." Suppose that in fact I do win. At the time when they hand me the check, I know that

I have won. I see the check, and I hear them telling me that I'm a winner. But what about the time *before* the winner is announced? At that time it is already true that I am going to win, and I believe at that time that I am going to win. But it is pretty doubtful that I already *know* that I am going to win. After all, my only evidence is a "feeling in my bones." Most people would say that this is not knowledge—it's just a hunch that turned out to be correct. So it appears that knowledge isn't just true belief. In this case, I have true belief, but no knowledge.

What would we have to add to true belief in order to get knowledge? How could we change the last lottery example so as to ensure that I do know that I am going to win? Here's one way. We can change the part about the "feeling in the bones." Let's suppose that I have bribed a lottery official. He has agreed to fix the lottery so that I will be a winner. I have very good reason to believe that he will go through with his part of the bargain. Suppose again that the winners haven't been announced, but I still believe that I am going to win. Once again, I am going to win. This time it seems that it would be correct to say that I know that I am going to win. The difference is that in this example I have good reason to believe that I will win. It's not just a hunch or a lucky guess. I'm not going on a feeling in my bones. In this case I know I have bribed an official, and I have reason to believe he will see to it that I win. So I have evidence to back up my belief.

So it appears that if a person knows something, he must also have evidence for it. A hunch, or a lucky guess that turns out to be correct is not knowledge. There must be some basis for the belief. There are a number of different expressions that philosophers use to indicate that a person's belief is more than just a hunch. We can say that such a belief is "justified," "grounded," "certain," "supported by the evidence," "warranted." So if S knows p, then S is justified in believing p.

Let us review the three main conclusions we have reached so far. First, we have seen that knowledge entails belief. This is sometimes called "the doxastic condition" for knowledge, and it can be put in this way: if S knows p at some time, t, then S believes p at t. Second, we have seen that knowledge entails truth. If S knows p at t, then p is true at t. This is sometimes called "the semantic condition." Finally, there is "the epistemic condition": if S knows p at t, then S is justified in believing p at t. So if you have knowledge, you have a justified, true belief.

For very many years, it was widely thought that this provides the basis for an answer to our original question about the nature of knowledge. Philosophers thought that it would be correct to say that knowledge is justified true belief.

SKEPTICISM

Sometimes when we say that a person is skeptical about something, we mean to suggest that she or he doubts the value of that thing. So, for example, to say that someone is skeptical about astrology would be to say that she or he doubts the value or usefulness of astrology. Such a person might be called a "skeptic." But there is another, somewhat technical use of the word "skeptic." In this technical sense, we can say that a person is a skeptic about something, provided that she thinks that no one has knowledge about that thing. Thus, if a person thinks that no one has knowledge about life on other planets, we can say that she or he is a skeptic with respect to life on other planets. This does not mean that the person doubts the value or usefulness of life on other planets. It just means that she or he thinks we don't know anything about that topic.

The word "skeptic" is the English version of a Greek word that was used to designate a certain group of ancient philosophers. Originally, the word suggested "one who observes," or "one who looks at." The skeptics were examining knowledge. However, the ancient skeptics had a very critical attitude about what constitutes genuine knowledge. Quite a lot of the things that others took to be knowledge, the skeptics regarded as non-knowledge. In time, the meaning of the word has shifted. So now when we say that someone is a skeptic, we usually don't mean that he or she is looking at knowledge. We usually mean that he or she denies the possibility of knowledge.

The ancient skeptics were particularly concerned to cast doubt on alleged knowledge gained by sense experience. They attacked this sort of knowledge-claim by appeal to arguments based on the fact that different people experience the same thing differently, or that the same person experiences the same thing differently on different occasions. For example, the same wine that tastes sweet to a healthy person tastes sour to someone with a cold. A tower that appears round to someone far away, appears square to someone nearby. From this variability in the deliverances of sense experiences, the skeptics concluded that one never gains real knowledge by sense experience.

Skepticism about the Future

One of the more popular targets for skeptics is our alleged knowledge of the future. Some have maintained that we have no such knowledge, and they have presented a puzzling and somewhat surprising argument to back up their claim. The argument begins with the seemingly innocuous fact that there are some things about the future that we don't know. For example, we can't predict with any assurance what the weather will be like on January 1, 2095. Other things about the future are just as hard to predict, even though they don't involve the distant future. Although astronomers can predict where Venus will be tonight, and what phase the moon will be in, no one can predict the time and location of the shooting stars that will be visible tonight. No one can predict such things, because no one knows where these various tiny objects are in space now, and no one knows how fast they are going, and no one knows what direction they are traveling in. They are so tiny that they cannot be observed until they hit the earth's atmosphere and burst into flames. So even though this is not a case that involves the distant future, just about everyone would agree that it is a case in which we are ignorant about something that is going to happen.

So let's agree that none of us knows when and where meteorites will fall. More particularly, none of us knows whether a large meteorite is going to strike the Statue of Liberty tonight. Such an event is not predictable on the basis of current astronomical knowledge.

However, certain things about falling meteorites are known. We know that large meteorites fall with tremendous explosive force. If a big meteorite hits hard enough, the impact will produce a large crater. Everything nearby will be destroyed, as if by a powerful bomb. So, if a large meteorite were to strike the Statue of Liberty tonight, it would surely wreck the statue. In that case, the statue would not be standing tomorrow. Since we don't know whether or not such a meteorite will fall, it seems to follow that we don't know whether the Statue of Liberty will be standing tomorrow.

I selected the Statue of Liberty merely as an example. I picked it because it is a well-known, large object. What I have said about it could just as easily have been said about any other similar object. It's not that the Statue of Liberty is especially vulnerable to meteorites. Since we evidently don't know whether or not the Statue of Liberty will be standing tomorrow, and every other structure is relevantly similar to the Statue of Liberty, we apparently don't know whether *any* large structure will be standing tomorrow. Indeed, a moment's reflection will show that virtually every event we expect to occur tomorrow might be disrupted by some cataclysm. You expect to see a sporting event tomorrow? What if the stadium is blown away by a freak tornado? You think you are going to meet a friend for lunch? What if an unpredictable earthquake annihilates the lunchroom?

Of course, some things cannot be disrupted in this way. No matter how many meteorites fall, two plus two will still equal four. Even if there is a huge earthquake, triangles will still have three sides and three angles. These things are necessary—they can't fail to be true. But the considerations mentioned above seem to show that there's reason to be skeptical about *contingent* propositions about the future; that is, ones that are neither necessarily true, nor necessarily false. Each such proposition is such that we can't really know that it's true. Thus, we seem to have an argument for skepticism with respect to future contingents. Our "innocuous" fact about the shooting stars seems to have led us to the conclusion that no one knows any contingent truth about the future!

Let us attempt to clarify the reasoning that brought us to this unexpected conclusion. We can do this by formulating an argument. The word "argument" here is another technical term. It does not mean what it means in ordinary English. When we speak of an argument in philosophy, we mean to indicate a collection of sentences of a special sort. In any such collection, the last member is supposed to be the "conclusion." Other members are the "premises." The premises, taken together, are supposed to prove that the conclusion is true. If the argument is a good one, the conclusion follows from the premises, so that if the premises are true, then the conclusion has to be true, too. Furthermore, in a good argument, the premises are true. So let's consider our argument for skepticism about the future.

Skepticism about the Future

1 I don't know whether a meteorite will hit the Statue of Liberty tonight.

2 If I don't know whether a meteorite will hit the Statue of Liberty tonight, then I don't know whether the Statue of Liberty will be standing tomorrow.

3 If I don't know whether the Statue of Liberty will be standing tomorrow, then no one knows any contingent truth about the future.

4 Therefore, no one knows any contingent truth about the future.

The first line of this argument is based on the fact that I don't know the positions and paths of movement of any meteors. They are too small to be seen prior to the time they enter the earth's atmosphere. Hence, I don't know in advance when and where one might come down and hit some object on the earth. For all I know for sure, one might hit the Statue of Liberty tonight. Then again, it might not. I just can't tell in advance. Thus, line (1) seems to be true.

Line (2) is based on the fact that if a big enough meteorite does hit the statue, the statue will be destroyed. Since I don't know whether or not the meteorite will fall, I don't know whether the statue will be standing. So line (2) seems to be true, too.

Line (3) is based on the fact that there's nothing special about the example I have selected. It's not that the Statue of Liberty is somehow especially vulnerable to meteorites, or that I am especially ignorant about the future. What's true of me is probably true of everyone else. If I don't know this specified contingent truth about the future, then no one else knows any other contingent truth about the future. So line (3) seems to be true.

I think it should be obvious that if lines (1), (2), and (3) are all true, then line (4) must be true as well. Anyone who admitted (1), (2), and (3), but denied (4) would be contradicting himself. Thus we can say that this argument is "valid." "Valid" is another technical term of philosophy. When we say that an argument is valid, we mean that its conclusion logically follows from its premises. In other words, if the premises are all true, then the conclusion must be true, too. So, in this technical sense, our argument for skepticism about the future is valid.

Soundness and Validity

It is extremely important to recognize that an argument can be valid even though its conclusion is false. Here, for example, is an argument of this sort:

1 All cows can fly.
2 Bossy is a cow.
3 Therefore, Bossy can fly.

This argument is valid, in our technical sense. If the premises were true, then the conclusion would have to be true, too. The conclusion follows from the premises. A person who admitted (1) and (2) but denied (3) would be contradicting himself. Of course, anyone who admitted (1) in this example would be a fool. If an argument is valid, but you want to reject the conclusion, then you must reject at least one of the premises—otherwise, you will be committed to a contradiction.

When we say that an argument is valid, we are *not* saying that each line follows from the one before. The premises may be logically independent of each other—none follows from any other. So, if an argument is valid, you can put the premises in any order you like and it will still be valid. The crucial thing is that all the premises, taken together, entail the conclusion. If all the premises are true, then the conclusion must be true, too.

As we have seen, an argument may be valid even though some of its premises are false. When this happens, the argument really doesn't establish its conclusion. Even though the argument is valid, the conclusion still might be false, since some of the premises are false. However, if an argument is valid, and all of its premises are true, then the conclusion must be true. Such an argument does establish its conclusion. Another technical term, "sound," is used for such arguments. We say that an argument is sound if and only if (*a*) it is valid, and (*b*) every premise is true. Obviously, if an argument is sound, then its conclusion is true.

Before we turn to a consideration of the question whether our argument for skepticism about the future is sound, I would like to introduce some other, similar arguments. Each of these is an argument for some other sort of skepticism. Once we have had a chance to think about these arguments, we will turn to evaluation. That is, we will try to figure out whether or not they are sound.

Skepticism about the Past

You might think that there is an important epistemological difference between the past and the future. You might think that there is more reason to be skeptical about the future than there is to be about the past. After all, future events haven't yet occurred, and there's always the chance that some unexpected catastrophe might prevent the things we expect. But past events have already occurred. They can't be "undone." The past is "fixed." So it might seem that there's less reason to be skeptical about the past. However, there is an interesting argument that seems to show that we don't have any knowledge of *past* contingents, either.

Some people think that the Bible is quite literally true. And they think they have found passages in the Bible that imply that the earth was created approximately four thousand years ago. Accordingly, these people believe that the earth was created four thousand years ago. Let's say that such a person is a "creationist." Others find this belief outrageous. They think they can refute it by appeal to empirical evidence. So, for example, someone might attempt to refute creationism by pointing out that there are fossils that seem to be millions of years old. "If the world is only four thousand years old, what's this fossil doing in this rock?" they ask. The creationist is utterly unmoved by such facts. According to him, when God created the world four thousand years ago, he created it complete with fossils. So the creationist maintains that on "day one" there were already fossils in the rocks, and that most of these fossils were fossils of animals that had never existed. Thus, the fact that there are fossils in the rocks now does nothing to show that the earth is more than four thousand years old.

Another scientist might try to refute creationism by pointing out that certain carbon atoms decay at known rates. By examining bits of matter containing carbon, it is possible to determine the date at which that bit of matter was part of a tree, or plant, or other living object. Using this method of carbon dating, scientists have shown that some objects are millions of years old. Hence, the world wasn't created just four thousand years ago. It is much older than that.

Once again, no sensible creationist should be troubled by such a naive objection. Obviously, the creationist should maintain that when God created the world, he created carbon atoms in various stages of decay. In places where he wanted objects to look very old, he created very decayed carbon atoms. In other places, he created less decayed carbon atoms. So the facts about carbon dating don't cast any doubt on the creationist hypothesis.

The creationist isn't silly enough to maintain that when God created the world, he created it "all brand new and shiny." Rather, when God created the world, he made it just as it would have been if it had been millions of years old. He created it complete with fossils, decayed carbon atoms, and perhaps with some "very old" plants and animals. No empirical evidence can refute this view.

Once you recognize this fact about creationism, you can begin to appreciate a far more radical hypothesis. How shall we refute the idea that the whole world came into existence just five minutes ago? Surely, a sufficiently powerful God could create a world with millions of dusty "old" photographs and newspapers, and with libraries full of "old" history books, and he could see to it that all of these bits of evidence correspond properly—just as if there really had been centuries of past history. Furthermore, he could create people of all "ages," and he could see to it that the "old" ones had lots of "memories" of various past events. Surely, if God wanted to, he could create thousands of people who seem to recall living through the Great Depression, even though none of them in fact had lived then, and even though the Great Depression never even occurred.

In *An Outline of Philosophy,* Bertrand Russell discussed an argument for skepticism about the past based upon just this point. He did not appeal to the idea that God created the world five minutes ago. He just introduced what he called an "awkward consideration." Here's what he said:

> there is one awkward consideration which the sceptic may urge. Remembering, which occurs now, cannot possibly—he may say—prove that what is remembered occurred at some other time, because the whole world might have sprung into being five minutes ago, exactly as it then was, full of acts of remembering which were entirely misleading.[2]

Let's say that "the Russell Hypothesis" is the view that the world sprang into being five minutes ago, exactly as it then was, full of misleading acts of "remembering." The skeptic can be viewed as challenging us to prove that the Russell hypothesis is false. How can we do this?

We cannot refute the hypothesis by hauling out an old diary, or last week's newspaper, or a faded photograph. Such things have no evidential value, since each of them, according to the hypothesis, was created just five minutes ago, when everything else was created. Nor would there be any point in gathering together a crowd of people who insist that they can recall something that happened a month ago. According to the hypothesis, when the world sprang into existence five minutes ago, it sprang into existence containing people with coordinated memories. So the fact that people now in fact do have these memories proves nothing. That's just how they'd be if the hypothesis were true. I think it will be found upon reflection that there simply isn't any way to prove that the Russell hypothesis is false. And this provides the crucial premise for our argument for skepticism about the past. Here's the argument:

Skepticism about the Past

1 I can't prove that the Russell hypothesis is false.

2 If I can't prove that the Russell hypothesis is false, then I don't know that I existed yesterday.

---

[2] Bertrand Russell, *An Outline of Philosophy,* London: 1927; George Allen and Unwin, p. 7.

3 If I don't know that I existed yesterday, then no one knows any contingent truth about the past.

4 Therefore, no one knows any contingent truth about the past.

We have already seen why the first premise here seems to be true. The second premise also seems quite plausible. If the Russell hypothesis is true, then I didn't exist yesterday—I was created just five minutes ago along with everyone else. Hence, if I don't know whether or not the Russell hypothesis is true, I don't know whether or not I existed yesterday. Thus, we have (2). The third premise here is relevantly like the third premise of the argument for skepticism about the future. The point in this case is that there is nothing epistemically special about me, or my alleged knowledge of my existence yesterday. If there is reason to suspect that I don't know that, then there is equally good reason to suspect that no one knows anything about the past.

The logic of the argument is clear enough. It certainly seems to be valid. Thus, if we are to reject the conclusion, we will have to find something wrong with one of the premises. But which one? Each seems pretty plausible.

A Theory of Perception

So we have seen an argument for skepticism about the future, and an argument for skepticism about the past. Perhaps someone will think that these arguments show that we can't know what's *going to happen*, and we can't know what *has happened*, but they leave open the possibility that we can know what *is happening*. However, there are plenty of other skeptical arguments designed to show that we can't know much about the present, either. Let us consider one of the most famous of these. To do so, we must first reflect on what happens when a person perceives an object.

Suppose I go into the back yard to admire my old blue truck. I stand before the truck, and look at it. Under normal conditions, I will see the truck. How does this happen? It is not necessary for us to understand all the subtle details of the process. We just need a general account of the main components. Virtually everyone would agree, I think, that what happens is something like this: sunlight is reflected off the surface of the truck. It scatters in all directions. Some of the reflected light heads straight for my eyes. It passes through the lens of my eye, and is focussed on the retina. When the light strikes the retina, it stimulates the light-sensitive nerves there. When these nerves are thus stimulated, a tiny electrical charge is created. The electrical charge goes down the optic nerve and into my brain, where it finally stimulates some part of my brain that is responsible for visual perception. Then I become aware of a visual image of the truck—I see it.

What's the relation between the visual image of the truck and the truck itself? In the first place, we have seen that the visual image of the truck is *caused* by the truck. More precisely, the image has the features that it has (shape, color, apparent size, etc.) because the truck has corresponding features. The visual image of the truck is blue, for example, because the truck is blue, and so the light reflected from its surface has a certain pattern of wavelengths—a pattern that causes blue visual images in normal observers.

Secondly, we can say that the visual image of the truck *represents* the truck for me. I am directly or immediately conscious of the visual image of the truck. I notice that this image has certain features, and I infer from this that the object causing the image must have corresponding features. I am not directly conscious of the truck. I know that the truck is blue because I see the blueness of my visual image of the truck, and conclude that the object causing this image must actually be blue. Of course, I'm usually not conscious of this reasoning. Usually it happens so fast and is so familiar that I pay no attention to it. Yet, in a proper account of perception, it must be mentioned.

What I have said about visual perception holds true, with suitable variation, for all other sorts of perception. Suppose, for example, that I have been hauling manure in my truck, and now I can smell it. In this case the process involves nerves in my nose instead of ones in my eyes, and it involves tiny molecules given off by the manure instead of lightwaves reflected from the surface of the truck. But the crucial element is the same. I am directly aware of an "olfactory image"—a smell. The smell is caused by the truck, and represents the truck. I am directly aware of the smell, and only indirectly aware of the truck. I infer that the truck has certain features by virtue of the fact that the smell has certain other features.

The diagram in Figure 2-1 illustrates this theory of perception. In the diagram, the physical object in the external world is represented as A—in this case, my truck. Light reflected from the surface of the truck, represented by B, heads for my eyes, C. The eyes are connected by nerves to the brain. When the nerves are stimulated properly, a visual image, D, arises in the observer. The observer, directly aware of the visual image, infers that there must be an object in the external world which has caused this image, and which is similar to the image in important respects. When all

FIGURE 2-1

this happens properly, and there really is a truck there, we say that the observer is seeing the truck.

We can generalize on this visual example. Let us use the term "sensation" to refer to mental images of all senses. Thus, we can say that a visual image is a sensation, but we can also say that a tactual, olfactory, or auditory image is a sensation, too. The fundamental principle here is that, in ordinary successful cases of perception, our sensations are relevantly similar to the objects in the external world that have caused them. By observing our sensations, and drawing the appropriate inferences, we come to know about the objects around us.

Many philosophers have endorsed this theory of perception. Indeed, it may seem odd to call it a "theory," since it is hardly more than a bunch of obvious facts. In any case, this view has come to be known as "the Causal-Representative Theory of Perception," and it is often associated with the great English philosopher, John Locke. In his *Essay Concerning Human Understanding,* Locke developed the theory in some detail, and used it as the basis for his subsequent reflections in epistemology.[3] In order to honor Locke, let us use his name in the name of the central principle of this theory:

Locke's Hypothesis: In standard cases of perception, our sensations are caused by objects that resemble them.

It is extremely important to recognize that Locke's hypothesis is not a necessary truth. Sensations could have been caused by objects quite unlike them. For example, we can easily imagine a person who, because of some problem in his nervous system, regularly misperceives colors. Perhaps red objects look green to him, and vice versa. Red objects look red to most of us only because most of us are fortunate enough to have properly functioning visual systems.

A more extreme sort of perceptual error can be imagined, too. Imagine a person whose optic nerve has been destroyed. Suppose neurologists find a way to splice tiny wires into the ends of the transmitter nerves. They may then send minute electrical charges down the wires, and thereby stimulate the person's brain in something like the way it would have been stimulated by incoming signals from the nerves in the retina. If the experiment works properly, they may cause the person to have visual experiences. Indeed, they might even find a way to attach the person to a computer so that his optic nerve would be stimulated in just the way it would have been stimulated by looking at a truck. The person then would have a sensation of a truck, but it would not at all resemble the thing that caused it. It wouldn't look at all like a computer. So it is clear that Locke's hypothesis is not a necessary truth. Our sensations might have been caused by things they don't resemble.

Skepticism about the External World

Now we must consider an extraordinarily puzzling question: How do we know that Locke's hypothesis is true? What reason do we have for thinking that our sensations in fact do resemble their causes?

---

[3] John Locke, *An Essay Concerning Human Understanding: In Four Books.* Printed by Eliz. Holt for Thomas Basset at the George in Fleet St., near St. Dunstan's Church, 1690. See especially Book II, Chapter viii, Paragraphs 11–26.

This may appear to be a very silly question. You might think that it's just obvious that my sensation of my truck looks very much like my truck. You might think that if I had any doubts about it, I could just look at the truck, and then compare my visual image of the truck with the truck itself. You might think I would then find that both are blue and shiny, and both are shaped in pretty much the same way, and they are alike in all the relevant respects. You might think that the same thing could be done for other people, and for other senses, and that the result would be that we would find that sensations generally do resemble the things that cause them. So experience, you might say, shows that Locke was right.

But this would be a terrible mistake. I cannot compare my truck with my visual image of my truck. For when I look at my truck, to see what color *it* is, all I will see will be yet another visual image of my truck. Whenever I attempt to perceive a thing, I will end up observing some sensation presumably caused by it. If Locke was right, my sensation will be relevantly like the external object that caused it—but if I'm looking for evidence that Locke's hypothesis is correct, I surely cannot simply assume that there is the alleged similarity. I have to find some way of checking on the external objects without allowing any sensations to mediate. But the theory itself entails that this cannot be done. We never perceive external objects directly. We always are directly acquainted with their "representatives." How, then, can we tell whether the representative (the sensation) is like the thing it allegedly represents?

Here's another proposal. I want to know whether my visual image of my truck is similar to the truck itself. I know how the image looks. I ask my wife to take a look at the truck, and to tell me how it looks. She describes the color and shape of the truck, and I listen carefully to what she says. In the end, I conclude that Locke was right—the cause of my sensation is quite similar to the sensation itself.

It should be obvious that this proposal is a hopeless failure. When my wife tells me that the truck is blue and shiny, she gets her information from perception. Her perception, like mine, is mediated by sensations. She is directly aware of some blue and shiny sensations, and she assumes that these are faithful representations of their cause, the truck. So when she tells me that the truck is blue and shiny, she is unconsciously appealing to Locke's hypothesis. She is inferring that the truck must be blue and shiny because it has produced some blue and shiny sensations in her mind. Clearly, then, her testimony does nothing to establish the truth of Locke's hypothesis.

A further point has to do with the question whether I can know that my wife has said these things. How do I know that she said that the truck is blue? Pretty clearly, I know it because I have heard her speak. But hearing is a kind of perception. So what really has happened is this: I have directly heard certain sounds. Assuming that these sounds were caused by something relevantly like them, I have inferred (via Locke's hypothesis) that my wife must be speaking to me, and that she must be saying that the truck is blue. However, if Locke's hypothesis is the doctrine in question, I surely have no right to make use of it in my search for evidence for it. Thus, I really don't know that my wife has spoken—or even that she exists!

The upshot here is that I simply cannot find evidence to support Locke's hypothesis. It remains an unjustified assumption. For all I know, my sensations might be caused by things utterly unlike them. I know what my sensations are like, but I don't know what the "external world" is like. A person in this epistemic situation is said to be "bound in by the circle of his own ideas." He knows what's going on in his own mind, but must remain in doubt about the external world. For all he knows, there is no external world.

Let us summarize these reflections by casting them into another skeptical argument, this one called "Skepticism about the External World":

1 I don't know that Locke's hypothesis is true.

2 If I don't know that Locke's hypothesis is true, then I don't know that my truck is here.

3 If I don't know that my truck is here, then no one knows any contingent truth about the external world.

4 Therefore, no one knows any contingent truth about the external world.

A REPLY TO THE SKEPTICAL ARGUMENTS

We have now considered three skeptical arguments. The first is designed to show that we don't know any contingent truths about the future. The second is designed to show that we don't know any contingent truths about the past. And the final argument is designed to show that we don't know anything about the external world. Looked at in another way, these arguments seem to show that we cannot depend upon perception, memory, or our powers of prediction. If the arguments work, we must conclude that none of these "faculties" is a source of knowledge.

Any sensible person will want to reject these arguments. The skeptical conclusions should strike you as being absurd. Of course we have knowledge of the past, and of the external world. Surely we can know some things about the future. So we have to find some way to rebut the arguments.

Over the years, various philosophers have attempted in various ways to avoid the skeptical conclusions of these arguments, and others like them. There is little agreement, however, about their proposals. I prefer not to enter into a long review of the things that have been said pro and con these replies. Instead, I want to present and explain what seems to me to be the most promising sort of answer. This answer was not given by Descartes, but is strongly suggested by certain remarks he made in other contexts. In any case, the answer is based upon an important Cartesian distinction—the distinction between *practical certainty* and *metaphysical certainty*. Let us now turn to that distinction.

Practical Certainty and Metaphysical Certainty

In some places,[4] Descartes draws the distinction by appeal to a distinction between two sorts of activity. On the one hand, there are all those activities involving "the practical needs of life," and on the other hand, there is an activity he calls "the search after truth." Descartes uses various other phrases to mark this distinction. In one place he calls the former "the practical life" and the other "the contemplation of

[4]HR I, 266.

truth."[5] And in yet another place he calls the former "the conduct of our life" and the latter "the search after truth."[6] In any case, the general idea is this: most of the time we are not engaged in philosophical reflections on truth and certainty. Rather, we are just going about the ordinary business of living. However, there are some occasions on which we are engaging in serious philosophical reflection about the nature and quality of our knowledge.

Descartes maintains that it is reasonable to expect no more than a fairly modest degree of certainty or evidence in the things we believe while engaged in the practical affairs of life. So, for example, if you are hungry, and you want to eat, and you have taken the normal precautions concerning the wholesomeness of your food, it is reasonable to believe that it is not poisoned. Of course, it *might* be poisoned, but it would be absurd to refrain from eating just because you haven't proven beyond the shadow of a doubt that the food is safe. If the food has been properly handled, and it looks and smells all right, then, for all practical purposes, you are justified in believing that the food is not poisoned.

Let us say that a belief is "practically certain" for a person at a time, if it is justified well enough for the ordinary affairs of life. Thus, under normal circumstances, we have practical certainty that our food is not poisoned. Our evidence is good enough to justify us in believing this for all practical purposes. Descartes sometimes says that such beliefs are "morally certain." When a proposition is not practically certain, when we don't even have the ordinary degree of evidence for it, we can say that it is "practically doubtful" or "practically uncertain."

On the other hand, if a proposition is sufficiently well justified to permit us to believe it while engaged in the search after truth, we will say that it is "metaphysically certain." This is a much higher grade of certainty, and requires much better evidence. In one place, Descartes suggests that when a belief enjoys this higher grade of certainty, there will not be "even the least ground of suspicion against it."[7] Such a belief will be "absolutely certain." When a proposition is not metaphysically certain, then we can say it is "metaphysically doubtful," or "metaphysically uncertain."

It should be clear, then, that not every practical certainty is a metaphysical certainty. That is, not everything that is well enough justified for the ordinary affairs of life will be well enough justified for a search after truth. Clearly, some of the things that we are justified in believing for all practical purposes are less than absolutely certain. There might be some slight reason to suspect that they are false. For example, consider again the proposition that this food is not poisoned. This belief is not *absolutely* certain. We could gain greater certainty about it if we were to send the food to a laboratory, and have it tested—or if we were to ask someone to eat some, and then wait to see whether or not that person dies. And furthermore, there is some slight reason to suspect that the food is poisoned—after all, *some* food is poisoned, and this is food. So it might be poisoned. Thus, the proposition that the food is safe is a practical certainty, but not a metaphysical certainty. It is justified well enough to permit us to believe it for practical purposes, but it is less than absolutely certain. There are some slight reasons to doubt it.

[5] HR II, 44.
[6] HR I, 219–220.
[7] HR II, 266.

Since there are two grades of certainty, or justification, and knowledge is defined in terms of certainty, or justification, it follows that there are two grades of knowledge. The lower sort of knowledge, the kind that requires only practical certainty, may be called "practical knowledge," while the higher sort of knowledge, the kind that requires metaphysical certainty, can be called "metaphysical knowledge."

We can say that a person, S, has practical knowledge of some proposition, p, at some time, t, provided that p is true at t, S believes p at t, and p is practically certain for S at t. Ordinary, everyday knowledge is practical knowledge. We can say that S has metaphysical knowledge of p at t provided that p is true at t, S believes p at t, and S has metaphysical certainty of p at t. Metaphysical knowledge is a sort of "super knowledge." It is knowledge beyond the slightest shadow of a doubt. There are not many things of which we have metaphysical knowledge—at any rate, it's not easy to think of many right off. It may be interesting to note that Descartes explicitly recognizes this distinction between practical and metaphysical knowledge. While commenting upon some particularly annoying objections, Descartes says:

> when I said "I know" I spoke only of the moral mode of knowing, which suffices for the regulation of life, and which I have often insisted is so vastly different from that Metaphysical mode of knowing which is here in question....[8]

A Reply to the Skeptics

Now that we have introduced the distinction between practical and metaphysical knowledge, let us return to the skeptical arguments, to see how this distinction will provide the basis for a possible reply. Let's focus on the argument for skepticism about the future.

The first thing to notice is that the word "know" appears several times in the argument. We have just seen that there is an important distinction between two sorts of knowledge. Accordingly, we must consider the effect on the argument of interpreting the word "know" in the two ways we have distinguished. First, let us assume that "know" is used throughout to express practical knowledge. In this case, the argument as a whole looks like this:

1 I don't practically know whether a meteorite will hit the Statue of Liberty tonight.

2 If I don't practically know whether a meteorite will hit the Statue of Liberty tonight, then I don't practically know whether the Statue of Liberty will be standing tomorrow.

3 If I don't practically know whether the Statue of Liberty will be standing tomorrow, then no one practically knows any contingent truth about the future.

4 Therefore, no one practically knows any contingent truth about the future.

In this form, the argument is still valid, and the conclusion is a truly shocking claim. However, now there is reason to doubt the truth of the first premise. According to that premise, I don't have the ordinary, garden variety of knowledge

[8]HR II, 278.

concerning the proposition that no meteorite will hit the Statue of Liberty tonight. Yet this seems wrong. I think I practically know that the statue will not be hit. After all, no large man-made structure has been hit by a meteorite in all of recorded history. Indeed, the chances that a large meteorite will hit any given spot on the earth on any given night are infinitesimally small. Going on this inductive evidence, I am justified, for all practical purposes, in believing that no meteorite will hit the statue. Hence, though the argument is valid, it is not sound. Line (1) is false.

Of course, I cannot *prove* that no meteorite will hit the statue tonight. There is some slight chance that one will. Hence, I do not have metaphysical certainty on this matter. I do not metaphysically know that no meteorite will hit the statue tonight. Thus, if we interpret the "know" in line (1) as expressing metaphysical knowledge, line (1) will be true. Furthermore, if we treat every other occurrence of "know" in the argument in the same way, the whole thing will be valid, and every premise will presumably be true. Hence, it may seem that we still have a proof of skepticism with respect to the future. That is, this argument seems to be sound:

1 I don't metaphysically know whether a meteorite will hit the Statue of Liberty tonight.

2 If I don't metaphysically know whether a meteorite will hit the Statue of Liberty tonight, then I don't metaphysically know whether the Statue will be standing tomorrow.

3 If I don't metaphysically know whether the Statue will be standing tomorrow, then no one metaphysically knows any contingent truth about the future.

4 Therefore, no one metaphysically knows any contingent truth about the future.

I am inclined to think that, when interpreted in this way, the argument is sound. It really does establish a sort of skepticism with respect to the future. Nevertheless, I think the sort of skepticism it establishes is hardly surprising or controversial. Whoever thought that we know, with absolute certainty, what's going to happen tomorrow? Who is silly enough to think that our knowledge of future contingents is perfect and unshakable? Surely, anyone who has given it any serious thought realizes that such things admit only of practical knowledge. So the argument shows that we don't have metaphysical knowledge of the future—but anyone who understands what metaphysical knowledge is already appreciates that fact. It's not disconcerting.

I think you will find, if you reflect upon the argument, that there is no way to revise the argument so that it will soundly lead to the conclusion that we have no *practical* knowledge of the future. I leave it to the interested reader to figure out why this is so. So the upshot is that if we take the argument to be about practical knowledge, it has a remarkable conclusion, but an indefensible premise. If we take it to be about metaphysical knowledge, it is sound, but the conclusion is not of much interest. If we try to retain the interesting conclusion, but make the premises all true, the argument will lose its soundness. In any case, we have no proof of any surprising form of skepticism.

I am convinced that the other skeptical arguments can be rebutted in much the same way. In each case, as I see it, the argument establishes, at best, that we lack metaphysical knowledge. So I am willing to accept the conclusion that we do not have perfect knowledge of the past—there is some slight reason to doubt beliefs based on memory. And I am willing to accept the conclusion that we do not have perfect knowledge of the external world. Perception does not yield absolute knowledge. Yet I think that memory and perception do yield practical knowledge—knowledge that is good enough for the ordinary affairs of life. In light of this, we may say that the arguments establish "metaphysical skepticism" about the past, the future, and the external world, but they do not establish "practical skepticism." Who could possibly care about this?

CARTESIAN SKEPTICISM

FUNDAMENTALS OF CARTESIAN EPISTEMOLOGY[1]

In Chapter 2, we considered three skeptical arguments. One of these purports to show that we have no knowledge of the past. Another purports to show that we have no knowledge of the future. The final argument purports to show that we have no knowledge of the external world. By appeal to the Cartesian distinction between practical and metaphysical knowledge, I tried to rebut the arguments. As I see it, the arguments show, at best, that we do not have *metaphysical* knowledge of the past, future, and external world. In other words, our knowledge of these things is less than perfect. It admits of some slight doubt. Since anyone who understands the difference between practical and metaphysical certainty would accept this point, the arguments are less shocking than they might at first have appeared. Who could possibly be upset to learn that our knowledge of the past, the future, and the external world is less than perfect?

Epistemic Purification

One person who was upset about this matter was Descartes. He wanted to have perfect knowledge of everything concerning which it is possible to have perfect knowledge. He wanted to have no beliefs that were merely practically certain. He wanted every one of his beliefs to be a metaphysical certainty. Thus, he was troubled by the fact that, as things stood, many of his beliefs were less than perfectly certain.

It is hard to say exactly why Descartes disliked having less than metaphysically certain beliefs. One suggestion is that if a person has a whole lot of merely practically certain beliefs, then it is likely that quite a few of those beliefs are in fact

---

[1] Reading Assignment: the *First Meditation*, Cress, 13–16.

false. However, since each of the beliefs is practically certain, they are all equally well justified. The person will not know which of his beliefs is mistaken. Some false beliefs may then serve as evidence for more general beliefs. The general beliefs, based as they are on faulty evidence, may also be erroneous. In this way, a few mistaken assumptions may serve to undermine the whole structure of the person's beliefs.

Perhaps this is the point Descartes is making in the opening passage of the *First Meditation,* where he says:

> Several years have now passed since I first realized how many were the false opinions that in my youth I took to be true, and thus how doubtful were all the things that I subsequently built upon these opinions. From the time I became aware of this, I realized that for once I had to raze everything in my life, down to the very bottom, so as to begin again from the first foundations, if I wanted to establish anything firm and lasting in the sciences.[2]

There is another, and perhaps more important reason for being upset about having merely practically certain beliefs. This can be brought out by appeal to an analogy. A person can go through life eating nothing but "junk food." He can fill his stomach with artificially flavored, artificially colored, and chemically preserved items purchased from vending machines. I suspect that it is possible for someone to live a long and healthy life on such a diet. However, many sensitive people prefer to eat more wholesome foods. They choose to avoid artificial flavorings and colorings, and to stick to fresh, unadulterated items. They may do this because they think it is more healthful. But they may also do it on aesthetic grounds. Naturally wholesome foods taste, smell, and look better than their artificial counterparts. It's no wonder, then, that some people feel better knowing that their stomachs are full of pure foods, not a mish-mash of chemicals. Even if there were no health benefits to be derived from doing so, they would still prefer, on aesthetic grounds, to eat only natural foods.

Similarly, a person might prefer, on aesthetic grounds, to have a mind full of perfect certainties. He or she might recognize that merely practical certainties would suffice for all the ordinary affairs of life (just as junk food might keep you alive), but might nevertheless want to avoid such imperfect beliefs. Perhaps there is something beautiful in having every one of your beliefs perfectly justified, so that there isn't the slightest reason to doubt any of them. Be this as it may, Descartes was not satisfied to go through life with a mind full of imperfect beliefs. He wanted his beliefs to be metaphysically certain.

Descartes' "Method of Doubt"

Let us say that a person is "epistemically purified" at a time, t, provided that everything he believes at t is a metaphysical certainty for him at t. I think it is correct to say that Descartes wanted to become epistemically purified. However, merely saying this about his aim is insufficient. It would be possible to become epistemically purified while having just a small number of beliefs, and it would be possible to do so while having a large number of beliefs. Obviously, the more beliefs one has

[2]Cress, 13.

(provided that each is metaphysically certain) the better off one is, epistemically speaking. So Descartes didn't merely want to become epistemically purified—he wanted to become "maximally epistemically purified." That is, he wanted to have the richest array of beliefs it would be possible for him to have, consistent with every one of them being metaphysically certain.

Descartes once compared himself to a man with a basket of apples.[3] Just as Descartes suspected that some of his beliefs were false, this man suspects that some of his apples are rotten. How can the man go about checking his apples? What procedures are available to him? One idea is this: he can remove the apples from the basket one by one. Each time an apple is removed from the basket, it can be checked to see whether it is rotten. If it's rotten, it can be discarded. If it is sound, it can be returned to the basket. At the end of the procedure, the man will have a basket full of sound apples.

That procedure has a few problems. One problem is that it will be very hard to tell when the procedure has reached its conclusion. Suppose there is a small rotten apple right down at the bottom of the basket. Suppose it is completely covered over by good apples, so that the man has no way of seeing it. He might think he has checked every apple in the basket, even though that one rotten apple is still there. So he might think that he has completed the process of purifying his apples, when in fact he hasn't. Another problem with this procedure is that one rotten apple may spoil many others. So long as the bad apples are left in the basket, there is the chance that they will ruin ones that might otherwise be good.

Similar problems would arise for Descartes if he were to try to sift through his beliefs in a similar way. Some unnoticed little metaphysical uncertainty might remain "at the bottom of the basket," potentially spoiling others. For this reason, Descartes proposed a more radical approach. He described it by appeal to the analogy of the apple-basket:

> in order to prevent there being any rotten apples among those of which our tub or basket is full, we should begin by turning them all out, and then fill up once more either by putting back again those in which there is no flaw or getting similarly sound ones from elsewhere.[4]

So the Cartesian procedure requires "turning them all out" as the first step. This means that we are to reject (so far as possible) all of our beliefs. We are to suspend judgment with respect to virtually everything. Once we have succeeded in thus emptying our minds, we can begin to re-evaluate our old beliefs. Ones that are found to be metaphysically certain are to be returned. We can begin believing them again. Ones that are found to be less than metaphysically certain are to be thrown out, just as rotten apples are thrown out. It is to be hoped that some pretty substantial number of beliefs will pass the test. Otherwise, we will end up with very few beliefs.

Two points should be made here. The first involves the notion of "suspension of judgment." When we suspend judgment on some former belief, we stop believing it. We do not start believing its opposite. Suppose you believe that the earth is round. Now you want to suspend judgment on this proposition. You stop believing that the earth is round. You do not start believing that the earth is of some other shape. You

---

[3] HR II, 282. The passage occurs in Descartes' commentary on the seventh set of *Objections*.
[4] HR II, 307.

simply adopt no opinion as to the shape of the earth. If someone asks you about the shape of the earth, you have to say, "I have no opinion on that question. I do not think it's round. I do not think that it's non-round. I have suspended judgment on the question of the earth's shape." Descartes does not suggest that we try to adopt the opposite of each of our old beliefs. He suggests that we suspend judgment.

The second point I want to make here involves Descartes' assumption that it is within our power to stop believing things that we now believe. This is a very controversial assumption. Many philosophers would insist that we don't have any direct power to stop believing things that we believe. Consider some belief that you have. For example, you probably believe that there are many people in the world. Can you stop believing that? Can you get yourself to withhold judgment on the question whether there are many people in the world? Of course, you can *pretend* that you don't believe it, and you can *say* that you don't believe it, but these facts are irrelevant. The question is whether you can actually stop believing it. I have to admit that I find it very hard to change my beliefs in any direct way. I can't get rid of a belief just by willing to be rid of it. I have to argue myself out of it, or somehow convince myself that it might really be a mistake.

I believe that my view on this question is pretty much like Descartes'. He also thought that a person needs to have a reason in order to stop believing something he or she already believes. If there is simply no reason to doubt a certain belief, then it is not in one's power to doubt it. Since Descartes' first goal is to suspend judgment on as many of his old beliefs as he can, he has to find reasons for doubting these things. For each of them, he has to discover some objection, some criticism, that shows that the belief is not as well justified as it might have been. If he can find such a reason for doubt, he will be able to suspend his judgment.

Descartes' Epistemic Principle

It will be useful, now, to formulate in a general way the fundamental principle guiding Descartes' efforts. As I see it, the principle tells us what we must do if we want to become maximally epistemically purified. And what it says is that, if we do have this goal, then, having selected an appropriate moment, we must "turn out all our apples." That is, we must suspend judgment on as many of our former beliefs as we can. Since, according to Descartes, we can suspend judgment on a belief only if it is less than perfectly certain, the result is that we are to suspend judgment on all such beliefs. So the Cartesian epistemic principle is this:

> Once in his or her life, a person who seeks maximal epistemic purification must suspend judgment on everything that is less than metaphysically certain.

It is important to recognize that this is a principle that cannot be acted upon with abandon. If you refrain from believing everything for which there is the slightest reason for doubt, you will surely refrain from believing lots of things you now believe. You may stop believing things that are directly related to the practical affairs of life. For example, you may stop believing that your food will nourish you. Perhaps then you won't be motivated to eat. You may stop believing that oncoming automobiles can injure you. Perhaps then you won't be motivated to look both ways before crossing. Descartes realized this. He knew that his project was not only difficult, but dangerous. He knew that it could reasonably be undertaken only when the conditions were just right. In the *First Meditation,* he says that he has found an opportune moment:

> The present is opportune for my design; I have freed my mind of all kinds of cares; I feel myself, fortunately, disturbed by no passions; and I have found a serene retreat in peaceful solitude. I will therefore make a serious and unimpeded effort to destroy generally all my former opinions.[5]

SKEPTICISM WITH RESPECT TO THE SENSES

Since Descartes wanted to suspend judgment with respect to as many as possible of his former beliefs, and he thought he could do this only if he could find reasons for such doubt, he felt that he had to find reasons for doubting those beliefs. He realized that it would be impossible to go through his beliefs one by one, and find a reason for doubting each of them individually. Rather, he had to find some reasons for doubting large classes of beliefs. At the beginning of the *First Meditation,* Descartes considers the idea that there is a single reason that suffices to cast every one of his former beliefs into doubt. This reason for doubt applies to every belief based upon sense perception. Everything that is derived from sense experience is such that this reason shows it to be less than perfectly certain. If every belief is based somehow on sense perception, then this reason for doubt applies to every belief. And what is this reason? Descartes explains it in this passage:

> Whatever I had admitted until now as most true I took in either from the senses or through the senses; however, I noticed that they sometimes deceived me. And it is a mark of prudence never to trust wholly in those things which have once deceived us.[6]

Descartes' point seems to be based on the fact that the senses sometimes deceive. This is undoubtedly true. If you don't believe it, stick your finger into the side of your right eyeball. Now press on your eyeball until you see double. Select some object that you are now "seeing twice." Your senses are telling you that there are two such objects there, but there is really just one. Hence, your senses are deceiving you. This shows that the senses sometimes deceive. Of course, many other experiments could have been used to establish the same point. A straight stick immersed in a glass of water looks crooked. A distant tower may look round, though it is really square. A traveler in the desert may seem to see an oasis, when it is just a mirage. So Descartes is surely right. The senses sometimes do deceive.

Descartes suggests that this fact casts doubt upon every belief based upon sense perception. Since the senses sometimes deceive, every proposition based on sense perception is less than perfectly certain. Each such proposition is such that there is some slight reason to doubt it. Take any belief based upon sense perception. It might be one that is erroneous. Hence, each such proposition is less than metaphysically certain, and so must be doubted by anyone undertaking a general overthrow of all previous beliefs in accordance with the Cartesian epistemic principle.

[5]Cress, 13.
[6]Cress, 13.

At this point, Descartes apparently assumes that every one of his former beliefs is based on sense perception. Hence, the fact that the senses sometimes deceive seems to give Descartes a reason to doubt everything he formerly believed. Since he had decided that this is the time to suspend judgment on everything that is less than metaphysically certain, he must now suspend judgment on every one of his former beliefs.

Descartes' reasoning here may be put into the form of an argument. I shall first present the argument, and then I will go back and explain the basis for each premise.

The Argument from Sense Deception

1 My senses sometimes deceive me.

2 If my senses sometimes deceive me, then every belief based on sense perception is less than metaphysically certain.

3 If every belief based on sense perception is less than metaphysically certain, then each of my former beliefs is less than metaphysically certain.

4 Now is the time when I must suspend judgment on everything that is less than metaphysically certain.

5 Therefore, now is the time when I must suspend judgment on each of my former beliefs.

The first premise of this argument is based on any of a number of little experiments anyone can easily perform. The bent stick in water, the finger in the eye, etc. all show that the senses sometimes deceive. So line (1) is pretty clearly true.

Line (2) is justified by appeal to the principle that we must never wholly trust anyone who has once deceived us. If the senses are known to deceive sometimes, then nothing they produce is wholly certain. Everything based upon sense perception is tainted. It comes from a questionable source. Thus, every such proposition is less than metaphysically certain.

Line (3) records Descartes' tentative assumption that every one of his former beliefs is derived from the senses. We will have more to say about this momentarily. For now, it is sufficient to see that if all sense-based propositions are uncertain, and all former beliefs are sense-based, then all former beliefs are uncertain.

As we saw earlier, Descartes has determined that now is the time for him to undertake the general overthrow of his former beliefs. Of course, he can only suspend judgment on beliefs for which there is a reason for doubt. But, now is the time to doubt every one of those. Line (4) records this procedural commitment. It may be viewed as an instance of the fundamental Cartesian epistemic principle, the principle that says that once in his or her life, a person who seeks maximal epistemic purification must suspend judgment on everything that is less than perfectly certain.

Line (5) validly follows from the earlier premises. It is the conclusion of the argument. If the argument is otherwise successful, it shows that Descartes is ready to "turn out all his apples." He has discovered a reason that casts doubt on all of his former beliefs, and so he can suspend judgment on them all. Then, perhaps, he can start to find some perfect certainties to take the place of his former uncertainties.

The Nature of Cartesian "Skepticism"

According to the interpretation I have proposed, the main point of this argument is somewhat different from the main point of traditional skeptical arguments, such as the ones discussed above in Chapter 2. Descartes does not use the argument to show that we really don't know as much as we might have thought. Rather, he uses the argument to show that all of his former beliefs are less than perfectly certain, and hence, since he is engaging in the process of epistemic purification, he must suspend judgment on such beliefs. It does not follow that ordinary people, who are not engaging in epistemic purification, really don't have ordinary knowledge of things based upon sense perception. For all Descartes has said, every such belief could be a quite satisfactory piece of practical knowledge. So he is not suggesting that ordinary people should stop believing the things they now believe, or that it is somehow irrational for them to hold the beliefs they do hold. He's trying to show that, if you have a higher epistemic standard, and want to have nothing less than metaphysical certainties, and the time has come for you to set about achieving this goal, then you must stop believing all the things you now believe.

Problems with the Argument from Sense Deception

Unfortunately, the first argument fails. There are several things wrong with it. In the first place, as Descartes points out, the fact that the senses sometimes deceive does not provide grounds for doubting all sense-based propositions. There is no reason here for Descartes to doubt that he has hands, or that he is seated by the fire. These beliefs concern things that are so easy to perceive, and that are so near and obvious, that there is no serious chance that the senses might be deceptive concerning them. So it appears that Descartes would have said that line (2) of our version of the argument is false. From the fact that the senses sometimes deceive, it does not follow that *every* sense-based belief is metaphysically uncertain.

Although Descartes did not say so, it appears to me that line (3) is also doubtful. Even if every sense-based belief were doubtful, some beliefs might still be certain, for some beliefs are apparently not based on sense perception. Consider, for example, the belief that three is a prime number. If you have the concept of primeness, and you know which number three is, you may be able to see that this is true. Your knowledge, in this case, is not based upon sense experience. If you were called upon to justify the belief that three is prime, you surely would not appeal to "how things look," or "how things smell." Propositions such as this are sometimes said to be knowable *a priori.* A person knows such a thing *a priori,* provided that he knows it, and his justification for believing it is independent of sense experience. If you have any *a priori* knowledge, then you have some knowledge that is not cast into doubt by the possibility of sense deception. In any case, line (3) seems to me to be open to question.

So the fact that the senses sometimes deceive does not give Descartes reason to doubt all of his former beliefs. It does not provide reason to doubt sense-based propositions concerning near and obvious objects, and it does not provide reason to doubt *a priori* propositions. There are other sorts of propositions that are not cast into doubt by the possibility of sense deception, but we won't discuss them until we come to the *Second Meditation.*

THE INSANITY ARGUMENT

In the passage immediately following the one we have been discussing, Descartes makes a number of comments about lunatics. He says that such people

> continually insist that they are kings when they are in utter poverty, or that they are wearing purple robes when they are naked, or that they have a head made of clay, or that they are gourds, or that they are made of glass.[7]

Many commentators have maintained that there is another argument in this passage. According to them, Descartes is claiming that he has no way of determining for sure that he is sane. Hence, for all he knows, he might be insane. The possibility that he is insane constitutes a reason for doubting all of his former beliefs. In light of this, none of those beliefs is beyond metaphysical doubt.

Let us say that a "criterion" for sanity would be an easily recognizable mark, or symptom, of sanity. To be a genuine criterion of sanity, such a mark would be present if and only if the person were truly sane. So, if you want to know whether or not a person is sane, and there is a criterion of sanity, then all you need to do is check to see whether the criterion is present. If it is present, the person is sane. If it is not present, the person is not sane. Since it would be relatively easy to determine whether or not the criterion is present, it would be relatively easy to determine whether or not the person is sane.

A good case can be made for the view that there is no criterion that you can use to determine whether or not you are sane. For consider any alleged mark of sanity. Now suppose you are insane, and you are checking to determine whether or not the mark is present in you. Since you are insane, you may very well conclude that the mark is present—it's typical of insane people to be deluded about themselves in this way. Hence, if you are insane, it may not be possible for you to determine whether or not the mark of sanity is present. Thus, you cannot use the alleged criterion, whatever it might be, to find out that you are insane. This gives us the crucial premise for our second Cartesian argument.

The Argument from Insanity

1 There is no criterion that I can use to determine whether or not I am insane.

2 If there is no criterion that I can use to determine whether or not I am insane, then every one of my former beliefs is less than metaphysically certain.

3 Now is the time when I must suspend judgment on everything that is less than metaphysically certain.

4 Therefore, now is the time when I must suspend judgment on every one of my former beliefs.

A Problem for the Insanity Argument

A careful scrutiny of the text of the *First Meditation* will reveal that neither this, nor any other argument based on the possibility of insanity is to be found. Descartes does not make use of or comment upon any such argument in the *Meditations*.

---

[7]Cress, 14.

There are some remarks about insanity in the paragraph we have been considering, but those remarks cannot be interpreted as the basis of a Cartesian skeptical argument. Rather, they are best understood as being a critical comment on the preceding argument—the argument concerning sense deception.

It may be useful to have the comments in question before us:

> But perhaps, although the senses sometimes deceive us when it is a question of very small and distant things, still there are many other matters which one certainly cannot doubt, although they are derived from the very same senses: that I am sitting here before the fireplace wearing my dressing gown, that I feel this sheet of paper in my hands, and so on. But how could one deny that these hands and that my whole body exist? Unless perhaps I should compare myself to insane people whose brains are so impaired...that they continually insist that they are kings when they are in utter poverty.... But they are all demented, and I would appear no less demented if I were to take their conduct as a model for myself.[8]

It should be clear that Descartes is not saying that for all he knows, he might be crazy. Rather, he is saying that only a crazy person would think that his senses could be deceiving him with respect to such matters as that he is seated before his fire, or holding a piece of paper in his hands. These things are based upon sense perception, and sense perception is sometimes deceptive. Nevertheless, one would have to be insane to think that his senses are deceiving him in these perfectly clear cases. The objects in question are too near and too large. There simply isn't any chance that they are being misperceived. So, on the interpretation I am proposing, these remarks about insanity should be viewed as a critical comment on line (2) of the argument from sense deception. Descartes is saying that the fact that the senses sometimes deceive does not give us reason to doubt all sense-based beliefs. Some sense-based beliefs are not cast into doubt by the fact that the senses sometimes deceive. You would have to be insane to think otherwise.

THE DREAM ARGUMENT

In the next paragraph, Descartes points out a very powerful reason for doubt. He remarks that he is accustomed to sleeping at night, and to experiencing in his sleep things as bizarre as those experienced by insane people. This, of course, serves to introduce the justly famous dream argument.

> How often has my evening slumber persuaded me of such customary things as these: that I am here, clothed in my dressing gown, seated at the fireplace, when in fact I am lying undressed between the blankets![9]

Descartes goes on to consider the suggestion that his present sense experiences are simply too distinct to be dream experiences. His head does not feel "heavy with sleep." Can't he know, then, that he is in fact not dreaming now? The answer, of course, is that he cannot know any such thing. For he can recall occasions in the past when he was deceived by just such experiences while dreaming. He concludes that "there are no definite signs to distinguish being awake from being asleep."

[8]Cress, 14.
[9]Cress, 14.

Making use of the technical terminology introduced above, we can rephrase the main point of Descartes' remarks. As I see it, he is suggesting that there is no criterion by which I can determine whether or not I am dreaming right now. If there were a criterion by which I could determine that I was not dreaming, then there would be some feature of my experience that would be present if and only if I were not dreaming. Furthermore, it would be relatively easy to determine whether or not the feature is present. What might such a feature be?

Some Proposed Criteria for Wakefulness

Some philosophers have suggested that our waking experiences have a kind of vividness that is absent from our dream experiences. When we are awake, and we are actually seeing some physical object in the external world, our visual imagery is bright, crisp, and sharply defined. On the other hand, when we dream, our visual imagery has a "dream-like" quality. It is hazy and blurred, especially around the edges. Thus, it might be said that *vividness* is a criterion by which we can determine that we are not dreaming. According to this view, you can always tell whether or not you are dreaming. Focus your attention on some object you can see. If the object seems bright and vivid, you are really seeing it, and you are awake. On the other hand, if the object seems hazy and blurred, then you are only dreaming that you see it. You are asleep.

If this claim about vividness were correct, then we could always tell whether or not we were dreaming. However, I think it is pretty obvious that the claim about vividness is not correct. Our dream experiences are sometimes quite vivid—even more vivid than ordinary perceptual experiences. Equally, our waking experiences are sometimes not very vivid at all. For example, if you are very tired, have had too much to drink, and are driving home on a foggy night, your visual experiences may be quite hazy and indistinct. Such experiences lack vividness. That provides good reason for you not to drive under such circumstances, but it doesn't provide good reason for you to think that you're really just dreaming!

Other philosophers have suggested that our waking experiences differ from our dream experiences since the former are "connected," whereas the latter are not. When we say that waking experiences are "connected," we mean to draw attention to the fact that the events and objects we observe seem to follow certain regular patterns. Things do not just "pop into existence" or "pop out of existence." Things do not change their locations without passing through the intervening space. If an object is observed in a certain spot at one moment, and nothing affects the object, it will be observed in the same location at the next moment. Dream experiences, it has been alleged, often lack this feature. In a dream, a person might suddenly see a tree, or a huge rock, where a moment ago there was nothing. A strange animal or even a monster might suddenly come into view, or inexplicably undergo some bizarre transformation. Thus, according to this proposal, the experiences we have in our dreams lack the coherence or connectedness of our waking experiences. If this is correct, then there is a criterion by which we can determine whether or not we are dreaming.

Of course, the second proposal is no more successful than the first. Our waking experiences are sometimes rather incoherent, and our dream experiences are sometimes as coherent as can be. To see that waking experiences can be incoherent, consider what happens at a good magic show. The magician makes it seem that objects just pop into existence from out of nowhere. You may rub your eyes in disbelief, but you know perfectly well that you are awake.

Equally, dream experiences might be quite coherent. A person could have a long dream in which objects behave in a quite regular and systematic way. Such dreams might be duller than average, but they are certainly possible.

A deeper problem for any proposed criterion for wakefulness has to do with whether it can properly be applied. Can I know that I have checked my experience for vividness, or connectedness, or whatever? This seems doubtful. To see why, suppose that in fact dream experiences do differ from waking experiences in some observable way. For example, suppose that dreams are always in black and white, while waking experiences are always in full color. (I realize that this is not a very plausible supposition.) Does this provide me with a criterion by which I can determine that I am not dreaming?

If I am awake, I can see that my visual experiences are fully colored. I can conclude that I am awake and hence, not dreaming. However, if I am asleep, it will not be so easy for me. Given our supposition, my visual imagery will all be in black and white. However, I may dream that I am checking it, and I may dream that I am finding it to be in color. After I wake up, I may realize my mistake, but during the dream, I may be utterly deceived. Thus, even if there is some feature that is present if and only if I am awake, this may fail to constitute a criterion for wakefulness. To be a criterion, it has to be a feature such that I can readily determine whether or not it is present. The problem is that, in a dream, I my think that I have made a proper determination, when in fact I have not.

This shows, by the way, why it's so pointless for you to pinch yourself to see if you're awake. You may dream that you are pinching yourself, and you may dream that you are finding yourself to be awake. Of course, if you are just dreaming that you are doing this, you are mistaken. In light of these considerations, it would appear that Descartes' suggestion may be right. Perhaps there is no criterion by which I can determine whether or not I am awake. We now have to consider how this claim figures in Descartes' argument.

Formulating The Dream Argument

It is important to recognize that, in the passage we are considering, Descartes does not present very much of the argument. What, then, is the relevance of the fact (if it is a fact) that there is no criterion for wakefulness? As I see it, it is this: if there's no criterion for wakefulness, then, for all I know, I might be dreaming right now. If I am dreaming, then many of the things that seem most certain are in fact false. For example, it seems perfectly certain that I am sitting up in a chair right now, but if this is all a dream, I'm probably in bed, and not sitting up in a chair. Thus, the fact that I might be dreaming casts some slight, metaphysical doubt on everything that seems most certain. If this is the time when I must refrain from believing everything that's less than perfectly certain, then this is the time when I must refrain from believing everything—for everything is less than perfectly certain.

In order to make discussion easier, let us consider a somewhat more formal reconstruction of the dream argument. On my interpretation, it goes as follows:

The Dream Argument

1 There is no criterion by which I can determine that I am not dreaming.

2 If there is no criterion by which I can determine that I am not dreaming, then everything I formerly believed is less than metaphysically certain.

3 Now is the time when I must refrain from believing everything that is less than metaphysically certain.

4 Therefore, now is the time when I must refrain from believing everything I formerly believed.

If interpreted in the way I have suggested, the dream argument is not a skeptical argument of the traditional sort. It is not designed to show that we really don't know the things we ordinarily take ourselves to know. So far as ordinary, practical knowledge is concerned, the argument is irrelevant. Rather, it is designed to show that even our most certain beliefs are less than perfectly certain—there is at least one slight reason to doubt them. This reason, of course, is that we might be dreaming. If we are undertaking a general overthrow of all our less-than-perfectly-certain beliefs, then we have reason to refrain from believing everything we formerly believed. If understood in this way, the dream argument seems to me to be extremely persuasive.

Descartes' Rejection of the Dream Argument

It is important to recognize, however, that Descartes *rejects* the argument. As he sees it, the possibility that he is dreaming *fails* to give him a reasonable basis for universal doubt. His objection to the argument seems to be based on a certain theory about dreams. According to this view, every visual image consists of various "simple and universal" images combined in some way so as to form some compound image. Perhaps the "simple and universal" images are the various colors, shapes, and sizes. In a dream, I may have a compound image that I have never experienced before. Thus, I may dream of a siren or a satyr, even though I have never seen any such thing. However, the simple components out of which these complexes are formed "are, as it were, like painted images, which could have been produced only in the likeness of true things."[10] And so he concludes that even if the compounds we experience in dreams are imaginary, nevertheless the simple elements of which they are composed must be based on realities.

The upshot is that Descartes rejects line (2) of the dream argument. He seems to be saying that the possibility that I am dreaming does not show that all of my former beliefs are less than perfectly certain. Some of those beliefs—ones having to do with "simple and universal" things—are not cast into metaphysical doubt by the fact that there is no criterion by which I can determine whether or not I am dreaming. He concludes by saying: "For whether I be awake or asleep, two plus three makes five,

---

[10]Cress, 14.

and a square does not have more than four sides: nor does it seem possible that such obvious truths can fall under the suspicion of falsity."[11]

It seems to me that Descartes' rejection of the dream argument is far too hasty. In a dream, I could easily make a mistake about "simple and universal things." I could dream that I have added two and three, and that I have found that their sum is six. I could dream that I have counted the sides of a square, and that I have found that it has five sides. Thus, It seems to me that no matter how certain I feel about some relatively simple matter, so long as I don't know for sure that I'm not dreaming, that matter is not perfectly certain. Be this as it may, Descartes was not satisfied with the dream argument. He went on to consider something he took to be an even more powerful reason for doubt.

THE DECEPTIVE GOD ARGUMENT

We now turn to the most important of the arguments of the *First Meditation*. This is the argument that finally convinces Descartes that he in fact does have reason to doubt just about everything he formerly accepted. The passage begins with these words:

> All the same, a certain opinion of long standing has been fixed in my mind, namely that there exists a God who is able to do anything and by whom I, such as I am, have been created. How do I know that he did not bring it about that there be no earth at all, no heavens, no extended thing, no figure, no size, no place, and yet all these things should seem to me to exist precisely as they appear to do now?[12]

Descartes' point seems to be that an omnipotent God would surely be powerful enough to cause an ordinary mortal such as Descartes to make the most outrageous of errors. An all-powerful God could easily make Descartes err with respect to the most obvious of perceptual matters. For example, such a God could make Descartes think he has a body, and lives upon an earth, when in fact he is just a bodiless spirit living in some nonphysical heaven. Equally, such a being could cause Descartes to err with respect to the "simple and universal" ideas mentioned above in connection with the dream argument. God could make Descartes think, for example, that there are five-sided squares, or that two plus three equals six. Thus, if there is a God, then there is a being powerful enough to make Descartes go wrong even with respect to the things that seem to him most certain. Since for all he knows there is a God, all such things are less than perfectly certain.

Some theists might insist that God would not lead Descartes into such wholesale error. Such deceit would be contrary to God's goodness. But Descartes rejects this reasoning. He points out that God allows us to be deceived at least some of the time. Thus, it appears that some deceitfulness is possible in God. Why not *total* deceitfulness?[13]

Descartes realized that some philosophers would not be moved by this argument, for they would simply reject the idea that there might be a God. If there is no God,

---

[11]Cress, 14.

[12]Cress, 15.

[13]Later on, Descartes discusses this point at some length. See below, Chapter 7, under "God and Knowledge."

then there is no deceitful God. In this case, there's no justification for universal doubt. For anyone in doubt about the existence of God, Descartes adds a certain complexity to the argument. He points out that if I haven't been created by an omnipotent God, then I must have come to be as I am by "fate or chance or a continuous series of events or by some other way."[14] Such causes as these are obviously less powerful than an omnipotent God would be. However, a less powerful cause would undoubtedly have a less perfect effect. So if I was created by something less powerful than God, then I was created by something that could easily have made me imperfect. One likely sort of imperfection would be intellectual imperfection. So if I was created by an imperfect cause, then I probably make lots of mistakes—even with respect to the things that seem most certain to me. The more imperfect my cause, the more likely it is that I am thus "epistemically defective." So even an atheist has some reason to doubt the things that seem most certain to him.

Formulating the Deceptive God Argument

The overall structure of the argument is only slightly more complex than that of the earlier arguments. The basic idea is this: there are two possible ways in which I might have been created. Either I was created by God, or I was created by something less powerful than God. If I was created by God, then I was created by a being powerful enough to make me go wrong even in what seems most certain. Hence, in that case, none of my beliefs is metaphysically certain. On the other hand, if I was created by something less perfect than God, then I was created by something weak enough to have made me epistemically defective. In this case, none of my beliefs is metaphysically certain. Hence, no matter how I was created, nothing is metaphysically certain. Every one of my former beliefs is thus cast into doubt, and should be discarded.

Let us attempt to summarize the main points of the argument as follows:

The Deceptive God Argument

1 Either I was created by God or I was created by something less powerful than God.

2 If I was created by God, then I was created by something powerful enough to make me go wrong in what seems most certain.

3 If I was created by something powerful enough to make me go wrong in what seems most certain, then everything I formerly believed is less than metaphysically certain.

4 If I was created by something less powerful than God, then I may have defective epistemic faculties.

5 If I may have defective epistemic faculties, then everything I formerly believed is less than metaphysically certain.

6 Now is the time when I must refrain from believing everything that is less than metaphysically certain.

---

[14]Cress, 15.

7 Therefore, now is the time when I must refrain from believing everything I formerly believed.

In my opinion, the deceptive God argument is the central argument of the *First Meditation.* It is the argument that finally convinces Descartes that he must withhold assent from all of his former beliefs. In other words, it is the argument that gives him reason to "turn out all his apples." In light of the importance of this argument, it may be worthwhile to study it in some detail.

First of all, we should recognize that, as formulated here, the argument is logically valid. If all the premises are true, then the conclusion must be true as well. Furthermore, each of the premises seems pretty reasonable.

The first premise says little more than that Descartes was created by something. Assuming that he was created by something, we can see that this "something" must either be omnipotent or less than omnipotent. Nothing can be more powerful than an omnipotent God. Even if Descartes created himself, still line (1) would be true—for in this case, Descartes would have been created by something less powerful than God—namely, Descartes himself.

The second premise is also quite plausible. An omnipotent being is one that can do anything that's possible. Surely it is possible for Descartes to be mistaken about the things that seem most certain. Therefore, if he was created by God, he was created by a being powerful enough to make him be mistaken about what seems most certain. This is not to say that God in fact wants Descartes to be mistaken. It is only to say that, if he exists, he is powerful enough to make Descartes err.

Line (3) merely points out that if Descartes was created by a God powerful enough to make him err with respect to the beliefs that are most certain, then each such belief is less than a perfect certainty. So, for example, consider the proposition that two plus three equals five. This may seem perfectly obvious. However, no matter how obvious it seems, it must be admitted that an omnipotent God would be powerful enough to make a falsehood seem just that obvious. Therefore, there is some slight reason to doubt that two and three equals five. Maybe God is deceiving us with respect to this matter. Hence, though this simple arithmetical truth is a practical certainty, it is not a metaphysical certainty. Apparently, similar reasoning would show that every other belief, no matter how strong the evidence, also fails to be metaphysically certain at this stage.

Line (4) takes up the other possibility concerning Descartes' creation. Maybe he was not created by an omnipotent God. Maybe he was created by chance, or fate, or a series of events. In this case he was created by something less powerful than God. This seems right. Since a less perfect cause would undoubtedly have a less perfect effect, it seems to follow that, if Descartes was created by some less perfect cause, then it is more likely that Descartes would be imperfect in various ways. In particular, he might have defective epistemic faculties. The epistemic faculties are the powers of perception and reasoning. To say that these faculties may be defective is to say that the beliefs acquired by their use may be false.

Obviously, if Descartes has some reason to suspect that his epistemic faculties are defective, then he has some reason to doubt even the most certain of the beliefs acquired by the use of those faculties. Every such belief is less than metaphysically certain because every such belief, no matter how clear it may seem, is the product of a belief-forming system whose reliability is questionable. Thus we have line (5).

As we have seen, Descartes has determined that the time is ripe for him to refrain from believing everything that is less than metaphysically certain. This is in accordance with his fundamental epistemic principle—once in his or her life, anyone who seeks maximal epistemic purification must suspend judgment with respect to everything that is less than metaphysically certain. The previous premises of the argument entail that everything is less than metaphysically certain, and so the conclusion follows that now is the time to suspend judgment with respect to everything formerly accepted. Descartes must turn out all his apples.

It would be a mistake to suppose that Descartes thinks that these considerations show that ordinary people don't know the things they take themselves to know, or that we are being irrational in believing the things that we believe. The deceptive God argument is not an old-fashioned skeptical argument. Rather, it is intended to show that the ordinary beliefs of ordinary people are (for the most part) less than perfectly certain. Every such belief is tainted by a slight reason for doubt. Until we know how we have been created, and by whom, our beliefs cannot be metaphysical certainties. If we wish to become epistemically purified, then we will have to select an appropriate time, and get rid of all these beliefs. If you aren't interested in epistemic purification, or if your time has not come, you certainly may go on holding your beliefs. But Descartes did care about epistemic purification, and he felt that his time had come. So he was convinced that he had to withhold assent from everything he formerly believed, no matter how reasonable such beliefs might have seemed.

THE EVIL DEMON

In the final paragraph of the *First Meditation,* Descartes mentions "an evil genius, as clever and deceitful as he is powerful, who has directed his entire effort to misleading me."[15] Descartes describes this demon as being very powerful —perhaps as powerful as God. But unlike God, this spirit is malicious. He delights in causing Descartes to make mistakes.

It is almost universally assumed that these remarks about the evil demon provide the basis for a final Cartesian skeptical argument. The fundamental premise of the argument is that, for all Descartes knows, there might be an evil demon such as the one imagined. If such a thing is a genuine possibility, then there is reason to suspect that even what seems most certain is really false. To see why, consider something that seems perfectly obvious. For example, consider the proposition that there is an earth. That surely seems to be true. However, a sufficiently powerful and sufficiently malicious demon could fool us into thinking that there is an earth when in fact there isn't. Perhaps we are really just bodiless spirits floating in space, and the demon has tricked us into thinking that we are embodied human beings walking upon a solid planet. Maybe this demon causes us to have all the sensory experiences we would have if there were an earth.

[15]Cress, 16.

Obviously, such speculations are utterly unfounded. There is no reason to suppose that there is such a demon, or that we are being deceived in the manner suggested. However, we cannot absolutely rule out the possibility that the demon exists as imagined. Thus, there is some slight reason to doubt that there is an earth. Equally, there is some slight reason to doubt just about every other seemingly well-justified belief. I of course am not suggesting that the possibility of the demon shows that we really don't know that there is an earth, or that all of our ordinary beliefs are epistemically worthless. All I am suggesting is that every such belief is made metaphysically uncertain by the possibility of the evil demon.

The argument as a whole may be formulated in this way:

The Evil Demon Argument

1 I cannot prove that there is no evil demon.

2 If I cannot prove that there is no evil demon, then each of my former beliefs is less than metaphysically certain.

3 Now is the time when I must suspend judgment on everything that is less than metaphysically certain.

4 Therefore, now is the time when I must suspend judgment on each of my former beliefs.

While this is a marvelous little argument, I do not think Descartes makes use of it, or anything relevantly like it, in the *Meditations*. A careful look at the text will reveal, I believe, that the evil demon hypothesis plays quite a different sort of role. It is not a premise in an argument. In order to understand the true function of the demon hypothesis, let us look more closely at the passage in which it is introduced.

The Role of the Evil Demon Hypothesis

After presenting and commenting upon the deceptive God argument, Descartes concludes:

> I have nothing to say in response to these arguments. At length I am forced to admit that there is nothing, among the things I once believed to be true, which it is not permissible to doubt—not for reasons of frivolity or a lack of forethought, but because of valid and considered arguments.[16]

However, Descartes points out that it is not so easy to doubt all of his former beliefs. In some cases, the beliefs seem so plausible and fitting that it is almost impossible to get rid of them. As Descartes says:

> For long-standing opinions keep coming back again and again, almost against my will; they seize upon my credulity, as if it were bound over to them by long use and the claims of intimacy.[17]

So Descartes faces a sort of psychological problem. He is convinced that there are reasons to suspend judgment with respect to all of his former beliefs. Now is the

[16]Cress, 15–16
[17]Cress, 16.

time when he is to undertake the suspension of judgment. However, he finds that he is unable to do so. The old beliefs "keep coming back." He finds himself believing the very things he has decided to reject. If you don't understand the difficulty, try to stop believing that there's an earth, and a sky, and trees and grass. I think you will find that it's not easy.

It is here that Descartes first mentions the demon. He says:

> Hence, it seems to me, I would do well to turn my will in the opposite direction, to deceive myself and pretend for a considerable period that they are wholly false and imaginary, until finally, as if with equal weight of prejudice on both sides, no bad habit should turn my judgment from the correct perception of things.... Thus I will suppose not a supremely good God, the source of truth, but rather an evil genius, as clever and deceitful as he is powerful,... has directed his entire effort to misleading me.[18]

I think it is clear that the evil demon hypothesis is introduced not as a premise in an argument, but as a sort of psychological tool—a pretense that will help Descartes to rid himself of his former beliefs. He pretends that he is being fooled by an evil demon, and that all his old beliefs are false. By concentrating on this pretense, he counteracts his natural tendency to fall back into his old pattern of metaphysically uncertain beliefs. After sufficient time, the pretense will have succeeded in getting him into a state in which he can suspend judgment on virtually everything he formerly accepted. He will have "turned out all his apples." The next stage in the process involves the search for some "sound apples," or metaphysically certain beliefs, to put back into his basket. We will consider that stage in Chapter 4.

---

[18]Cress, 16.

THE COGITO

WHAT IS THE COGITO?[1]

"I think, therefore I exist" (or, in Latin, *Cogito, ergo sum*) is undoubtedly one of the most widely known and often quoted of philosophical remarks, and Descartes is the man who said it. Although the *Meditations* is Descartes' most famous philosophical work, the remark in question does not appear there. To find the famous words, one must look into Descartes' *Discourse on Method*,[2] or his *Principles of Philosophy*.[3] Other remarks, apparently with just about the same meaning, however, can be found near the beginning of the *Second Meditation*.

The phrase, "Cogito, ergo sum" is sometimes called "the Cogito." If we understand the name in this way, we will have to say that the Cogito does not appear in the *Meditations*. However, since relevantly similar words do appear in the *Meditations*, it would be convenient to use the name in some other way. Let us agree to use the name "the Cogito," to refer to the third paragraph of the *Second Meditation*. So, for our purposes here, the Cogito is the passage beginning with the words: "But on what grounds do I know that there is nothing over and above all those which I have just reviewed...," and ending with the words: "...one must come to the considered judgment that the statement 'I am, I exist' is necessarily true every time it is uttered by me or conceived by my mind."[4]

In the two paragraphs immediately preceding the Cogito, Descartes reviews his epistemic situation. He thinks he has discovered that every one of his former beliefs

---

[1] Reading Assignment: the first three paragraphs of the *Second Meditation*, Cress, 17.
[2] HR I, 101.
[3] HR I, 221.
[4] Cress, 17.

is less than metaphysically certain. Each one of those beliefs is cast into doubt by the fact that Descartes might have been created by a deceitful God, or by some relatively imperfect sequence of accidents. In either case, no matter how certain a belief seems, it still may be false. In accordance with his fundamental epistemic principle, Descartes has decided to suspend judgment on all these beliefs, even though many of them are sufficiently well justified for ordinary purposes. We may assume that Descartes has succeeded in withholding his assent from all of these former beliefs. His mind is now empty. It's like the basket from which all the apples have been removed.

At this point, Descartes starts to search for some proposition that he can accept. To be acceptable for Descartes under these circumstances, a proposition has to be metaphysically certain. It must be utterly beyond doubt. There must be no reason at all to suspect it of falsehood. If no such proposition can be found, the Cartesian enterprise will end in failure. He will have to acknowledge that, if he is to have any beliefs, he will have to have metaphysically uncertain beliefs. Epistemic purification will be beyond his powers.

The first proposition that Descartes considers at this point is the proposition that God exists. Maybe it will turn out to be the first metaphysical certainty. After all, Descartes finds various thoughts going through his mind, and so maybe God is "instilling" those thoughts in him. That would show that God exists. But Descartes immediately rejects this proposal. "But why should I think that, since perhaps I myself could be the author of these things?" Descartes is not *denying* the existence of God. Rather, he is pointing out that the proposition that God exists is not perfectly certain. Since he is searching for a belief that is perfectly certain, this one won't do.

Almost by accident, Descartes is led to consider the proposition that he himself exists. "...am I not at least something?" He then considers some possible reasons for doubt, to see whether any of these casts doubt upon his own existence. The first of these is the extremely unlikely possibility that he has no sense organs and no body. But he finds that this does not cast any doubt on the proposition that he exists. "Am I so tied to the body and to the senses that I cannot exist without them?"[5]

Descartes next recalls that he has persuaded himself that "there is nothing at all in the world: no heaven, no earth, no minds, no bodies." He then asks himself whether it would follow from this (admittedly far-fetched) assumption that he himself also does not exist. His answer is: "But certainly I should exist, if I were to persuade myself of something." His point seems to be this: if he persuades himself that nothing exists, then surely he himself does exist—since he is persuaded of something. If he is persuaded of something (whether it is true or false), he must exist in order to be persuaded.

Finally Descartes considers the evil demon hypothesis. He has decided to pretend that there is an evil demon, expending all his energies in deceiving Descartes. "Then there is no doubt that I exist, if he deceives me. And deceive me as he will, he can never bring it about that I am nothing so long as I shall think that I am something." Once again, the point is that if he is deceived, whether by God or by some other

[5]Cress, 17.

deceiver, then he must exist. After all, if you don't exist, you can't be deceived. Thus, the evil demon hypothesis does not cast any doubt upon Descartes' belief in his own existence.

Descartes concludes this passage by announcing that he has found his first metaphysical certainty.

> Thus it must be granted that, after weighing everything carefully and sufficiently, one must come to the considered judgment that the statement "I am, I exist" is necessarily true every time it is uttered by me or conceived in my mind.[6]

In another place Descartes seems to make virtually the same point:

> And hence this conclusion *I think, therefore I am*, is the first and most certain of all that occurs to one who philosophizes in an orderly way.[7]

Puzzles about the Cogito

In spite of its appearance of simplicity and clarity, the Cogito is really quite a puzzling passage. In order to see how puzzling it is, let us consider a few questions concerning it. The most crucial question, as I see it, is this: precisely what is the "first certainty" allegedly uncovered in the Cogito? Is it "I exist," or is it "if I think, then I exist," or is it "I think, therefore I exist"? Perhaps it is something else, not mentioned here. In any case, the second question has to do with the reasons Descartes gives for thinking that this belief, whatever it may be, is his first certainty. Does he maintain that it is certain because it has been *proved to be true*, or because it is simply *seen to be true*, or perhaps for some other reason? What is Descartes' justification for making his claim about the first certainty? If we conclude that the first certainty is supposed to be certain because it has been proved to be true, then we must ask some questions about the proof. What are the premises? What justifies Descartes in accepting them? What justifies him in thinking that they entail the first certainty?

I have assumed that the central claim of the Cogito is that something is *certain*. However, it should be pointed out that, in the passage we have been considering, Descartes does not say that "I am, I exist" is certain. Rather, he says that it is "necessarily true." So we have to consider a question about the alleged status of the thing discovered in the Cogito. Is "I exist" (or whatever) supposed to be *certain*, or *true*, or *necessarily true*?

So we have three main questions:

1 What is the first truth of the Cogito?
2 What status does Descartes claim for this first truth?
3 What reasons are given for supposing that the first truth has the status claimed for it?

Since the Cogito marks the first forward step in the Cartesian philosophical procedure, and since he places such great emphasis upon it, we should attempt to

[6]Cress, 17.
[7]HR I, 221.

come to some conclusion about its meaning. We have to try to settle upon some clear, precise answers to the questions mentioned above. It must be admitted, however, that even though scholars have studied this passage for more than three centuries, there is still very great disagreement about its interpretation. Thus, it is unlikely that any answers suggested here will be acceptable to all readers. Nevertheless, we have to consider some proposals.

THE INFERENTIAL INTERPRETATION OF THE COGITO

One of the most important interpretations of the Cogito is based on the idea that, in the Cogito, Descartes infers that he exists, and thereby becomes metaphysically certain of this conclusion. Let us consider this proposal first.

Some Arguments

At the beginning of the Cogito, Descartes considers and rejects a little argument for the existence of God. The argument is based on the fact that various thoughts are going through Descartes' mind. If these thoughts are "instilled" in him by God, then God must exist. Descartes rebuts this argument by pointing out that he himself might be the author of the thoughts. This consideration leads him to ask a question: "Am I not at least something?" The answer, though not stated here, is perfectly obvious. Of course he is something. He exists. So, while he cannot take "God exists" as his first certainty, perhaps he can take "I exist" as his first certainty.

The next few lines seem to contain several little arguments. The first of these is suggested by the following passage:

> But I have already denied that I have any senses and any body. Still, I hesitate; for what follows from that? Am I so tied to senses and body that I cannot exist without them?[8]

Perhaps Descartes meant to suggest this argument:

1 I deny that I have a body and senses.
2 If I deny that I have a body and senses, then I exist.
3 Therefore, I exist.

The second argument is much more clearly presented. It is contained in this passage:

> But I have persuaded myself that there is nothing at all in the world: no heaven, no earth, no minds, no bodies. Is it not then true that I do not exist? But certainly I should exist, if I were to persuade myself of something.[9]

If we abbreviate Descartes' claim slightly, we can put it into the form of an argument as follows:

1 I am persuaded that there is nothing in the world.
2 If I am persuaded that there is nothing in the world, then I exist.
3 Therefore, I exist.

[8] Cress, 17.
[9] Ibid.

Descartes then goes on to present a third and a fourth argument, each very much like the preceding two:

> But there is a deceiver (I know not who he is) powerful and sly in the highest degree, who is always purposely deceiving me. Then there is no doubt that I exist, if he deceives me. And deceive me as long as he will, he can never bring it about that I am nothing so long as I shall think that I am something.[10]

The third argument, then, is this:

1 I am deceived by something.
2 If I am deceived by something, then I exist.
3 Therefore, I exist.

And the final argument is this:

1 I think that I am something.
2 If I think that I am something, then I exist.
3 Therefore, I exist.

Toward the end of the *Second Meditation*, there is a somewhat puzzling passage in which Descartes discusses a piece of wax.[11] One of the main points he apparently wants to make in this passage is that it is easier for a person to know that he himself exists than it is for him to know that an external object, such as a piece of wax, exists. In this context, Descartes produces an argument strikingly similar to the four I have just mentioned. He points out that when he seems to see a piece of wax, he cannot be absolutely certain that the wax really exists. "For it could happen that what I see is not truly wax."[12] He goes on to say, however, that when he thinks he sees wax, he *can* be absolutely certain that he himself exists. The argument here seems to be this:

1 I think I see wax.
2 If I think I see wax, then I exist.
3 Therefore, I exist.

The Cogito Argument

These arguments share a common pattern. In each case, the first premise is a proposition to the effect that Descartes is thinking in some way or other. Either it says that he is believing something, or that he is seeming to see something, or that he is denying something. Each of these is some sort of psychological fact about Descartes, and each can easily enough be viewed as a form of thought—if we use "thought" in a slightly wider sense than we usually do.

The arguments are also alike with respect to their second premises. In each case, it is a premise that links thinking in some way or other to existing. Each is apparently based on the idea that is I am thinking in any way, then I must exist.

[10] Ibid.
[11] Cress, 20–23.
[12] Cress, 22.

Finally, the arguments all have the same conclusion—"I exist." And in each case, the conclusion validly follows from the two premises. Let us then formulate one central argument that displays the common features of all these arguments from the *Second Meditation*. We can call this "the Cogito Argument."

1 I think.
2 Whatever thinks exists.
3 Therefore, I exist.

Many scholars maintain that, in the Cogito, Descartes makes use of the Cogito argument in order to reach his first metaphysical certainty. That certainty, of course, is the fact that he himself exists. Since this conclusion, "I exist," is deduced, or inferred, from some other premises, this interpretation of the passage is generally called "the Inferential Interpretation of the Cogito."

If a person comes to know a thing because he has inferred it from some other things, then he must have known those other things. Similarly, if a person comes to be metaphysically certain of a thing because he has inferred it from some other things, then those other things must have been metaphysically certain. Thus, if Descartes came to be metaphysically certain of his own existence as a result of inferring it from some premises, those premises must have been metaphysically certain to start with. Anyone who adopts the inferential interpretation of the Cogito must explain why the premises of the Cogito argument were metaphysically certain for Descartes.

Let's consider the first premise, "I think," first. Why should we view this as being metaphysically certain for Descartes? The answer, I believe, turns on a remarkable feature of thought. If you think you are walking, you might be mistaken. Maybe you are only dreaming that you are walking. However, if you think you are thinking, you must be right. You cannot think that you are thinking, if you are not thinking. So if an evil demon causes you to think that you are thinking, he won't cause you to make a mistake. You will be right. You will be thinking. If, in a dream, you think that you are thinking, you will be right. There is no possibility of error here. You cannot make a mistake if you think you are thinking.

This point can be put in another way. If you think you are thinking, then there is absolutely no reason for you to doubt that you are thinking. To see this, let's suppose you think you are thinking, and let's see whether any of the main reasons for doubt make this belief any less certain. Consider, for example, the possibility that you are dreaming. Does that give you any reason to doubt that you are thinking? Obviously not. For if you are dreaming, then you are thinking—dreaming is a way of thinking. Since "I am dreaming" entails "I am thinking," the possibility of dreaming does not cast doubt on the fact that you are thinking. If anything, it makes it *more* certain. Consider, next, the possibility that you are being deceived by an evil demon. Does that cast doubt on the fact that you are thinking? Once again, it does not. To be deceived about something is to believe a falsehood about it. To have a belief is to think in a certain way. Hence, if you are deceived, you are thinking. So if a demon, or even God, is deceiving you, you are thinking. Hence, the possibility that you are being deceived does not cast any doubt on the fact that you are thinking.

Further reflection on this point will reveal that you can never have good reason to doubt that you are thinking, if you think you are thinking. Hence, "I think" can be a metaphysical certainty. According to the inferential interpretation of the Cogito, "I think" was a metaphysical certainty for Descartes at the time of the Cogito. That explains how it could be used in the Cogito argument.

In a variety of places, Descartes discusses a very plausible metaphysical principle. The principle says that if a thing has any properties at all, it must exist. Put in another way, the principle says that if a thing does not exist, it cannot have any properties.[13] Since "being thoughtful" or "thinking" is a property, it follows that whatever thinks, must exist. How could a thing have the property of being thoughtful, if it were not there to have it? So, according to the inferential interpretation, we can say that (2) of the Cogito argument was a metaphysical certainty for Descartes because it is an instance of an obviously true principle about properties.

Finally, we must say that Descartes was metaphysically certain that the Cogito argument was valid. Otherwise, he would not be able to gain metaphysical certainty of the conclusion by use of the argument. Since the argument is of a fairly obviously valid form, this may seem a reasonable claim.

Now let us summarize the main elements of the inferential interpretation of the Cogito. They are as follows:

> In the Cogito, Descartes achieves his first metaphysical certainty, which is the fact that he himself exists. This fact becomes metaphysically certain for Descartes because he infers it from two premises, each of which is already metaphysically certain for him, and he does it by means of an argument whose validity is metaphysically certain for him.

So we can see, then, how the inferential interpretation provides answers to our three main questions concerning the Cogito. First, there was the question about the identity of the "first truth." According to this interpretation, the first truth that comes to one who philosophizes in an orderly way is "I exist."

The second question was the question about the status assigned to the first truth. On the inferential interpretation, it is alleged that "I exist" becomes *metaphysically certain* in the Cogito.

The third question has to do with the reason Descartes gives for saying that "I exist" is metaphysically certain. On the inferential interpretation, the answer is that "I exist" becomes metaphysically certain because it is validly inferred from two other premises, each of which was already metaphysically certain for Descartes, via an argument whose validity was metaphysically certain for Descartes.

SOME PROBLEMS FOR THE INFERENTIAL INTERPRETATION

Although many philosophers are inclined to accept it (or something relevantly like it), and although it has a superficial appearance of plausibility, the inferential interpretation of the Cogito is simply unacceptable. It faces a multitude of objections, some of which are, in my opinion, unanswerable. Let us review some of the main objections.

---

[13]See, for example, *Principles* XI, HR I, 223. I take it that "no qualities pertain to nothing" means "what's nonexistent has no qualities." I recognize, of course, that the principle admits of other (less plausible) interpretations.

Objection A

Perceptive readers will surely have noticed that there is an internal inconsistency in the version of the inferential interpretation that I have presented. On the one hand, according to that theory, "I exist" is the first metaphysical certainty that Descartes achieves in the *Meditations*. On the other hand, it is alleged that he derives this certainty from two other propositions, each of which was metaphysically certain before "I exist" was. Clearly enough, it is impossible for "I exist" to be the *first* certainty if two other things are certain before it is!

There are a variety of ways in which we can modify the inferential interpretation in an attempt to avoid this objection. We might simply delete the claim that "I think" and "Whatever thinks exists" were certain before "I exist" became certain. This proposal simply doesn't work, however. The problem is that if the premises of the Cogito argument were not metaphysically certain to start with, it would be impossible to make the conclusion certain by inferring it from them. You can't come to know that a conclusion is true by inferring it from a set of premises unless you already know that the premises are true.

Another way to answer Objection A would involve deleting the claim that "I exist" is the first metaphysical certainty achieved in the *Meditations*. We could drop that point, and say instead that "I exist" is the third, or the fourth, or the tenth certainty that Descartes achieved as he attempted to refill his basket of beliefs.

This proposed modification is hardly an improvement. One new difficulty is this: Descartes surely sets out in the Cogito to find a metaphysical certainty. Right before the passage we have been considering, he says, "Surely great things are to be hoped for if I am lucky enough to find at least one thing that is certain and indubitable."[14] So it appears that he is looking for a metaphysical certainty. At the end of the Cogito, he seems to have found it. He says:

> Thus it must be granted that, after weighing everything carefully and sufficiently, one must come to the considered judgment that the statement "I am, I exist" is necessarily true every time it is uttered by me or conceived by my mind.[15]

Isn't he saying, in a somewhat obscure way, that he has discovered his first certainty, and that it is "I am, I exist?"

Objection B

A second problem is closely related to the first. It has to do with whether the second premise of the Cogito argument really could have been metaphysically certain for Descartes at the moment in question. Could he have been absolutely certain of the principle that whatever thinks, exists?

To say that premise (2) was a metaphysical certainty for Descartes at the time in question is to say that he had absolutely no reason to doubt it. It appears to me that Descartes did have some reasons to doubt (2). One of these reasons is that God, or and evil demon, might be deceiving him into thinking that (2) is true. Another is that he might just be dreaming that (2) is true. A final reason, perhaps not so interesting

---

[14]Cress, 17.
[15]Ibid.

as the others, is this: other people, in the past, have made mistakes with respect to metaphysical principles relevantly like (2). So, even though it seems pretty certain to Descartes, couldn't he be making a mistake with respect to (2)?

Perhaps we can drive this point home more persuasively if we recall that Descartes is entertaining the hypothesis that God might be a deceiver. Descartes has admitted that God could make him go wrong while counting the sides of a square, or adding two and three. Surely, if God could make Descartes err with respect to such simple matters as these, he could make Descartes err with respect to a rather abstract metaphysical principle such as "whatever thinks, exists." Thus, it appears that premise (2) of the Cogito argument was *not* metaphysically certain at the time of the Cogito. Hence, contrary to what the inferential interpretation says, Descartes could not have used (2) in an effort to make some later conclusion metaphysically certain.

A closely related point has to do with the question whether Descartes could have been metaphysically certain of the validity of the Cogito argument. It seems pretty clear that the argument is valid, but that's not the point here. The question is whether Descartes could have been metaphysically certain of its validity. It seems to me that he could not have been. Surely, he had some reasons to suspect that it was invalid. We have just reviewed some of these. Perhaps God is deceiving him into thinking it is valid. Perhaps he is just dreaming that it is valid. Perhaps he was created by a series of accidents, and has defective epistemic faculties. Though none of these is a very likely possibility, none can be ruled out at this stage. Each casts some slight doubt on the belief that the Cogito argument is valid. Hence, it is not metaphysically certain that it is valid. In light of this, Descartes cannot use the argument to make "I exist" become metaphysically certain.

Objection C

One of the most striking and perplexing objections to the inferential interpretation of the Cogito was presented by the British philosopher, Bertrand Russell. Russell suggested that there is a serious problem with premise (1) of the Cogito argument:

> Let us begin by examining Descartes' view. "I think, therefore I am" is what he says, but this won't do as it stands. What, from his own point of view, he should profess to know is not "I think," but "There is thinking".... He would say that thoughts imply a thinker. But why should they? Why should not a thinker be simply a certain series of thoughts, connected with each other by causal laws?[6]

In order to understand Russell's objection, we have to reflect on some topics in metaphysics. According to an ancient and still popular view, there is an important distinction between "substances" and "properties." Substances are concrete individual things, such as my truck, the moon, or the Sphinx. Properties are abstract things. Some examples would be the property of being blue, the property of being old, the property of being magnetic. "Quality," "characteristic," "feature," and "attribute" are sometimes used as synonyms for "property."

Consider the statement: "My truck is blue." This statement is about a certain substance, my truck. It says that the truck has a certain property, blueness. The

[6]Bertrand Russell, *An Outline of Philosophy*, London: George Allen and Unwin, 1927, p. 7.

statement is true if and only if the substance in question has the property in question. A person knows that the statement is true if and only if he knows that the substance, my truck, has the property, blueness. Merely knowing that *something* is blue would not be sufficient for knowing that the statement is true. You also have to know which thing it is that has blueness. So if you merely saw a blue blur flashing down the highway, you would not have enough evidence to conclude that the statement is true. All you could say with confidence is that something is blue.

As I understand it, Russell's objection is based on just this point. The statement, "I think," also involves a substance and a property. The substance here is the "self" or "mind," and the property is thoughtfulness, or "being a thing that thinks." Russell is suggesting that Descartes has no direct knowledge of the substance involved in the statement "I think." Russell is prepared to admit that Descartes knows that some thinking is going on, but he is not prepared to admit that Descartes knows *who* or *what* (if anything) is doing the thinking. Descartes, according to Russell, has no direct awareness of the self, or mind. He is merely assuming that there is a self, or mind, that somehow bears, or supports the property of thinking.

If you want to pursue this point a bit further, perhaps you should try a little experiment. Look as carefully as you can into your own experiences. Reflect intently on how you feel, and what you see. Perhaps you see various colors, and feel warmth, or chilliness. Maybe you can feel some pressure on some parts of you body. These are all properties that you are experiencing. Now look even closer, and see if you can see a "self" or an "ego" or a "me" that is the subject of all these experiences. If Russell is right, you will not find any such entity. At best, you can assume that it is there, serving as a support for all the properties that you can experience.[17]

It should be clear that, if Russell is right, the inferential interpretation of the Cogito is ruined. We have to say that Descartes was not metaphysically certain of the first premise of the Cogito argument. At most, Descartes was entitled to an argument such as this one:

1 Something is thinking.
2 If something is thinking, then something exists.
3 Therefore, something exists.

It is not clear to me that Russell is right. I find his objection extremely puzzling. I acknowledge that it is impossible for me to observe my "self," but it often seems to me that I can nevertheless know with absolute certainty that I am thinking. It is not clear to me how I do this. I leave it to the interested reader to reach his or her own assessment of Objection C.

Objection D

A final, rather impressive objection was originally developed by Baruch Spinoza (1632–1677). As a young man, Spinoza had studied Descartes' philosophy with

---

[17] My interpretation of Russell's point is derived from a famous passage of David Hume's *Treatise of Human Nature*, Book I, part iv, section 6. There, Hume claims that when he enters most intimately into what he calls *himself*, he always stumbles on some particular perception or other of heat or cold, light or shade, love or hatred, pain or pleasure. He claims that he never can catch himself without a perception, and never can observe anything but the perception.

great care. He was considered to be an expert on Cartesianism. When he was asked to tutor a friend, he wrote a very penetrating and insightful exposition and commentary on the *Meditations*. In the first section of that book, Spinoza discussed the Cogito. He presented an interesting objection that goes right to the heart of the inferential interpretation.

Spinoza says:

> ...it must first of all be observed that the statement *I doubt, I think, therefore I am* is not a syllogism, whose major premise has been omitted. For, if it were a syllogism, the premises ought to have been clearer and better known than the conclusion itself, *therefore I am*: and so *I am* would not be the first basis of all knowledge; besides, it would not be a certain conclusion, for its truth would depend on universal premises that the author had long since called into question.[18]

In order to understand this objection, let us consider an analogy. Suppose you have been to a riotous party, and have had far too much to eat and drink. The next morning, you wake up feeling horrible. You go to the bathroom to get an aspirin. While in the bathroom, you see yourself in the mirror. You look terrible. Furthermore, you have the aspirin bottle in you hand. Consider this little argument:

1 I look horrible, and I have an aspirin bottle in my hand.
2 If I look horrible, and I have an aspirin bottle in my hand, then I have a headache.
3 Therefore, I have a headache.

I am convinced that you could not come to know that you have a headache by the use of the argument. The problem is not that the argument itself is defective. It is that you would unoubtedly know that you have a headache before you could go through the various steps of the argument. Furthermore, you would already be so certain that you have a headache that you could not increase your certainty by the use of this argument. Your knowledge of your headache would not be based on evidence such as that contained in premises (1) or (2) of the argument. Your knowledge that you have a headache would be more direct. The headache itself is all the evidence you need for the conclusion that you have a headache.

As I understand him, Spinoza wants to make something like this point concerning the Cogito argument. Perhaps there is nothing wrong with the argument itself. The problem is that Descartes could not have used that argument to come to know that he exists. He undoubtedly knew that he existed before he made use of that (or any other) argument. His knowledge of his own existence could not have been dependent upon any premises. He knew immediately, and without evidence, that he existed.

So Spinoza means to criticize a fundamental feature of the inferential interpretation of the Cogito. He wants to point out how absurd it is to suppose that Descartes could have become certain of his existence by inferring it from other premises. As Spinoza sees it, no inference could possibly increase Descartes' certainty concerning his existence. Each of us can be perfectly certain of his or her own existence without

---

[18] Baruch Spinoza, *Principles of Cartesian Philosophy*, translated by Harry E. Wedeck, London: Peter Owen Ltd., 1961, pp. 12–13. It must be admitted that Spinoza makes a variety of points in this passage, and the one I draw out is a bit hard to find. Nevertheless, I'm pretty sure Spinoza wanted to make this point, too.

inference. That I exist is a fact I can know directly, without making use of any premises.

I am inclined to think that Spinoza's point is correct. I acknowledge that when I am thinking, I can know directly and without further evidence that I am thinking. "I think" enjoys a special epistemic status. However, "I exist" seems to have about the same status. I can know directly and without further evidence that I exist. Thus, there is no reason to go to the trouble of attempting to infer the latter from the former. "I exist" can be perfectly certain without inference.

In light of all these objections, I think it is clear that we must seek a better account of what's going on in the Cogito. We have seen that there are profound difficulties in the inferential interpretation. But if the passage does not contain an inference, what does it contain?

A NEW INTERPRETATION OF THE COGITO

The *Meditations* was not Descartes' first serious philosophical work. More than a dozen years before he wrote the *Meditations*, he had written his *Rules for the Direction of the Mind.*[19] In the *Rules*, Descartes drew an important distinction between two different ways in which a person can come to know something. He went so far as to say that these two ways are the only sure roads to knowledge.[20] The two methods are "intuition" and "deduction."

Intuition and Deduction

Sometimes, when you get to know a new thing, you get to know it because you see that it follows from some other things you already knew. For example, suppose you know that the murderer was left-handed, and you know that only the butler is left-handed. Putting two and two together, you conclude that the butler is the murderer. In this case, you come to have some knowledge by deduction. Knowledge by deduction is *derived* knowledge. In order to gain some knowledge by deduction, you must already have some previous knowledge. Otherwise, from what could you derive the new knowledge?

It is hard to see how *all* of a person's knowledge could be deductive. Surely, if a person has any knowledge at all, some of it must be nonderivative. Descartes maintained, in the *Rules*, that this nonderivative knowledge is "knowledge by intuition." When we say that a person knows something by intuition, we do not mean that he or she "just has a funny feeling that it is true." Rather, we mean that he or she "sees" it to be true, in the way that you can just "see" that 2 is greater than 1, or that if some number, n, is greater than another, m, then m is less than n. These are things that are known directly. We don't get to know them by deducing them from simpler things that we previously knew.

In the *Rules*, Descartes gave an account of knowledge by intuition:

> By *intuition* I understand, not the fluctuating testimony of the senses, nor the misleading judgment that proceeds from the blundering constructions of imagination, but the con-

[19] HR I, 1–77.
[20] HR I, 7.

ception which an unclouded and attentive mind gives us so readily and distinctly that we are wholly freed from doubt about that which we understand. Or, what comes to the same thing, *intuition* is the undoubting conception of an unclouded and attentive mind, and springs from the light of reason alone; it is more certain than deduction itself, in that it is simpler....[21]

I think we have to face up to the fact that this explanation of intuition is a bit hard to follow. One main point seems to be that when you know a thing by intuition, you do not know it on the basis of sense perception. Furthermore, when you know a thing by intuition, you know it directly, not by deriving it from any previously known facts. The basic idea here seems to be that, if you focus your attention on a sufficiently simple fact, and you understand the concepts involved in that fact thoroughly, and the truth of the fact is driven home to you so clearly that you are unable to doubt it, then you may be intuiting it. In that case, you have some knowledge by intuition.

Descartes went on to give an extremely important example of something that can be known by intuition. He says:

Thus each individual can mentally have intuition of the fact that he exists, and that he thinks; that the triangle is bounded by three lines only, the sphere by a single superficies, and so on.[22]

It seems perfectly clear that, at least in the *Rules*, Descartes wanted to maintain that each of us can have knowledge by intuition of his or her own existence. This suggests another interpretation of the Cogito—the intuitional interpretation.

The Intuitional Interpretation of the Cogito

According to the intuitional interpretation of the Cogito, Descartes' fundamental claim in the Cogito is that he is metaphysically certain that he exists, and he is certain of it because he has intuited it.

We can see that this interpretation differs in one main respect from the inferential interpretation. Both interpretations give the same answer to the first question, "What is the first truth?" They both say that it is "I exist." They also agree on the answer to the second question. The status assigned to "I exist" is the same—metaphysical certainty. The two interpretations differ, however, on the third question. Whereas the inferential interpretation says that "I exist" became metaphysically certain because it was *inferred*, the intuitional interpretation says it became metaphysically certain because it was *intuited*.

The intuitional interpretation is clearly superior to the inferential interpretation in a few respects. As we saw, anyone who accepts the inferential interpretation is going to have a hard time explaining how "I exist" can be the first certainty, if it is derived from two previous certainties. This is no problem for the defender of the intuitional interpretation. On the intuitional interpretation, "I exist" is the first certainty. "I exist" is alleged to be certain, not because it has been deduced from earlier premises, but because it has been intuited. Hence, there is no embarrassing

[21] HR I, 7.
[22] HR I, 7.

question about the epistemic status of the premises from which the first certainty is derived. Equally, no question arises about the epistemic status of the argument by which it is derived. There is no such argument.

Furthermore, the defender of the intuitional interpretation does not have to answer Spinoza's objection. That objection was based on the fairly plausible claim that I cannot gain any greater certainty of my own existence by seeing that it follows from a bunch of premises. Even before I make use of any argument, I will be as certain as can be that I exist. On the intuitional interpretation, there is no argument. It is not alleged that Descartes became certain of his existence because he derived it from some premises. It is alleged that he became certain of his existence because he simply "saw" that he existed.

Problems for the Intuitional Interpretation

Nevertheless, the intuitional interpretation faces insurmountable obstacles. One main problem is that it just does not fit the text of the *Meditations*. If we look closely at the Cogito, we will find that Descartes simply does not say that he has intuited anything. Furthermore, there are many expressions that indicate inference. For example, we find him saying that *if* he is persuaded, *then* he exists; *if* he is deceived, *then* he exists, etc. These remarks surely suggest that "I exist" is being deduced, not intuited.

A second problem with the intuitional interpretation is that it fails to explain adequately why "I exist" is metaphysically certain for Descartes. We might think that Descartes becomes metaphysically certain of his own existence simply because he has intuited it, but this seems pretty implausible. An omnipotent God, if he wanted to, could surely make Descartes think he was intuiting something, when that thing was really false. An evil demon undoubtedly could make Descartes think that he was intuiting that a square has three sides. Indeed, Descartes himself seems to make this very point just a few pages later, when he says:

> I am constrained to admit that, if he wishes, it is very easy for him to cause me to err, even in those matters that I think I have intuited as plainly as possible with the eyes of the mind.[23]

In light of this, we have to acknowledge that merely intuiting a thing cannot make it metaphysically certain, for no matter how obvious it may seem, one must always admit that it might be false—maybe a deceitful God is just making it seem to be true. Until he knows for certain that God is not a deceiver, Descartes cannot be absolutely sure even of the deliverances of intuition. These things are subject to some slight metaphysical doubts. Thus, the intuitional interpretation seems unacceptable. It does not provide a satisfactory account of the reason why "I exist" was metaphysically certain for Descartes.

THE EPISTEMIC DISCOVERY INTERPRETATION OF THE COGITO

I am inclined to believe that the most plausible interpretation of the Cogito is one according to which the crucial activity of the Cogito is neither *inference* nor

---

[23]Cress, 24.

intuition. Rather, it is *discovery*. As I see it, Descartes is telling us that he has discovered a belief that is metaphysically certain. The belief, obviously, is the belief that he exists. This belief is metaphysically certain, not because it has been derived from indubitable premises, and not because it has been intuited. Rather, it is metaphysically certain simply because there is no reason to doubt it.

As we have already seen, Descartes has decided to suspend judgment with respect to everything that admits of the slightest doubt. He thinks he has found some extremely powerful reasons for doubt. These include the dream hypothesis, the deceptive God hypothesis, and (perhaps) the evil demon hypothesis. These reasons for doubt seem at first to be so powerful as to cast all of Descartes' former beliefs into doubt. Hence, he has attempted to suspend judgment with respect to everything he formerly believed.

At the beginning of the Cogito, Descartes is searching for something to believe. In order to be believable in these circumstances, a proposition must be absolutely certain. There must be no reason at all to doubt it. Descartes first considers the proposition that God exists, but he finds that it is less than absolutely certain. Then he stumbles upon the proposition that he himself exists. It seems to be a likely candidate. Maybe he can accept it as his first certainty. However, before he can put this belief back into his "basket," he must check to see whether there is any reason to doubt it.

In an effort to see whether there is any reason to doubt "I exist," Descartes reviews the most powerful sources of doubt. First he recalls the fact that his senses sometimes deceive him. In light of this, he has been persuaded to suspend judgment with respect to all sense-based beliefs. He is imagining that there is no heaven, no earth, no bodies, etc. He wants to see whether this hypothesis casts doubt on his own existence. His answer is that it does not: "But surely I should exist, if I were to persuade myself of something." As I see it, Descartes is pointing out that this first reason for doubt (the fact that his senses sometimes deceive him) is not a reason for doubting that he himself exists. After all, if one proposition entails another, it cannot also be a reason for doubting that other. "I am deceived by my senses" entails "I exist."

The next important source of doubt is the hypothesis of an external deceiver—either God or something less powerful than God. This hypothesis casts doubt upon and enormous range of beliefs. Does it cast doubt upon "I exist"? Descartes' answer, once again, is that it does not. "Then there is no doubt that I exist, if he deceives me." Since "Someone is deceiving me" entails "I exist," the latter cannot be cast into doubt by the former. Hence, the possibility of a powerful deceiver does not make "I exist" metaphysically uncertain.

Equally, the dream hypothesis fails to cast doubt upon Descartes' existence. Clearly, "I am dreaming" entails "I exist." Therefore, the possibility that he is dreaming does not constitute a reason for Descartes to doubt that he exists. Rather, the more reason he has for thinking that he is dreaming, the more confident he can be that he *does* exist. So, though he doesn't mention this fact in the Cogito, it should be clear that the dream hypothesis does not serve to make "I exist" any less certain.[24]

---

[24] A similar point can be made about the insanity hypothesis, too. If you are insane, you must exist. Hence, the possibility of insanity does not cast doubt on one's existence.

The conclusion is that there is no reason—not even an outlandish or far-fetched reason—for Descartes to doubt that he exists. As he says in another context, "all the most extravagant suppositions brought forward by the skeptics were incapable of shaking it."[25] Therefore, he can accept "I exist" as his first metaphysical certainty. Since it is perfectly certain, he can admit it as his first new belief. He has thus started to "refill his basket."

If we accept the epistemic discovery interpretation of the Cogito, we will be able to provide a reasonably satisfactory account of the little arguments that appear in the passage. As I see it, Descartes does not present these arguments in an effort to prove that he exists. Rather, he presents these arguments in order to show that the main sources of doubt entail "I exist," and therefore cannot serve to make "I exist" any less certain. For example, consider the deceptive God hypothesis. It is clear, I think, that this is a valid argument:

1 Some powerful deceiver is deceiving me.
2 If some powerful deceiver is deceiving me, then I exist.
3 Therefore, I exist.

Clearly, Descartes could not use this argument to prove that he exists. One perfectly obvious problem is that the first premise is extremely implausible! However, he can use this argument to show that the deceiver hypothesis, premise (1) here, entails "I exist." If (1) entails "I exist," then (1) cannot provide reason to doubt "I exist."

Let's summarize the epistemic discovery interpretation by seeing how it answers our three questions about the Cogito. The first question was the question about the identity of the first truth. On this view, we say that the first truth is "I exist." The second question has to do with its status. According to the epistemic discovery view, its status is metaphysical certainty. And why is it metaphysically certain? Because there is simply no reason to doubt it.

Objections to the Epistemic Discovery Interpretation

The epistemic discovery interpretation of the Cogito is open to some objections, too. One problem is that it is hard to see how Descartes could have been so certain that there were *no* reasons for him to doubt his own existence. After all, he only considered a few of the most obvious sources of doubt. Isn't it possible that there is some other hypothesis, not mentioned here, that does serve to cast "I exist" into doubt? I do not know how best to answer this objection. Perhaps Descartes thought he could just see that nothing could possibly cast doubt upon his own existence. My own view is that if he did think this, he was right. Nothing could possibly give me good reason to doubt that I exist.

Anyone who reads Descartes' other major philosophical works will find another problem for this interpretation of the Cogito. In those other works, there are passages that correspond very closely to the Cogito of the *Meditations*. It will be found, I fear, that the epistemic discovery interpretation does not provide a very plausible account of any of those other passages. In some of them, Descartes seems

[25] HR I, 101.

to be inferring "I exist" from "I think." In others, he seems to be claiming that he can intuit "I exist." In yet others, he seems to be making still other claims about his own existence. Thus, it is important for me to be clear about my own thesis. I only mean to suggest that the epistemic discovery interpretation is the best interpretation of the Cogito of the *Meditations*. I do not mean to suggest that it is the best interpretation of the corresponding passages in the other works.[26]

[26]Although I will not attempt to defend these views here, perhaps I should mention how I would interpret the corresponding passages from the other works. The passage in the *Rules* (HR I, 7) is best understood in accordance with the intuitional interpretation. The passage in the *Discourse* (HR I, 101) seems to be explainable by a version of the epistemic discovery interpretation, but the thing that is discovered is not "I exist." It seems to be "I think, therefore I am." The passage in the *Principles* (HR I, 221) is confused, but seems to contain some elements best explained by the inferential interpretation. Finally, in the *Search After Truth* (HR I, 316), we seem to have a pretty straightforward inference from "you doubt" to "you exist."

PHILOSOPHICAL THEOLOGY

Part Two of this book is about "philosophical theology." This is the philosophical study of the nature and existence of God. The question of God's existence and nature arises sooner or later for virtually every thoughtful person. For most of us the issue is a very personal and emotional matter, primarily concerning faith and religion. We may ask ourselves whether we should adopt the religious tradition that we have inherited, or whether we should follow a path different from that of our parents. In this context, we may begin to wonder whether there really is a God, and, if so, what sort of God it may be.

For Descartes, however, the question of God's existence and nature arises in a different context. For him, it is a fundamentally *epistemological* issue. As we have seen, of all the skeptical arguments available to him, none impressed Descartes more than the deceptive God argument. The possibility that there might be no God, or that there might be a deceptive God, cast doubt on all but a very few of Descartes' former beliefs. In order to overcome this doubt, Descartes felt that he had to prove, first, that God exists, and, second, that God is no deceiver. Unless he can prove these things, he tells us, he can never be certain of anything.

Part Two contains four chapters. In Chapter 5, I describe Descartes' post-Cogito epistemic situation more carefully, and explain why he wants to prove the existence of God. I go on to give a detailed account of a traditional concept of God, and to present and evaluate some fairly simple-minded arguments for the existence of God. In Chapter 6, I discuss some of the most important traditional arguments for the existence of God. I suspect that Descartes was aware of arguments relevantly like the ones I discuss, even though he didn't make use of them.

In Chapter 7, we return to the *Meditations,* to see Descartes' proofs of the existence of God. Descartes argued for the existence of God in two main ways. One of these is generally considered to be a form of the "Cosmological Argument" (or "Causal Argument"), and the other is a form of the "Ontological Argument." These arguments are presented, explained, and evaluated in Chapter 7. In the final section of Chapter 7, I return to Descartes' epistemic concerns. I try to explain how the proof of the existence and non-deceptiveness of God provides Descartes with the means to increase his stock of metaphysical certainties.

The final chapter of Part Two is about "Atheology"—philosophical arguments *against* the existence of God. The most famous problem for theists is, of course, the problem of evil. If there is a God, why is there so much evil in the world? I discuss this and other atheological arguments, and try to show how theism can be defended.

Let us begin, then, by reflecting on Descartes' epistemic status at the end of the Cogito.

PHILOSOPHICAL THEOLOGY

DESCARTES' EPISTEMIC STATUS AFTER THE COGITO[1]

At the beginning of the *Third Meditation,* Descartes gives a sort of "status report." He summarizes what he has accomplished so far. I think it will be useful to take the trouble to study this summary fairly closely. We might expect that Descartes' view is that he has so far discovered just one metaphysical certainty—"I exist." We will find, however, that Descartes thinks he has found quite a few other certainties, beyond this one. We will have to consider whether he is justified in this belief. A second reason to study the summary is this: if we understand the summary, we will be better able to understand why Descartes proceeds to consider the question of God's existence and nature.

Here is the passage in which Descartes presents his status report:

> I am a thing that thinks, that is to say, a thing that doubts, affirms, denies, knows a few things, is ignorant of many things, wills, rejects, and also imagines and senses. As I observed earlier, although these things that I sense or imagine may perhaps be nothing at all outside me, nevertheless I am certain that these modes of thinking—which I call sensations and imaginations—insofar as they are only modes of thinking, are within me. In these few words I have summed up what I truly know, or at least what, so far, I have observed that I know.[2]

What Descartes Can Know with Certainty

It seems to me that Descartes means to maintain that he has discovered metaphysical certainties of two main sorts. The first sort, somewhat overlooked here, consists of

[1] Reading Assignment: the first four paragraphs of the *Third Meditation,* Cress, 23–24.
[2] Cress, 23.

just one belief, and that is the belief that he himself exists. As we saw in Chapter 4, it is not entirely clear *why* he thinks this is a metaphysical certainty. Nevertheless, it is clear that he does think that he is entitled to believe that he exists. I think he's right. He has no reason to suspect that he is mistaken about his own existence.

The second main sort of metaphysical certainty consists of facts about Descartes' current mental states—what he calls "modes of thinking." Let us assume that Descartes was sitting at a desk, writing. He was having various visual and tactual experiences. He seemed to see the desk, writing paper, pen, and ink bottle. He seemed to feel the pen in his hand, and the chair beneath him. Perhaps he felt the warmth of the morning sunshine as it fell upon his arm. In this case, a number of facts would have been metaphysically certain for Descartes. Here are a few:

1 I now seem to see a desk.
2 I now seem to feel a pen.
3 I now seem to feel warmth as if it were in my arm.

It is important to understand just what is meant by a claim such as (1). (1) merely says how things *seem* to Descartes. (1) can be true even if there is no desk before Descartes. So if he is just dreaming that he sees a desk, or if he is having a hallucination, or even if he is being deceived on the grand scale by God or some deceiver, still he can be sure that (1) is true.

Let's compare (1) with a genuine perceptual proposition. That would be:

4 I now see a desk.

It should be clear that (4) cannot be true unless there actually is a desk near Descartes, and he has suitable sense organs, and they are operating properly, etc. So, if there is any doubt about any of these things, Descartes cannot be metaphysically certain that (4) is true. Obviously, for someone in Descartes' epistemic situation, there is plenty of doubt about these things, and so (4) is not a metaphysical certainty for Descartes at the beginning of the *Third Meditation*. However, if Descartes has the internal, mental experiences that are associated with seeing a desk, and he uses (1) merely to express this fact, then he can be metaphysically certain of (1). He can say, "I don't know whether there is really a desk here, or even if I have eyes to see one if it is here. But it certainly does *seem* to me now that I am seeing a desk.' Similar comments hold for (2) and (3).

(1), (2) and (3) may be said to report facts about Descartes' current psychological state, and each of them is metaphysically certain for Descartes. We might think, therefore, that Descartes can be metaphysically certain of all current psychological facts about himself. However, this would be a mistake. To see why, we need only reflect on such psychological facts as these:

5 I now know that there is a desk before me.
6 I now seem to see the pen with which I wrote a letter to Princess Elizabeth last week.
7 I am now sad because of the death of my daughter, Francine.

While these sentences pretty clearly express psychological facts about Descartes, the facts in question are not so immediately knowable. If (5) is true, then there must in fact be a desk in front of Descartes. Since there is some slight reason to doubt whether there is really a desk there, there is some slight reason to doubt (5). Hence, it is not a metaphysical certainty for Descartes. Sentences (6) and (7) have similar problems. (6) entails the existence of Princess Elizabeth, and (7) entails that Descartes had a daughter, Francine, who died. While these entailments may have been true enough, they are things that Descartes could not have known with metaphysical certainty at the time in question. Hence, (6) and (7) could not have been known with metaphysical certainty, even though they are, at least in part, statements about Descartes' current psychological state.

In light of all this, I think we should say that the second class of metaphysical certainties consists of facts about Descartes' current "immediately accessible" mental states. These are states such as the ones indicated by (1), (2), and (3). If Descartes is in such a state, he can know directly and with absolute certainty that he is in it. No such state entails the existence of any contingent substance aside from Descartes himself. I am sorry to have to admit that I cannot give a fully adequate account of what I mean by "immediately accessible mental state." I trust that the general idea is sufficiently clear.

We should also recognize that, among these immediately accessible mental states, there are such states as believing, denying, willing and imagining. Thus, some other metaphysical certainties for Descartes might be:

8 I now believe that there is a desk before me.
9 I now deny that squares have five sides.
10 I now imagine that there is an evil demon.

As I see it, Descartes can also be absolutely certain about each of the facts mentioned here. Each of these involves a "propositional attitude"—a way of conceiving of some proposition. In (8) the attitude is belief, in (9) it is denial. I think that, when I believe something, I can know that I am believing it. Of course, from the fact that Descartes can know (8) with absolute certainty, we should not infer that he can know with absolute certainty that:

11 There is a desk before me.

He can't.

We should not forget the most general of psychological facts Descartes can know. This, of course, is the fact that he is thinking. When a person is thinking, he or she can know immediately and with absolute certainty that he or she is thinking.

What Descartes Cannot Know

These considerations naturally lead to some further questions about Descartes' epistemic status. What sorts of facts are *not* metaphysically certain for Descartes? What sorts of things are subject to doubts, and hence not worthy of belief in the current circumstances?

One very important class of uncertainties is the class of facts about the "external world." Any proposition that entails the existence of a desk, chair, pen, ink bottle, or house is such a proposition. Equally, a proposition that entails the existence of the earth, or the sun, or the moon would have to be viewed as being metaphysically uncertain. Furthermore, propositions about Descartes' body, such as "I have a hand" or "I have sense organs," are about the external world, and unworthy of belief in the present context. For each such proposition, Descartes can think of many reasons for doubt.

Another important class of uncertainties consists of contingent propositions about the past. Descartes' evidence for any such proposition involves his memory, and surely God could make him seem to remember things which in fact did not occur. Hence, he has reason to be suspicious about any contingent proposition about the past.

Contingent propositions about the future are unacceptable, as well. As we saw in Chapter 2, our evidence for any such proposition is always less than absolutely conclusive. There is always some slight reason to doubt that things will turn out as we expect them to. Hence, if Descartes is suspending judgment with respect to everything that admits of the slightest doubt, he must suspend judgment with respect to every contingent proposition about the future.

It appears that Descartes wants to go even further. He wants to reject even very simple truths of arithmetic and geometry. Even these necessary truths admit of some slight doubt, as Descartes makes clear in this passage from the fourth paragraph of the *Third Meditation*:

> When I considered something very simple and easy in the areas of arithmetic or geometry, for example that two plus three together make five, and the like, did I not intuit them at least clearly enough that I might affirm them to be true? To be sure, I did decide later on that I must doubt these things for no other reason than that it entered my mind that some God could have given me a nature such that I might be deceived—even about matters that seemed most evident. For every time this preconceived opinion about the supreme power of God occurs to me, I am constrained to admit that, if he wishes, it is very easy for him to cause me to err, even in those matters that I think I have intuited as plainly as possible with the eyes of the mind.[3]

Descartes' point is clear and plausible. Even when he intuits a necessary truth, he still has some slight reason for doubt. The reason for doubt is that he may have been created by a God who chooses to cause him to err. If he was created by such a powerful deceiver, then his power of reasoning may be inherently defective. In this case, he could go wrong even with respect to the things that he thinks he sees most clearly. So, at this early stage of the *Meditations,* Descartes cannot believe even such a simple fact as:

12 $2 + 3 = 5$

He cannot believe (12) because he has decided to suspend judgment on everything that admits of the slightest doubt. (12) is slightly doubtful because, no matter how clearly he sees it to be true, God (or an evil demon) might be deceiving him about it.

The Impact of the Deceptive God Hypothesis

I think the possibility of a deceptive God serves to make very many beliefs metaphysically uncertain. This would include necessary truths of arithmetic and geometry,

---

[3]Cress, 24.

as we have seen. Presumably, it would also include such "analytic" truths as that all mothers are female, and that a square has four sides. It would undoubtedly include metaphysical principles such as "every event has a cause," "no substance can both have and lack a given property at the same time," and "what goes up must come down." If Descartes is to remain true to his fundamental epistemic principle, he must suspend judgment with respect to all such propositions. Obviously, this doesn't leave much to be believed.

Now we can see why it is so important for Descartes to prove that God exists, and that he is no deceiver. For until this powerful source of doubt is removed, it is hard to see how Descartes can regain his old beliefs. He will be like a man who has dumped out all of his apples—good and bad alike—and who now finds that he cannot put even the good ones back into his basket. From a certain perspective, we might say that such a man is worse off for the effort. Whereas he formerly had a lot of good apples (admittedly mixed in with some bad ones) now he has very few apples indeed (although they are now all good ones).

Descartes clearly recognized the importance of establishing the existence and veracity of God. He says:

> I ought at the first opportunity to inquire if there is a God, and, if there is, whether or not he can be a deceiver. If I am ignorant of these matters, I do not think I can ever be certain of anything else.[4]

Thus, the time has come for us to consider whether or not there is a God, and if so, what sort of God it may be.

FUNDAMENTALS OF PHILOSOPHICAL THEOLOGY

Descartes developed and defended some rather interesting arguments for the existence of God. We will have to study these fairly closely. However, before we turn to Descartes' arguments, it will be useful to consider some of the traditional arguments that were available to him. Some of these are easier to understand than the arguments Descartes used, and reflection on them will serve as a good preparation for the study of Descartes' arguments. So, in the remainder of this chapter, we will consider some of the fundamentals of philosophical theology, and some fairly unsophisticated arguments for the existence of God. In Chapter 6, we will consider some of the most important standard arguments for the existence of God. Finally, in Chapter 7, we will return to the *Meditations,* to see how Descartes tried to establish the existence of a non-deceptive God.

Reason to Believe in God

The question that confronts us, then, is whether there is any good reason to believe in God. We have to be clear about what's meant by "good reason." You might think that one good reason to believe in God is this: if you believe, you will be happier. Belief in God will support you in times of trouble. You will therefore avoid despair

[4]Cress, 24.

and the feeling that "life is meaningless." Since you will be better off in these ways if you believe in God, you have good reason to believe in God.

Belief in God undoubtedly does have these good consequences in many cases, and many people do have this sort of good reason to believe in God. If you are such person, I hope you will believe in God. However, there is another way to understand the expression "good reason to believe in God." Sometimes, when we seek a good reason to believe something, we are looking for a conclusive argument for that thing. That is, we are looking for some known facts which, when put together, show that the thing in question is true.

To see the difference between these two concepts of "good reasons," consider the case of a man who has been hauled up before the Inquisition. The Inquisitors demand to know whether he believes in God. They threaten to torture him if he proves to be an atheist. Such a man has good reason (of the first sort) to believe in God! If he doesn't, he'll be tortured. However, the threats of the Inquisitors do not constitute any *argument* for the existence of God. They do not help the man to come to know that God exists, and they do not give him any deeper understanding of the nature of God. So, using "good reason" in the second sense, we can say that such a man has not been given good reason to believe in God.

If we are looking for good reasons of the second sort, we are looking for a conclusive argument for the existence of God. That's what we're doing here. We are not attempting to catalogue the benefits of faith. We are attempting to discover whether there is evidence on the basis of which it can be shown that God exists, or whether, by the use of our intellects, we can come to know that God exists. Even if we should fail in this, it might still be the case that belief in God is so beneficial that we would be fools to give it up. In that case, our belief in God would be beneficial, but rationally unfounded.

This distinction between two senses of "reasons to believe" may help to shed light on an often misunderstood argument originally presented by a French philosopher and mathematician, Blaise Pascal. Pascal, who lived at about the same time as Descartes, tried to show that it is far more reasonable to believe in God than it is to disbelieve. His argument has come to be known as "Pascal's Wager." It is based on certain very natural assumptions. First, we assume that if you believe in God, and God actually exists, then you will be rewarded in heaven. This will be very good for you. On the other hand, if you don't believe in God, but God exists, then you will be punished in hell. That will be very bad for you.

However, if God does not exist, then it won't make much difference whether you believe or not. Assuming that the hedonistic life of the atheist is slightly more fun than the ascetic life of the theist, we may suppose that, if God does not exist, you will be slightly better off if you don't believe.

These facts can be summarized in the "utility matrix" that appears in Table 5-1. This is a little chart that shows how well off you will be under each of the four main possibilities Pascal mentioned. Notice that in the upper left box the number is +1,000. That indicates how well off you will be if God exists, and you believe in God. In the upper right box we find a −6. That indicates the slight loss of value for you if you waste your time believing in God, when God does not exist. The −1,000 in the lower left box represents the pain of going to hell in case God does exist, but you

TABLE 5-1

	God exists	God does not exist
You believe	+1,000	-6
You disbelieve	-1,000	+6

don't believe it, and the +6 in the lower right box indicates that you will enjoy a little harmless pleasure if there is no God, and you live a carefree life.

I think it should be pretty obvious that in this case it is more reasonable for you to believe in God than to disbelieve. You can get the best outcome only if you believe, and you risk the worst outcome only if you disbelieve. Furthermore, the worst that can happen to you if you believe is not too bad, while the worst that can happen to if you disbelieve is terrible. Thus, assuming that it is just as likely that God exists as it is that he doesn't, it is clearly more reasonable for you to believe than to disbelieve.

We can explain more precisely why belief is the more reasonable course of action in this case, if we make use of a certain technical term—"expected utility." To find the expected utility of a course of action, you must first determine the main possible outcomes of that course of action. For each possible outcome, find the likelihood of that outcome, and the value of that outcome. Multiply these together. Then add up all the products. The result is the expected utility of the course of action. The most reasonable course of action is the one with the highest expected utility.

In the current example, there are two courses of action: believing in God, and disbelieving. If we assume that the chances that God exists are 50/50, the result is that the expected utility of believing in God is +497. We get this figure by multiplying the probability that God exists (.5) by the value of believing in God if he exists (+1,000), and then adding this to the result of multiplying the probability that God does not exist (.5) by the value of believing in God when he doesn't exist (−6). Since 500 minus 3 equals 497, the expected utility of belief in God in this case is +497.

On the other hand, the expected utility of *not* believing in God is −497. We get this figure by adding together (.5 × −1,000) and (.5 × +6). The rational course of action is assumed to be the one with the higher expected utility. Since +497 is much greater than −497, you have very good reason to believe in God.

I think that there is nothing wrong with this line of reasoning. It does show (given the assumptions) that we all have reason to believe in God. The problem is that it only gives us reason *in the first sense* to believe in God. It just shows that we might be better off believing in God. It does not provide evidence, or proof of the existence of God. It does not make it seem more likely that God exists. It gives us no argument for the conclusion that God exists. Hence, it does not give us reason *in the second sense* for believing in God.

If we put ourselves in the position of someone like Descartes, who wants to know whether or not God exists, Pascal's wager is utterly irrelevant. No amount of reflection on it will get us any closer to knowing that God exists. For our purposes, it is about as useful as the instruments of torture that terrified people during the Inquisition.

An Argument from Meteorology

One of the most popular arguments for the existence of God is based on the fact that we are sometimes awed and overwhelmed by the enormous power of certain natural phenomena such as the movement of the tides, or the changing of the seasons, or the rebirth of plants and animals in the springtime. Sometimes, when we are thus awed and overwhelmed, we begin to feel that there is some sort of powerful entity directing the natural phenomena. We feel that there must be some great source of energy in the universe—something strong enough to make the tides rise and fall, something strong enough to make the seasons change. We decide to use the word "God" to refer to this great source of energy, and so we conclude that God exists. Since quite a few people have reasoned in this way, we should attempt to formulate the argument clearly, and evaluate it.

In one form, the argument looks something like this:

The Argument from Meteorology

1 The tides go in and out, the seasons change, the wind blows, etc.
2 If the tides go in and out, the seasons change, the wind blows, etc., then there is some great source of energy in the universe.
3 If there is a great source of energy in the universe, then God exists.
4 Therefore, God exists.

The first premise of this argument is obviously true. We can observe the tides and the winds without any great trouble. Anyone who has taken a holiday at the seashore knows that (1) is true.

Line (2) is also quite plausible. If you consider the amount of water that moves when the tide changes, you will realize that it takes a lot of energy to change the tides. Equally, if you consider how much damage can be done in a severe wind storm, you will realize that there's a lot of energy behind the winds, too. All this energy can't just spring up out of nowhere. It must have a source.

Many people choose to identify that source as "God." That is, they choose to use the word "God" to refer to a great source of energy in the natural world. Since there is little doubt that such a source of energy exists, they conclude that God exists. This view of things is formulated in line (3). If the word "God" means the same as "great source of energy in the universe," then line (3) is true.

As formulated here, the argument from meteorology is valid. Nevertheless, it should be clear that there is something terribly wrong with the argument. The facts mentioned in (1) and (2) surely do not settle the issue of God's existence. Surely, an atheist can acknowledge that something makes the tides change! So what, exactly, is wrong with the argument?

As I see it, the problem here has to do with the word "God." If we use this word simply to mean "great source of energy," then I think the argument is perfectly sound. The facts mentioned in the premises really do show that there is a great source of energy in the world. If we choose to use the word "God" in this sense, then we may say that the argument shows that God exists. However, if we do use "God" in this sense, we must realize that there is no reason to say that God is a supernatural being of any sort, that he is in any way conscious or thoughtful, or that he has any sort of moral authority. For all this argument shows, God might turn out to be the sun or the moon! Indeed, I suspect that God (in this sense) would have to be the sun or the moon, since they are primarily responsible for the movements of the tides, and the winds. Thus, while the argument may be sound, it is extremely misleading. A careless reader might think it has something to do with some sort of divine, supernatural being. Of course, it has nothing to do with any such thing. It does not serve to establish the existence of the entity in which we were originally interested.

On the other hand, we might choose to use the word "God" in some other way. We might suppose that "God" refers to some sort of divine, supernatural being that does have moral authority. In this case, it is not at all clear whether line (3) is true. We need to know much more about this alleged "God" before we can determine whether or not "God exists" follows from "there is a great source of energy in the world." On the face of it, there seems to be no obvious connection.

The failure of the argument from meteorology shows that we have to come to some more explicit and satisfactory understanding of our concept of God before we can properly evaluate arguments about God's existence. Just what sort of entity are we talking about when we say that God exists? And what sort of entity do we deny when we say that God does not exist? What is the nature of the supposed entity about which atheists and theists disagree? Until we clarify this point, our discussion is likely to be vague and inconclusive. There will be no way to decide what evidence counts in favor of, or against, the existence of God, until we know what sort of thing this "God" is supposed to be.

ANALYZING THE CONCEPT OF GOD

The concept of God, according to one of the grandest Western theological traditions, is the concept of a "supreme being"—a being that is, in every respect, perfect. Let us attempt to clarify this notion of God.

Consider the property of being powerful. This is a property that comes in various degrees. Some things are more powerful than others. If a thing were perfect with respect to power, it would have power "in the highest degree." That is, it would be as powerful as it is possible for anything to be. This consideration naturally leads to the idea that a thing has a perfection if it has some property "in the highest degree." Of course, not just any property will do here. We don't want to say that a thing has a perfection because it has ugliness in the highest degree, or because it has greediness in the highest degree. Rather, we want to say that a thing has a perfection if it has, to the highest degree, some property that is good to have, such as power, or wisdom.

Here, then, is a preliminary definition of "perfection":

D1 F is a perfection = df. F is the highest degree of some property that (*a*) comes in degrees, and (*b*) is good to have.

Now we can see why a being that is powerful in the highest degree has a perfection—omnipotence. This is because the property of being powerful comes in various degrees, and is good to have. Omnipotence is the highest degree of power-fulness, and so omnipotence is a perfection. Perfect ugliness, on the other hand, is not a perfection. Ugliness comes in various degrees, and perfect ugliness may be the highest degree of ugliness. But since ugliness is not good to have, perfect ugliness is not a perfection. Similarly for perfect greediness.

We might think, then, that we can say that "supreme being" means "being with all perfections." In other words, we might define "supreme" as follows:

> **D2** x is supreme = df. x has all perfections.

Using this concept of supremacy, we could go on to say that our concept of God is the concept of a supreme being—a being having all perfections. In other words, the idea is that God is an entity that has the highest degree of every property that is good to have, and that comes in degrees.

This account of the concept of God is on the right track, but it is not quite correct. There is a slight problem concerning the definition of "perfection." To see the problem, consider the property of *getting good gas mileage*. That's a good property to have—especially for cars and trucks. Furthermore, it is a property that comes in various degrees, since some cars get better gas mileage than others. Given D1, it would follow that *getting infinite gas mileage* is a perfection. But surely, we do not want to count this among God's perfections. A supreme being is supposed to be outstanding in many respects, but gas mileage is not one of them.

I believe we can solve this problem by appeal to a distinction. Let us distinguish between properties that are *extrinsically* good to have, and properties that are *intrinsically* good to have. We can say that a property is *extrinsically* good to have if it is good to have because of its results, or consequences. Extrinsically good properties are ones that may be worthless in themselves, but are valuable because of what they lead to. On the other hand, we can say that a property is *intrinsically* good to have if it is good in itself, for its own sake, and not because of its results or consequences. I do not think that the property of getting good gas mileage is intrinsically good to have. It is only extrinsically good to have. It is good to have that property, not for its own sake, but because of its consequences—if a car gets good gas mileage, then it won't cost so much to run. And, as a result of that, its owner will be able to use his or her money on other, more satisfying things than gasoline.

Making use of this distinction, we can revise D1 slightly. The new definition is:

> **D1′** F is a perfection = df. F is the highest degree of a property that (*a*) comes in degrees, and (*b*) is intrinsically good to have.

On the new definition the property of getting infinite gas mileage no longer counts as a perfection. That surely is an improvement. As before, we can say that a supreme being is one that has all perfections, and we can say that our concept of God is the concept of a supreme being. I think this is satisfactory for our present purposes. However, we still need to say more about these alleged perfections. Which properties, exactly, are we ascribing to God when we say that he has all perfections?

Omnipotence

I have already mentioned one of the most important properties generally ascribed to God. That, of course, is the property of *omnipotence*. Omnipotence is the highest degree of powerfulness. Powerfulness clearly does come in various degrees. Some things are more powerful than others. Furthermore, a case can be made for the view that it is good in itself to be powerful. If so, then the highest degree of powerfulness would be a perfection according to D1′. (Of course, it must also be admitted that a pretty good case can be made for the view that powerfulness is only extrinsically good. If powerfulness is only extrinsically good, then omnipotence is not a perfection, on D1′.)

We must not think of God's power as any sort of physical strength. When we say that God is omnipotent, we do not mean to suggest that God has huge rippling muscles. Rather, we mean to suggest that God "can do anything." This concept of omnipotence may be defined as follows:

> **D3** x is omnipotent = df. For any state of affairs, p, x can make p occur.

In other words, an omnipotent being is one that can make anything happen. Consider the state of affairs of the Red Sea being parted. If God is omnipotent, he can make this state of affairs occur. Similarly for the state of affairs of the world being created in seven days. For any state of affairs you can think of, an omnipotent being (if there is one) can make it happen.

Definition D3 is open to a very serious objection. It is generally assumed that some states of affairs are impossible. For example, consider the state of affairs of some triangle having four sides, or the state of affairs of there being colorless blue frogs. In each case, the state of affairs seems to involve a contradiction—if the figure is a triangle, it must have three (and not four) sides; if the frog is blue, then it has a color (and is not colorless). It is hard to see how such impossible states of affairs could occur. Since they are impossible, they can't occur. Nothing could make them happen—not even the most powerful of all possible beings.

While some theologians and philosophers[5] have apparently wanted to defend something like D3, I think we will make better progress if we demand less of an omnipotent being. Let us say instead that an omnipotent being is one that can make happen anything that is possible. In other words:

> **D3′** x is omnipotent = df. For any state of affairs, p, if p is metaphysically possible, then x can make p occur.

When we say that a state of affairs is metaphysically possible, we mean that we can conceive of its occurrence; its occurrence does not entail any contradiction; we can imagine a possible world in which it happens. Thus, miracles such as the parting of the Red Sea, and the creation of the world in seven days are metaphysically possible, but absurdities such as there being a four-sided triangle are not. According to D3′, an omnipotent being is able to make happen anything that is metaphysically possible. Such a being does not have to be able to do the metaphysically impossible. The inability to do such things does not detract from its omnipotence.

---

[5]Including, perhaps, Descartes himself. In a number of letters, Descartes apparently said that each thing that in fact is a contradiction is such that God could have made it a truth. See, for example, the letter of May 2, 1694 to Mesland, which can be found in *Descartes: Philosophical Letters,* translated and edited by Anthony Kenny, Oxford: Oxford University Press, 1970, pp. 150−151.

Omniscience

A second traditional perfection is "omniscience." Loosely, we may think of an omniscient being as one that is "all knowing." However, we must not suppose that an omniscient being literally knows *everything*. The problem is that if a thing is known, it must be true.[6] Since some things must be false, it follows that some things cannot be known. Not even God can know that $2+3=4$, or that there are four-sided triangles. At most, we can insist that an omniscient being must know everything that is true. In other words:

> **D4** x is omniscient = df. For any proposition, p, if p is true, then x knows p.

If there is an omniscient being, then that being knows everything that is true. If some proposition is false, then that being does not know that proposition. Not even God can know that my truck is green (since it is not green). Of course, if some proposition is false, then an omniscient being will know that it is false. So if there is a God, and he is omniscient, then he knows that the proposition that my truck is green is false. (Of course, it is true that the proposition that my truck is green is false.)

Many people feel that knowledge is good only because of its consequences. If some bit of knowledge is entirely useless, and its possession does not make the knower any happier, or richer, or better off in any other way, these people are prepared to say that there's nothing good about having that knowledge. In itself, just knowing things, on this view, is worthless. The only value of knowledge is in its consequences. Other people feel that, even when it doesn't have any beneficial results, it is better to know than to be ignorant.

To clarify your own view on this question, you can try a little thought experiment. Imagine two possible worlds. Imagine that you exist in each of the worlds, and are just as happy and rich in the one as you are in the other. Suppose that the worlds are as alike as possible, except that in one your beliefs are mostly true, and you have considerable knowledge. In the other, your beliefs are mostly false, and you are extensively deceived. In order to make the experiment worthwhile, you must be sure that you are imagining worlds that are otherwise as alike as possible. You must imagine that your knowledge in the first world does not have any good results, and you must imagine that your ignorance in the other world does not have any bad results. The worlds must differ only with respect to the amount of knowledge you have (and whatever is logically entailed by this difference).

Some people will say that "where ignorance is bliss, 'tis folly to be wise." They will see no reason to prefer the world in which they have knowledge. Others will say that "knowledge is its own reward." They will prefer the world in which they have knowledge, even if that knowledge does not produce any further good. For my own part, I think I'd rather have the knowledge—but it's hard to tell, since in real life knowledge is almost invariably useful. In any case, my point here is this: if knowledge is intrinsically good to have, then omniscience is a perfection. In that case, any supreme being would have to be omniscient.

---

[6] The analysis of knowledge was discussed earlier, in Chapter 2.

Omnibenevolence

A third traditional perfection of God is *omnibenevolence,* or perfect goodness. The idea here is that there are various grades of moral excellence. Some things are morally better than others. The highest grade of moral excellence is a perfection, since it is (allegedly) intrinsically good to be morally excellent. Therefore, a supreme being, if there is one, would be pre-eminent with respect to virtue, too.

There are some serious puzzles about God's virtues. If you think about it for a moment, you will realize that it's doubtful that God has the traits that are thought to be virtues for people. For example, consider faith or piety. faith is usually counted among the virtues, but does it make any sense to say that God is faithful (using as our definition for faithful "full of or characterized by faith")? What is God supposed to believe in? An even more difficult case is chastity. Many people maintain that chastity is a virtue. But surely, it is nonsense to suppose that God could be chaste. Being chaste requires refraining from improper sexual activities, but God is probably not the sort of entity that could engage in such activities anyway. Clearly enough, if God is a nonphysical entity, "he" has no body and no sex. What would then be involved in his chastity? The upshot is that we cannot just say that an omnibenevolent being is one that has the ordinary human virtues, but just to a greater extent. Rather, we have to construct a concept of perfect virtue that will be more fitting to a divine entity.

One way in which we can do this is based upon the notion of preferences. A greedy or selfish person may prefer a certain distribution of wealth even though he realizes that it is not the best distribution. He may prefer it because, under that distribution, he himself gets a disproportionately large share of the wealth. A foolish person might prefer a certain state of affairs, failing to recognize that it is much worse than some of its alternatives. A morally perfect being would never have failings of these sorts. Such a being would always prefer the better to the worse, and would never prefer something unless it was for the best. Such preferences would always accord properly with the true values of things. Let us say that this is the crucial feature of omnibenevolence—always and only preferring the better to the worse:

> **D5** x is omnibenevolent =df. For any states of affairs, p and q, x prefers p to q if and only if p is intrinsically better than q.

I cannot prove that omnibenevolence is a perfection. However, it seems reasonable to suppose that it is. Many people feel that it is good to have your preferences match the values of things—even if there is no payoff involved. If they are right, then omnibenevolence is intrinsically good to have. Furthermore, it is pretty clear that omnibenevolence is the highest degree of a certain property—preferring the good to the evil. If both of these points are correct, then omnibenevolence is a perfection, and so any supreme being would have to have it.

Necessary Existence

The final traditional perfection is a bit harder to explain, since it requires an understanding of a concept that is alien to most of us nowadays. I suspect that most people would say that *existence* is not a property that comes in various degrees. Nothing "exists more" than anything else. We don't normally speak of one thing "existing to a greater degree" than another. However, there is a highly respected metaphysical tradition according to which there would be nothing wrong with such talk. According to this tradition, there are various grades, or degrees, of existence.

We may be able to grasp this notion if we think of it in terms of "ontological independence"—the ability of a thing to exist in its own right. Some things allegedly have very little ontological independence. They cannot exist unless several other things exist, and are properly related. For example, consider a football game. Unless there are several players, a suitable field, and a ball; and unless the players come together at the appropriate time, and interact properly, the game will not exist. The game depends for its existence on many other individuals. The same sort of remark could be made for a corporation, or a nation, or an orchestra. Such things have a relatively low grade of ontological independence. They are not very "real."

An individual substance, such as a football player, or a trombone, might seem to be more real. Such entities can exist pretty much on their own, whether or not other players, or other instruments exist. Such entities are "contingent existents," since it is not necessary that they exist, and it is not necessary that they do not exist. If they exist, it is a mere matter of fact that they do.

Presumably, such things cannot create themselves. If some contingent existent exists, something must have caused it to exist. Therefore, such things are not utterly independent ontologically. They depend upon their creators. If there were a thing that could "create itself," or that did not need to be created, it would have a higher grade of ontological independence. Presumably, if there were a "necessary existent," it would have the highest grade of ontological independence. It would be able to exist no matter what happened.

The point of all this is to make sense of the idea that there are grades of existence, or reality. Each such grade is characteristic of a certain type of entity. The lowest grade is had by events, or "modes." An intermediate grade is had by contingent substances. The highest grade would be had by a necessary substance.[7]

Some philosophers have maintained that existence itself is a good thing. Of course, if you don't exist, nothing good can happen to you. Existence seems to be a necessary condition for every valuable thing. However, this only shows that existence is extrinsically good—a condition without which it is impossible to enjoy anything good. It does not show that existence is good in itself. To establish this latter claim, we would have to show that, even when it does not lead to, or cause, or provide the condition for any other good thing, existence still is valuable. It is not clear how this could be shown. One problem is that it is pretty hard to compare the value of an existent thing with the value of a nonexistent thing. Nonexistent things don't exist. How can we determine the value of a thing if it isn't there? How can such a thing be compared with an existent thing?

Here's a possible test: suppose you are offered the choice of having one or the other of two gold coins. Each coin is exactly like the other with respect to weight, purity, design, age, etc. The only difference between the coins is that one of them

[7]For a more detailed account of this notion, see below, Chapter 7 under "A New Causal Principle."

exists and other does not. Which would you rather have? It has been suggested that if you prefer the existent coin, it must be because you think existence is good in itself. For my own part, I am inclined to think that there is something fishy about the proposed test.[8]

If we assume that it is intrinsically good to exist, and we accept the doctrine that there are grades of existence, we will reach the conclusion that the highest possible grade of existence is a perfection. In this case, we will say that "necessary existence" is one of God's properties. We can define this concept as follows:

> **D6** x is a necessary existent = df. For any time, t, it is metaphysically necessary that x exists at t.

Some Other Properties of God

It seems to me that we should add one more perfection to this catalogue of divine properties. I am inclined to accept the view that pleasure is intrinsically good. It is pretty obvious that pleasure comes in various degrees, or grades. Therefore, it would seem that the highest possible grade of pleasure would have to be a perfection. In this case, God would be the happiest of all possible entities.

In addition to these perfections, there are some further properties generally ascribed to God. One of these is *creativity*. A thing is creative, in this special sense, if it has created everything else. More exactly, we should say that a thing is creative if every contingent thing is ontologically dependent upon it. Descartes seems to have thought that each contingent thing is brought into existence by God. This is not a very surprising view. What is surprising, however, is Descartes' idea that each contingent thing needs to be kept in existence by God. If God were to stop "conserving" a thing, it would just slip out of existence. I don't know whether we should understand creativity in this strong way, or whether it is sufficient to define it in a more familiar, weaker way. Perhaps it doesn't matter. In any case, we will say that a thing is creative, provided that all contingent existents depend upon it for their existence.

Although many people have accepted polytheistic religions, the God of Western theology is typically thought to be the sole or unique supreme being. If there were two supreme beings, neither of them would answer to the traditional concept of God. So let's add *unity* to our catalogue of divine attributes. By this I do not mean that God is just one thing—God would be just one thing even if there were a dozen other beings just as powerful as he is. Perhaps I can explain divine unity by saying that a thing has divine unity provided that nothing other than it has all the perfections.

Some theologians would insist that in order to be God, an entity would also have to be *incorporeal*. That is, they would say that God is not a physical object of any sort. He is a "spiritual" entity. This doctrine seems to run counter to the Christian view that (at least for a period of time) God lived here on earth in the body of a man.

---

[8] We will consider this problem more carefully later on, in the section on Descartes' ontological argument for the existence of God. See Chapter 7 under "An Objection to the Ontological Argument."

In order to avoid squabbling over details, let us agree to put this property into special category. It is not clear whether, in order to count as God, a thing has to be incorporeal.

There are, of course, many other properties that have been ascribed to God. Some say that God is jealous. Others say that God is merciful. Some say that God is male. Others say that God is female. Many would insist that since God is incorporeal, it makes little sense to ascribe any sex to him.[9] I think it would be best to remain neutral with respect to these further properties. For our purposes here, it will be sufficient to think of God as an omniscient, omnipotent, omnibenevolent, creative, necessary being. We will also assume that God is unitary. Some will go on to assume that God is incorporeal, but, as I mentioned above, this may be a bit controversial.

Now, armed with this concept of God, we can return to our original question: is there any good reason to suppose that any such entity exists?

SOME POPULAR ARGUMENTS

There are very many different arguments for the existence of God, and these can be catalogued in a variety of ways. My plan here is to discuss some of the weaker arguments first, and then, in Chapter 6, to turn to some of the more impressive attempts. If you have a clear understanding of the defects of the weaker arguments, you may be better able to appreciate the ingenuity and subtlety of the more powerful ones. So let's turn to a popular, but not very successful line of reasoning.

The Argument from Scripture

Even the most superficial glance at a copy of the Bible will reveal that there are quite a few references to God in that book. Many biblical statements entail the existence of God. For example, in one place in the Bible, it is said that God created heaven and earth.[10] If God never existed, he could not have done this. Hence, the statement entails that God existed.

To simplify, let's suppose that the Bible actually says that God exists. Some people apparently think that this provides the basis for an argument for the existence of God. Their reasoning can be displayed as follows:

The Argument from Scripture

1 The Bible says that God exists.
2 What the Bible says is true.
3 Therefore, God exists.

It is important to understand why this argument fails. The problem is not a logical one—the argument is valid. Nor is it that the premises are false. For all I

---

[9]My own view is that if there is a God, he is essentially incorporeal. Thus, he is neither male nor female, Nevertheless, when I need a pronoun to refer to God, I use "he" rather than "she" or "it." I do this because such sentences with "it" or "she" seem quite jarring and are often a bit hard to understand. I hope no one will be offended or misled.

[10]Genesis 1:1.

know, they might both be true. The problem is an epistemological one. It has to do with our reasons for accepting the second premise.

Suppose I believe in God. Suppose I also think that the Bible is the work of writers who were inspired by God. Since they had divine inspiration, what they wrote was all true. It was "the word of God." For this reason, I believe that everything the Bible says is true. Thus, I accept (2). It would be pointless for me then to make use of the argument from scripture in an effort to come to know that God exists. After all, I accepted premise (2) only because I already assumed God exists.

An argument such as this one is said to "beg the question." One of the premises is epistemologically dependent on the conclusion. In order to know that the premise is true, we'd first have to know that the conclusion is true. Since there is no independent way of being sure that the conclusion is true, we have no way of establishing the truth of the premise. In this case, we cannot extend our knowledge by the use of the argument.

The problem can be made clearer, perhaps, by considering what an atheist would say about this argument. If the atheist were reasonably clear-headed, and he were willing to discuss the question, he would undoubtedly attack line (2). He would say that, in his opinion, there is no more reason to believe what is said in the Bible than there is to believe what is said in the *Iliad* or *The Lord of the Rings*. Surely, it would be irrational to try to convince such an atheist by telling him that line (2) must be true, since the Bible is the inspired word of God. Since he doesn't believe in God, he will not be moved by this consideration to accept line (2) of the argument.

In light of this, we can see that the argument from scripture is quite worthless. Atheists will reject the second premise, and so will be unmoved by the argument. Theists will accept the second premise, but they accept it only because they already believe in God. They cannot increase their knowledge by the use of the argument. Agnostics, who are unsure about the existence of God, will be unsure about the truth of the second premise. Thus, the argument cannot rationally influence anyone's belief in God.

The Argument from Consent—I

When I was a child, I was required to undergo a certain amount of religious education. Although I don't recall much of what I was taught, I do have a pretty clear recollection of one of the textbooks. I think it was called *One God*. It was an elementary book in comparative religion. Each chapter presented an account of the main features of some religious tradition. The overall theme of the book is suggested by the title. As I understood it, we were supposed to come to the conclusion that all people, in spite of minor variations in detail, share a common belief in a single divine being. (There was also the suggestion that, where religious traditions differed, my own was generally closest to the truth, and the others were wrong.)

I think that my classmates and I were expected to understand that, since the belief in God is universally accepted, there must be something in it. If there were no God, why would everyone believe that there is? So the message is clear—since everyone believes in God, God must exist. This argument is generally known as "The Argument from Consent" or "Consensus Gentium" (Latin for "the agreement of the people"). It can be put in this way:

1 Everyone believes that God exists.
2 If everyone believes that something is true, then it is true.
3 Therefore, God exists.

In this form, the argument is valid. Beyond this, however, nothing good can be said about it. Neither premise is worthy of acceptance. Since there are very many atheists and agnostics, line (1) is clearly false. Since it is possible for everyone to be mistaken about something, there's no good reason to accept (2).

The Argument from Consent—II

I think that there is a somewhat more plausible line of reasoning that might be suggested here. This is based on the fact that belief in God is very widespread. Very many people, in widely varying circumstances, have accepted this belief. So here we have a certain fact. This fact needs to be explained. Why have so many people believed in God? One explanation presents itself as most reasonable—this belief is so widespread because it's true. People believe in God because God actually exists. This provides the basis for a more sophisticated version of the argument from consent:

The Argument from Consent—II

1 Belief in God is very widespread.
2 The best explanation for the fact that belief in God is very widespread is that God exists.
3 If belief in God is very widespread, and the best explanation for this is that God exists, then God exists.
4 Therefore, God exists.

This version of the argument is also valid. It is better than the first version, since here there are at least two true premises. As I see it, (1) and (3) are probably true.

Nevertheless, the argument is inconclusive. The problem is in line (2). According to line (2) the actual existence of God provides the best explanation for the fact that so many people believe in God. But this is implausible. Even if God does exist, how could this explain the fact that people believe in God? Surely we cannot suppose that the mere existence of an entity causes people to believe in that entity. Furthermore, there may be a quite satisfactory "naturalistic" explanation for this belief in God. Perhaps we should explain this belief by appeal to the fact that every person starts out very weak and small. As infants, we are awed and impressed by the apparent strength and wisdom of our parents. When we grow up, the remnants of this belief may remain. We continue to believe that there is a wise and powerful being who stands in judgment over us. Since no ordinary human being seems to be wise and powerful enough, we imagine that there is a god.[11]

---

[11]One of the most famous advocates of this sort of naturalistic approach is Sigmund Freud. See his *The Future of an Illusion,* translated by W. D. Robson-Scott. Garden City, New York: Doubleday Anchor Books, 1957.

If there is some such naturalistic explanation for the belief in God, and if this explanation is better than an explanation based on the idea that God actually exists, then line (2) is false. Atheists must conclude that there is some such explanation. Theists, if they want to endorse this argument, have to give some account of the way in which the existence of God serves to explain why so many people believe in God. Agnostics should realize that the argument is valid, but that line (2) is open to serious doubts.

The Mystical Approach

Quite a few people have reported having experiences of a strange and impressive sort. Some have said that they "saw God." Others claim to have been "in communion with God." Sometimes these people stress the notion that they experienced some sort of unity, or "oneness" with God. Generally, people who claim to have had these experiences insist that the experiences were so unusual that it is impossible to describe them in ordinary language. For this reason, such experiences are often said to be "ineffable," or incapable of being described in ordinary language.

In many cases, the experience is life-altering. After having undergone it, the person changes in important respects. A man who has led a fairly ordinary life may, after one of these experiences, become deeply religious. Perhaps he will give up his wordly goods, and devote himself to works of charity, or even to a life of meditation and prayer.

It is clear that such experiences can easily cause someone to believe in God. However, since we are interested in rational proof of the existence of God, we must consider whether any facts about such experiences provide the basis for an argument for the existence of God.

Sometimes, after having had such an experience, people will claim that they "know" that God exists. If we ask them how they know this, they may say, "I know that God exists, because I have seen God." The argument here seems to be:

The Argument from Mystical Experience—I

1 Some people have seen God.
2 If some people have seen God, then God exists.
3 Therefore, God exists.

It should be obvious that if God is a nonphysical entity, then (1) cannot be true. At best we could see "messengers" of God, or "manifestations" of God. God himself would not be something visible. Even if it should turn out that God is visible, it is very hard to determine in advance what God looks like. Thus, when seeing something very odd and striking, it is hard to determine whether that thing is God. How can mystics be sure that the thing they are seeing is really God? And even if they have some way of being sure, how can the rest of us be sure? Merely taking their word for it cannot be sufficient. Even an honest mystic might be mistaken.

Sometimes the argument takes another form. Sometimes mystics claim that they have had a weird and supernatural experience. This experience is so odd, so overpowering, and so "otherworldy," that it cannot be explained by naturalistic science. In order to explain how this experience is possible, we must assume that God somehow caused it. We must conclude that if there were no God, then such experiences as this one would never occur.

In order to facilitate discussion of the argument, let us formulate it more clearly. Here is one version:

The Argument from Mystical Experience—II

1 Some people have had mystical experiences.

2 Mystical experiences are explainable only on the assumption that God exists.

3 If some people have had mystical experiences, and such experiences are explainable only on the assumption that God exists, then God exists.

4 Therefore, God exists.

In this form, the argument is valid. Lines (1) and (3) seem to be true. As you may have guessed, I'm not too impressed by line (2). For one thing, I find it difficult to understand how the existence of God would serve to explain why people have mystical experiences. If you think that there is some such explanation, you should attempt to formulate it clearly and precisely. Merely saying, as some have, that "God works in mysterious ways," is worthless here. Such statements, even if true, are not explanations. They are just admissions of our inability to explain things we assume to have been done by God. In the present context, we are looking for an explanation of the mystical experiences.

Secondly, it seems to me that as psychology progresses, we may find that there are quite adequate naturalistic explanations for mystical experiences. The fact that such experiences follow certain fairly standard patterns, and the fact that the administration of psychoactive drugs can induce these exeriences (or ones relevantly like them) strongly suggest that a neurological explanation will eventually be found. Until we are quite confident that no such explanation can be found, I think we must suspend judgment on line (2), and the argument from mystical experience as a whole.

With this we conclude our consideration of some of the more popular arguments for the existence of God. In Chapter 6, we will turn to some arguments that deserve somewhat more serious attention.

TRADITIONAL ARGUMENTS FOR THE EXISTENCE OF GOD

COSMOLOGICAL ARGUMENTS

If you ask theists to give an argument for the existence of God, chances are they will mention something about the creation of the world. Perhaps they will spread their arms, pointing to the trees, houses, mountains, and fields in the vicinity, and say, "if there's no God, then who created all this?"

This rather sketchy little argument can be developed along a number of different lines. No matter how it is developed, however, the argument will contain two essential features. First, it will have a premise affirming the existence of some contingent thing. It might be the earth, or the whole solar system, or it might be something less grand—such as some person. Second, it will have a premise that appeals to some sort of principle about causation. The principle will state that things such as the one mentioned in the first premise couldn't exist unless they were created. Somehow, it will be alleged, these facts about causation lead to the conclusion that there must be a God. Hence, God exists. Arguments based on these fundamental ideas are called "Causal Arguments" or "Cosmological Arguments."

Although the general idea behind this sort of argument is relatively familiar, one can easily run into serious trouble when trying to formulate it precisely. So let's start by considering a version of the argument that illustrates a number of traps into which we might fall, if we are not sufficiently careful when dealing with a cosmological argument.

A Naive Version of the Cosmological Argument

In one of its simplest forms, the Cosmological Argument starts from a premise that I know to be true—"I exist." As we saw above in Chapter 4, Descartes also thought that he knew that he existed. You undoubtedly know that you exist, too. While it is not easy to say just how we come to know of our own existence, I think is pretty clear that we can have this bit of knowledge.

The second premise here is going to be a causal principle that is sometimes known as "The Principle of Universal Causation." For the purposes of the present argument, we need to put this principle into a form in which it says that concrete individual things, such as myself, are caused. When we say that such a thing is caused, we mean to suggest that it is created, or brought into being. When we speak of "the cause" of some thing, we refer to the thing that caused it. Thus, if I make a statue, I am the cause of the statue. If two people get together and conceive a child, the parents are the causes of the child. Let's put the principle in this form: "everything that exists has a cause."

It is not easy to say exactly what we mean when we say that something *causes* something. However, most of us would probably agree that part of what we mean is summed up in the claim that it is impossible for a cause to come into being *after* its effect. If A is the cause of B, then A must exist before B begins to exist. It would make no sense to say that a certain statue was created by a certain sculptor, even though the statue already existed at the time of the birth of the sculptor. How can the statue be created by the sculptor, if the sculptor doesn't yet exist? In general, then, we can say that causes must precede their effects in time. The cause must come before the effect. This will be the third premise in our cosmological argument.

So we know that something exists, and we have assumed that everything that exists must have a cause that comes before it. This seems to imply that there must be a great sequence of causes and effects. Each member of the sequence is caused by the preceding member of the chain, and each member of the sequence causes the succeeding member. Now, a question arises concerning the first member of the causal sequence. Where did it come from? What caused it? One possible answer is that the first member "caused itself." Since no contingent entity can cause itself to come into existence, the first cause must be a necessary existent. We can call this "God." In light of all this, we may conclude that God exists.

The whole argument, when tidied up, looks like this:

The Cosmological Argument (Naive Version)

1 I exist.
2 Everything that exists has a cause.
3 Causes precede their effects.
4 Therefore, there is a self-caused first cause (from 1, 2, 3).
5 If there is a self-caused first cause, then God exists.
5 Therefore, God exists (from 4, 5).

The first line of this argument needs no explanation. Each of us can know that he or she exists. The second line is a fairly plausible metaphysical principle about causation, the principle of universal causation. Things cannot begin to exist unless something makes them exist. (3) is "analytic"—that is, it is true simply by virtue of the meanings of the terms it contains. We wouldn't call something a "cause" of a certain effect, unless that cause came before that effect in time.

Line (4) is an intermediate conclusion, or "lemma." It is not the final conclusion of the argument, but it is not a premise, either. It is a line that is supposed to follow from some earlier lines. From the strictly logical point of view, there is really no reason to include a lemma in an argument. If the argument is valid with it, the argument will be valid without it. However, it is often useful to include a lemma when we formulate an argument, since it may help to make the structure of the argument clearer. That's why (4) is included here.

The reasoning behind line (4) was mentioned above. Something exists. Everything has a cause. Causes come before their effects. Therefore, there must be a long sequence of causes and effects. This sequence has to begin somewhere. Something must be the first member, and that thing must be self-caused. Thus, there must be a self-caused first cause. That's what (4) says.

Line (5) is a consequence of some reflections on the concept of God. God is suppposed to have the highest possible degree of ontological independence. Anything that depends upon some other thing for its existence would be less than maximally ontologically independent. hence, God cannot be caused by anything else. God must be self-caused. Similarly, God is supposed to be creative. Other things are supposed to depend upon God for their existence. Thus it is fitting to suppose that if there is some self-caused entity that has caused everything else, then that entity must be God. Hence, if there is a self-caused first cause, God exists.

Problems for the Naive Version

Earlier, I said that this version of the cosmological argument illustrates a number of traps into which a theist might fall. The argument is indeed defective in several ways—some of which may already be obvious. I believe it will be useful to reflect on some of these defects. Once they are understood, we may be better able to appreciate the reasons for the complexity of some of the more successful versions of the cosmological argument.

The main flaw in the argument, as I see it, is that (4) simply does not follow from (1), (2), and (3). In fact, if you put (1), (2), and (3) together, you may derive the *negation* of (4)! If something exists, and everything has a cause, and causes come before their effects, then there cannot be a first cause.

In the first place, to say that something is a "first" cause is presumably to say that it is a thing that causes the existence of later things, but which is itself not caused. The principle of universal causation (line(2) here) says that there can't be any such thing. Each thing is such that something must cause it.

Secondly, line (3) says that the cause of a thing must precede that thing in time. Obviously, nothing can precede itself in time. Therefore, nothing can be the cause of itself. Hence, if (3) is true, (4) must be false. There cannot be a self-caused entity. The upshot is that if lines (1), (2), and (3) are true, then there is no self-caused first cause. These considerations show, I believe, that we must be rather more careful if we are to do justice to the ideas behind the cosmological argument.

A More Sophisticated Cosmological Argument

Gottfried Wilhelm Leibniz (1646–1716) developed some rather interesting versions of the cosmological argument. His versions differed in several important respects from the naive version we have already considered. For one thing, Leibniz did not make use of the principle of universal causation. Rather, he made use of a closely related metaphysical principle of his own—"The Principle of Sufficient Reason." We will consider that principle in a moment. A second difference has to do with Leibniz' conception of God. For Leibniz, God was an "extramundane necessary existent." In other words, God is thought of as a substance that exists necessarily but outside of the temporal and spatial order of the universe. We cannot locate God at any of the points of time and space with which we are already familiar. God exists, but not "in the world." A final important difference between the arguments is that Leibniz' version is valid.

Let us use the expression "the world" to indicate the sum total of all the contingent things that exist, have existed, or will exist. Thus, the earth is just one of many things that are contained in the world. Even though we don't know exactly what there is in the world, we know that the world exists. Furthermore, since every part of the world is contingent, it's reasonable to suppose that the world itself is contingent, too. This gives us our first premise for Leibnizian cosmological argument:

1 The world exists and is contingent.

The second premise in our argument is going to be a version of Leibniz' principle of sufficient reason. Leibniz formulated this in a variety of ways. In one place, he put it this way:

> nothing ever takes place without its being possible for one who knew everything to give some reason why it should have happened rather than not.[1]

In another place, he puts it in these words:

> nothing happens without a sufficient reason why it should be thus rather than otherwise.[2]

Leibniz suggests that while a necessary entity might serve as its own explanation, this could never happen in the case of a contingent thing. In order to understand why a contingent thing is as it is, we must look beyond that thing—perhaps to its cause, or to the purposes of its creator. Let us say, then, that the sufficient reason for a contingent thing must always be sought in something "independent" of that thing. Two things are independent of each other, provided that neither is part of the other. Using this new terminology, we can formulate one version of the principle of sufficient reason in this way:

2 For each contingent thing, there is some independent sufficient reason why it is as it is, rather than otherwise.

It is important to understand (2) properly. (2) does not imply that people in fact know why things are as they are. (2) just says that for everything that happens, there

[1] *Leibniz: Philosophical Writings,* edited by G. H. R. Parkinson, translated by Mary Morris and G. H. R. Parkinson, Totowa, N. J.: Rowman and Littlefield, 1975, p. 112. In subsequent footnotes, I shall refer to this book as "Parkinson."
[2] Parkinson, 211.

is a reason—not that people know what that reason is. So (2) is consistent with the fact that there are "mysteries"—things we currently can't explain. What (2) implies is that there is no contingent thing that is in principle inexplicable. Everything is such that, if only we knew enough about it, we could understand why it happens as it does. Nothing is utterly and in principle unintelligible.

Furthermore, according to (2), for each contingent thing, the facts that explain it are "independent" of it. That means that no contingent thing either is or contains its own sufficient reason. We must always look beyond a contingent thing in order to understand fully why it is as it is.

I find the principle of sufficient reason quite plausible. It represents a fundamental article of faith for anyone who thinks that "the world makes sense." If you think that every natural phenomenon is such that it is in principle possible to come to an understanding of it, then you should look favorably upon the principle of sufficient reason. If you reject the principle of sufficient reason, then you must maintain that some things that happen are in principle inexplicable. No matter how much we learn about them, we can never explain why they happen as they do. Such events, if there are any, must be uncaused, too; for if there were a cause, then the event would be explainable by appeal to facts about the cause. It is hard to imagine what such an event would be like.

If you put (1) and (2) together, you can derive the conclusion that there is something that (a) is independent of the world, and (b) constitutes a sufficient reason for the world's being as it is. What could this be? Since every contingent thing is a part of the world, and this reason is not a part of the world, the reason for the world must be a noncontingent thing. In other words, it must be a necessary being. Furthermore, this necessary being must be responsible in some way for the world's being as it is. If there were a creator who created the world as it is because he wanted it to be that way, then this creator would be responbsible for the world's being as it is. We could then explain why the world is as it is by saying that this entity made it that way. That would give a sufficient reason for it to be that way.

The more we learn about this entity, the more it sounds like God. It is a necessary being. It created the world, It has some sort of consciousness (since it has preferences). Leibniz concluded that if the world has an independent sufficient reason, then God exists. That is the third line of the argument.

We are now in a position to state our version of Leibniz' cosmological argument. We'll call it "The Argument from Sufficient Reason":

1 The world exists and is contingent.
2 For each contingent thing that exists, there is some independent sufficient reason why it is as it is rather than otherwise.
3 If there is some independent sufficient reason why the world is as it is rather than otherwise, then God exists.
4 Therefore, God exists.

I wish I could now cite three or four places where Leibniz clearly presented just this argument. Unfortunately, I cannot do so. In fact, I don't know of any place where Leibniz presented exactly this argument. The claim I want to make here is that there are many passages in Leibniz' writings in which he strongly suggests this argument. One of the best of these passages is from a short work called "A Specimen of Discoveries About Marvelous Secrets of a General Nature." Leibniz says:

> If there were no necessary being, there would be no contingent being; for a reason must be given why contingent things should exist rather than not exist. But there would be no such reason unless there were a being which is in itself, that is, a being the reason for whose existence is contained in its own essence, so that there is no need for a reason outside it. Even if one went on to infinity in giving reasons for contingent things, yet outside their series (in which there is not sufficient reason) a reason for the whole series must be found. From this it also follows that the necessary being is one in number, and is all things potentially, since it is the ultimate reason of things....[3]

I leave it to the reader to determine whether the argument from sufficient reason, as I have formulated it, can be found in this passage (or any other in Leibniz). For present purposes, it is not really important whether Leibniz developed the argument or not. What's important is whether or not it's a good argument.

An Evaluation of the Leibnizian Argument

One good feature of the argument is that it is valid. The conclusion really does follow from the premises. In this respect, it is a genuine advance over the naive argument presented earlier. Another good feature of the argument is that the first premise is clearly true. Since "the world" just means "the sum total of all the contingent things that exist," it is reasonably clear that (1) is true.

There is also some plausibility in line (3). If there is a necessarily existent, extramundane entity that somehow explains why the world exists, then that entity would surely be godlike. Of course, it might not be omnibenevolent, and it might fail to be omniscient, but it would have at least some of the divine perfections. Thus, it would be a rather important entity in any case, even if it were not God.

Line (2), as I see it, is the troublesome premise. Some people will simply deny it. They will maintain that some things happen without any reason. According to these people, the world is, at least in part, "meaningless" or "absurd." There is no reason for things to be as they are. Nothing caused them to be as they are, and they could just as well have turned out otherwise. This view may be called "Existentialism." It should be recognized, however, that this term has also been used for a variety of other doctrines as well.

Here's a test that you can apply to yourself to see whether you accept the principle of sufficient reason or not. Imagine that an important public figure has been found dead. It's not clear whether he was assassinated, whether he committed suicide, or whether he died of natural causes. Pathologists are called in to determine the cause of death. They perform a careful autopsy, and issue their final verdict. They claim that there was no cause of death. At first, people think that they mean they haven't found any cause of death, but the pathologists insist that that's a misunderstanding of their report. They claim that it would be impossible for anyone to find any cause

---

[3] Parkinson, 76–77.

of death in this case, because in fact there was no cause of death. Others suppose that what they really mean is that the public figure simply "gave out"—he got too old and decrepit, and died because of a general breakdown of his internal systems. But the pathologists deny this, too. They point out that "old age" is a possible cause of death. There was *no* cause of death in this case. The public figure did not die because of old age, general decrepitude, or anything else. He simply died for no reason at all.

If you understand what the pathologists in the story have said, and think they might be right, then you may be willing to reject the principle of sufficient reason. You, apparently, can make sense of the idea that some contingent events occur for no reason at all. If, on the other hand, it seems to you that the imaginary pathologists' report must be wrong—that there must be a cause of death, even if no one can determine what it is—then you probably accept some version of the principle of sufficient reason.

There is one final critical comment that may be made concerning the argument from sufficient reason. Some critics might feel that the principle of sufficient reason is true, but only on a "local" scale. That is, they might feel that every contingent event *in* the world can be explained—perhaps by appeal to its cause. However, they might doubt that the principle of sufficient reason holds on the "global" scale. They might say that the world as a whole has no cause, and no reason. It's just a huge accident that there is any world at all. It seems to me that this position may require scrutiny, since it seems to allow us to retain everything sensible about the principle of sufficient reason while rejecting its application to the world as a whole. Thus, it would enable a critic to deny line (2) of the argument, while maintaining that there is a sufficient reason for everything that occurs in the world.

Leibniz, of course, rejected this approach. His comments on it can be found scattered through his writings. One good place to look is in the essay mentioned above.[4] Another interesting essay is "Primary Truths."[5]

This is not the place for any extended discussion of the merits of various forms of the principle of sufficient reason. It is time for us to consider a final, somewhat less complex version of the cosmological argument.

The Big Bang Argument

In recent years, a novel form of causal argument has emerged. This argument is based on some exciting new ideas in physics, the most crucial of which is the idea that the universe began with a "big bang." But what reason is there for assuming that the universe did begin in this way? It seems that there are three main sorts of evidence.[6]

The first sort of evidence is rather indirect. Apparently, astronomers have believed for some time that the galaxies are steadily moving away from each other.

---

[4]Parkinson, 75–86.
[5]Parkinson, 87–92.
[6]I have relied throughout this section on Paul Davies, *The Edge of Infinity*, Oxford: Oxford University Press, 1983. See esp. Chapter 8.

This can be explained by appeal to Einstein's theory of the expanding universe. If space itself is expanding, it's no wonder that the things in it are getting further apart. However, it is natural to assume that, if space is steadily expanding, then, at some time in the past, it must have been more compressed. Carrying this back to its limits, one reaches the conclusion that at some time in the very distant past, all the matter and space that existed must have been crammed together at a point. Furthermore, we are told that, at that moment, all the matter and space began to expand explosively.

The second sort of evidence was discovered by some Bell Telephone Company experimenters in 1965. While at work on some problems concerning satellite communications, they noticed that there is a certain amount of energy emanating from the most distant edges of the observable universe. It does not seem that this energy is radiating from any star or galaxy. Rather, it seems to be fairly uniformly distributed all around the outer limit of observability. Where is this energy coming from?

The final sort of evidence concerns the relative amounts of different sorts of matter in the universe. If the physicists assume that there was an enormously hot original explosion, and that temperatures quickly began to fall, they can calculate the sorts of matter that would have been produced out of the orginally chaotic mish-mash of particles. The relative proportions of various sorts of matter that they actually find correspond nicely to the ones they would expect, if there had been such an explosion.

All of this evidence suggests, then, that the physical universe began with a colossal explosion. Perhaps this explosion serves to explain the energy noticed by the astronomers. Maybe, as they peer out into space, they are observing the remnants of an ever-receding shockwave—a shockwave caused by the original "big bang." Similarly, maybe the universe is expanding as a result of this big bang. Maybe all the matter in the universe is flying outward, away from the place where the explosion occurred.

Some astronomers and physicists have accepted the big bang hypothesis. As they see it, the universe came into being with an enormous explosion. All the matter that exists began to exist in one location. Enormous forces blasted it out in all directions. As the matter spread out in space, it cooled and formed stars and planets. These are still expanding, and will go on expanding until all the energy from the original big bang is dissipated. Perhaps then the universe will lapse into nonexistence.

Such theorizing drives us to consider a deeper question: what caused the big bang? The answer cannot come from physics or astronomy, since (if there was a big bang) no physical objects existed before the big bang. Whatever caused the big bang, therefore, must be a nonphysical substance. Furthermore, since the big bang is supposed to be the most gigantic explosion in the history of the universe, its cause must be an entity of extraordinary power. This entity, by causing the big bang, brought the physical universe into existence. In light of all this, we can see that the cause of the big bang must have been a nonphysical, omnipotent, and creative being. That sounds a lot like God. What else could have caused the big bang?

So here we have a new cosmological argument. It may be formulated as follows:

The Big Bang Argument

1 The universe began with a big bang.
2 If the universe began with a big bang, then something must have caused the big bang.
3 The only thing that could have caused the big bang is God.
4 If God caused the big bang, then God exists.
5 Therefore, God exists.

Although this argument has attracted a fair amount of attention in recent years, I think it is really quite worthless. Careful inspection will reveal that none of the interesting premises is adequately justified.

In the first place, the astronomers are not entirely convinced that the universe began with a big bang. It has been suggested that the universe has no beginning in time, but that it goes through a cycle of expansion and contraction. The contractions are powered largely by gravity, which draws all the matter together in an ever more massive lump. At the end of the contractive phase, all the matter in the universe is jammed together at a point. Other forces then take over, causing a huge explosion, and leading to the expansive phase of the cycle. On this view of things, the big bang is not a unique event marking the beginning of the universe. It is just one of a series of big bangs, each of which marks the beginning of a new expansive phase in the endless and beginningless history of the universe. If this alternative cosmological picture is closer to the truth, then line (1) of the argument is false.

Even if we assume that there was a big bang, it is not entirely clear that it makes sense to speak of the "cause" of that event. Usually, when we speak of a cause, we have in mind some event that occurs earlier in time than its effect. But the big bang, if it occurred, occurred at the beginning of time. There was no "before." Perhaps it is such an anomalous event that our ordinary assumptions about cause and effect simply do not apply. Thus, line (2) is questionable.

Even if we assume that there was a big bang, and that it was caused, still there is no reason to believe that the cause of the big bang must have been omniscient, omnibenevolent, or omnipotent. Indeed, it is very difficult to reach any firm conclusions about the nature of the cause of the big bang, assuming that there was such a thing. In any case, I think that we should be pretty skeptical about line (3) of the argument, too.

So my conclusion with respect to the big bang argument is that, in spite of its popularity, it is not very successful. Let us turn, then, to another sort of argument for the existence of God.

ARGUMENTS FROM DESIGN

One of the most powerful sources of belief in God is the observation of "design" or "purpose" in nature. Arguments based on such considerations are now generally called "Arguments from Design," or "Teleological Arguments." Although many philosophers and theologians have formulated versions of the so-called "Argument from Design," no one has ever done it better than William Paley did in his *Evidences of the Existence and Attributes of the Deity*, which was first published in 1802. Thus, I will let Paley be our guide in the discussion of this argument.

An Argument about a Camera

Suppose you and a friend are walking through the woods one day, and you spot a shiny black object on the ground. As you get closer, you see that it is a camera—let's suppose it is a fairly new 35 mm single lens reflex model of some brand not previously known either to you or to your friend. Suppose you examine the camera, and you find that most of the components seem to be in good working order. There is a lens on the front, a viewfinder, a light meter that automatically sets the shutter speed, etc.

You observe that the various parts of the camera are constructed in such a way as to enable it take pictures. The lens on the front is put in just the right spot. Light coming through it will be focused on the film in the back. The film spools are just where they have to be in order to advance the film after a picture has been taken. The light meter is positioned just where it needs to be in order to adjust the exposure. Even the lens cap and the shoulder strap make their contribution to the overall usefulness of the device.

Let us suppose that, having observed all this about the camera, you exclaim, "Somebody must have designed this camera!" (I admit that it is a bit difficult to understand *why* you would say such a thing, but let's suppose you do. It makes the story more relevant to my present purposes.) You have reached this conclusion, we may imagine, by means of a little argument. The argument is this:

The Camera Argument

1 The parts of the camera are so arranged as to enable it to achieve its purpose.
2 If the parts of the camera are so arranged as to enable it to achieve its purpose, then somebody designed the camera.
3 Therefore, somebody designed the camera.

Suppose your friend is unconvinced. She doesn't think that you are entitled to your conclusion. "Wait a minute," she says, "what about this viewfinder? I think there is a crack in it." Sure enough, upon closer inspection, you find a small crack in the lens of the viewfinder. Nevertheless, you stand your ground. You still think that the camera is the product of some designer. Perhaps it was originally designed and constructed properly, and then it broke. Maybe somebody dropped it.

Your friend then points to a little lever on the side of the case, and demands to be told what purpose it serves. You admit that you haven't any idea. "That settles it," she says. "You agree that this part serves no identifiable purpose. Therefore, the camera was not designed by anyone." This strikes you as a terrible objection. You realize that even it some parts have no identifiable purpose, still it is clear enough that the whole thing is designed for a purpose. Thus, somebody must have designed it. So you reply, "Maybe those parts do serve a purpose, but we just can't figure out what it is. Maybe the designer just put them there as a joke. It doesn't matter. The camera as a whole is clearly designed to take pictures, and so somebody must have designed it."

Your skeptical friend has one last objection. She demands to be told how the camera was produced. She insists that if you cannot explain how the various parts were constructed, and how they were fastened together, then you have no right to say that the whole thing was designed.

This objection also strikes you as silly. Even though you don't know much about the methods by which the camera was produced, still you think you can see that it was designed and produced somehow. It is so clearly a purposeful human artifact that it doesn't much matter how it was produced. So you stand by your argument. The camera is fitted together so as to fulfill its purpose, and so somebody must have designed it.

An Argument about an Eye

This little tale about the camera is introduced in order to bring to light some important general considerations. These considerations have to do with the observability of design and purposiveness in nature. To see the relevance of all this to philosophical theology, let us construct a somewhat different version of the story. Let us suppose that, instead of a lost camera, you and your friend are contemplating the human eye. You look at a diagram of the eye (perhaps like the diagram in Figure 6-1), and notice that the lens is placed just where it needs to be in order to focus light on the retina. You see that the light-sensitive cells on the retina are spread out just where the light will fall. You notice that the iris of the eye can open and close to accommodate dimmer or brighter light, and you see that the eye is made so that it can focus on near or distant objects more or less "automatically." In these respects, the eye is at least as well designed as the camera.

Furthermore, there are some respects in which the eye is clearly superior to any camera. For one thing, if you scratch the lens of a camera, the scratch will just stay

FIGURE 6-1

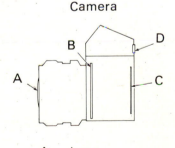

Camera   Eye

A — Lens   A — Cornea
B — Shutter   B — Lens
C — Film   C — Iris
D — Viewfinder   D — Retina
                                          E — Optic nerve

there until you get a new lens. On the other hand, small scratches on the lens of a living human eye will heal themselves. Given sufficient time, the lens may be just as good as new, if the healing process is successful. Another advantage of the human eye over the camera has to do with lens cleaning. If your camera lens gets dusty, you need to clean it with a little brush or a soft cloth. Your eye, however, has a built-in lens cleaning system. Tears are automatically spread over the surface of the eye, and the eyelids blink. That keeps the lens clean and dust-free. In these respects the eye seems to be even better designed than the camera.

If our little argument about the camera was a good one (and it seems to me that it was), then this little argument about the human eye seems also to be a good one:

The Eye Argument

1 The parts of the human eye are so arranged as to enable it to achieve its purpose.

2 If the parts of the human eye are so arranged as to enable it to achieve its purpose, then somebody designed the human eye.

3 Therefore, somebody designed the human eye.

Someone could object to line (2) here, pointing out that many people need glasses. Indeed, some people have such bad eyes that they can't see at all. Doesn't this cast doubt on the claim that the eye has been designed?

As we saw above in connection with the camera, the fact that there are imperfections in a thing does not show that it hasn't been designed. There are plenty of ways in which to explain such flaws. Maybe the designer originally designed the eye properly, but the eye was subsequently misused. Maybe it was strained, or injured. Another possibility is that although the eye was properly designed, it may have been improperly "manufactured." Maybe the processes by which eyes come into existence are inherently liable to go wrong in various ways. "Quality control" isn't perfect. Hence, though some eyes are defective, still it is reasonable to maintain that somebody designed them.

A second objection might be that eyes have some apparently useless parts. These do not serve any identifiable purpose. For example, why should some eyes be blue, and others brown? This variation in color does not seem to make the eyes see any better. Does this make line (2) any less plausible?

A defender of the argument would surely insist that, just as in the case of the camera, the objection is unsuccessful. Maybe eye color does serve a purpose, but we just haven't discovered what it is. Maybe eye color doesn't contribute to the central purpose of eyes (seeing), but the designer thought it would make eyes more interesting, or prettier. So the presence of a few inexplicable features does not cast significant doubt on the conclusion. The eye is the product of some designer.

The third objection is no more successful. We may not know how cameras are produced, but we know that they must be produced somehow. The designer's plan has been embodied in a physical object. Similarly for eyes. There are great mysteries about the means of production. But the evidence of design seems so obvious that we are justified in reaching our conclusion anyway. Somebody must have designed the eye.

The point of all this should be clear. We have argued for the view that somebody designed the eye. Who could this be? Surely not some team of optical engineers in some camera factory! Perfectly satisfactory eyes existed before the principles of optics had even been discovered. Indeed, perfectly satisfactory eyes existed long before there were any human beings. Thus, the designer of the eye cannot be human.

Paley's Argument from Design

Paley once said that contemplation of the human eye is the surest cure for atheism. Thus, it's clear that he thought that only God could have designed the human eye. Many others have agreed.

Furthermore, it must be admitted that if God did design the human eye, or anything else for that matter, then God must have existed at some time in the past. In order to design something, you must exist. But our concept of God is the concept of a necessary being—a being that necessarily exists at all times. Hence, if God ever existed in the past, then he must exist at all times, including the present time. Therefore, God exists.

Let us now formulate the argument as a whole. We call it "The Argument from Design, Version A."

1 The parts of the human eye are so arranged as to enable it to achieve its purpose.

2 If the parts of the human eye are so arranged as to enable it to achieve its purpose, then somebody designed the human eye.

3 Only God could have designed the human eye.

4 If God designed the human eye, then God exists.

5 Therefore, God exists.

In this form, the argument is valid. Premise (1) is derived from observation. If you study an eye closely, you will just see that it is at least as well designed as any camera. Premise (2) is relevantly like premise (2) of the eye argument. If a thing is organized in such a way as to achieve some purpose, then somebody (or something) must be responsible for its being so. Line (3) can be defended in a variety of ways, but most of these boil down to a simple question: "if God didn't design the eye, then who did?" Line (4) is based on our concept of God as a necessary being. If a necessary being exists at any time, then it must exist at all times. Such a being, once in existence, cannot stop existing. Thus, if God ever did anything, God must exist now.

Objections to Paley's Argument

The argument from design has been subjected to a substantial amount of criticism. Some have even attempted to mock and ridicule it. Of course, mockery and ridicule do not serve to refute an argument. To refute it, we have to show either that it is invalid, or that it has a defective premise. In the version presented here, the argument is valid. So we must see what can be said against the premises.

One premise that is surely open to objection is (3). There is really no justification for supposing that only God could have designed the eye. We must recall here that we are using the word "God" in such a way that nothing will count as God unless it is the supreme being. It must be omniscient, omnipotent, omnibenevolent, and necessarily existent. Isn't it clear that a non-supreme being could have designed the eye almost as easily as a supreme being? Can't we imagine that eyes were designed by some lesser deity, perhaps called "Oculus," who is less than omniscient, less than omnipotent, less than omnibenevolent, and only contingently existent? Surely, even if we agree that some deity is responsible for the eye, there is simply no reason to suppose that that deity answers to our concept of God.

We can go even further than this. As marvelous as eyes may be, it certainly seems that they are not entirely perfect. As we get older, many of us begin to experience problems with our eyes. Our vision begins to fade. Furthermore, there are many eye diseases, such a glaucoma, that cause lots of trouble for many people. Surely if eyes had been designed by an omniscient, omnipotent, and omnibenevolent creator, he could have made them a little better. Such defects and imperfections seem to point to a less-than-supreme designer (assuming there is a designer at all).[7]

A Deeper Problem about Purposes

I think there is another problematic premise in this argument. The premise I have in mind is (1), and the objection has to do with whether the eye has a purpose. It may be a bit difficult to explain the objection, but I think it is worthwhile to try. First, however, let me digress.

In the area where I am currently living, it is pretty easy to find tiny chips of flint in the earth. Some of these chips are believed to have been manufactured by ancient people. They allegedly were made by hammering large flints until chips broke off, and then by shaping the chips by striking them with smaller "hammer stones." Once the chips had achieved the proper shape and size, they were fastened onto a stick, so as to make a crude saw for sawing wood. Although no such saw has ever been found (the wooden part would surely have rotted thousands of years ago) it has been shown that it is possible to make such a saw using these chips as teeth.

One of the confusing things about these chips is that they look very much like chips that have been formed in the ordinary course of nature by erosion, or jostling in the bottom of a fast-running stream, or freezing and thawing. Some archeologists have insisted that all of the chips are in this way purely natural stones, none having been made by ancient people for any purpose. Others feel that some of the chips are natural, and some are manufactured items.

Suppose we find one of these little stones. Suppose it is one whose origins are in dispute. Some think it manmade, others think it natural. Nevertheless, we can all agree that this stone is suited for use as a sawtooth. By virtue of its shape, its size,

---

[7]An amusing discussion of the design argument can be found in H. L. Mencken's marvelous essay, "The Cosmic Secretariat," which is included in the anthology *A Mencken Chrestomathy,* New York: Alfred A. Knopf, 1956, pp. 67–69. Mencken focuses his attention on such things as flat feet, decayed teeth, and the human appendix, and concludes that there must have been a committee of incompetent deities in charge of the design of the human body! A more serious, but no less incisive discussion can be found in David Hume's *Dialogues Concerning Natural Religion,* 1752 (available in *Dialogues Concerning Natural Religion,* edited by Norman Kemp Smith, Edinburgh and New York: Nelson, 2nd edn., 1947).

and its hardness, this little chip surely can be used as a sawtooth to help cut wood. If someone wanted to cut wood in this rather crude manner, and he knew how to put together such a saw, he could use the chip. Let us say, then, that the chip *can be used for a purpose.*

However, there is disagreement about whether it was originally made by somebody who intended that it be used for any purpose. It might have come about by the unconscious operations of purely natural forces. It might have the shape, size, and hardness that it has purely as a result of the way it was jostled and bounced in some ancient stream-bed. So there is disagreement about whether the chip *was made for a purpose.*

I think you can see that if the chip was made for a purpose, then somebody designed it. If somebody wanted a sawtooth, and intended to turn a piece of flint into a sawtooth, and so chipped and hammered away on this chip of flint, then he or she counts as the designer of the chip. Even if the maker was just following somebody else's directions for the manufacture of sawteeth, still I think it is clear that if the chip was made for a purpose, somebody designed the chip—maybe it was the person who directed the efforts of the person who actually handled the chip.

On the other hand, from the mere fact that the chip can be used for a purpose, we cannot conclude that it was designed. It might just be good luck that it has the right size, shape, and hardness. So long as we can think of some purely natural processes that can account for the chip being as it is, we do not have to conclude that it was manufactured. Thus, there is an important difference between two concepts of purpose. On the one hand, there is the concept of *being such that it can be used for a purpose,* and on the other hand, there is the concept of *being made for a purpose.* Now let's return to the point. What has all this to do with the argument from design?

When, in the first premise of the argument from design, we say that the parts of the eye are so arranged as to enable it to achieve its purpose, our statement is ambiguous. It might mean (1a) that the parts of the eye are so arranged as to enable it to achieve the purpose *for which it was made,* or it might mean (1b) that the parts of the eye are so arranged as to enable it to achieve the purpose *for which it can be used.*

Once we see that premise (1) is ambiguous in this way, we can see that there are really two possible interpretations for the argument as a whole. If we use (1a), and make other necessary changes, then the argument looks like this:

1a The parts of the eye are so arranged as to enable it to achieve the purpose for which it was made.

2a If the parts of the eye are so arranged as to enable it to achieve the purpose for which it was made, then somebody designed the eye.

3 Only God could design the eye.

4 If God designed the eye, then God exists.

5 Therefore, God exists.

The problem with this version of the argument is clear. Line (1a) is open to objection. Unless we already know that there is a divine creator (whether Oculus or God) we have no way to establish that eyes were made for a purpose. No matter how useful and intricate the eye may be, we cannot conclude that it was made for a purpose until we have some independent way of establishing that somebody originally created it intending that it be useful for some end. The mere fact that it is quite useful does not establish this premise. Perhaps some natural processes will account for the fact that eyes have the complexity and usefulness that they are found to have.

In its second version, the argument goes this way:

1b The parts of the eye are so arranged as to enable it to achieve the purpose for which it can be used.

2b If the parts of the eye are so arranged as to enable it to achieve the purpose for which it can be used, then somebody designed the eye.

3 Only God could design the eye.

4 If God designed the eye, then God exists.

5 Therefore, God exists.

I think that (1b) is pretty nearly true.[8] The eye can be used for seeing, and its parts are so arranged as to make it suitable for that. So we can use our eyes for a purpose. However, as we saw above, it does not follow from this that somebody designed the eye. If the eye came to have its shape, size, and other features as a result of purely natural processes, then we can avoid the inference to an original designer of eyes. Many philosophers feel that there is a purely natural explanation for the fact that eyes, and other organs, are so useful. The explanation, of course, is the Darwinian explanation based on the principles of natural selection. Thus, it is clear that there is no defense for line (2b). The second version of the argument also fails.

The upshot of all this is that we have to be very careful when we speak of "purposes" in nature. If we believe in God, we may think that eyes and other organs have been created for some purpose. We can suppose that God intended all of this to be useful for some end. Our religion may purport to tell us what this purpose is. However, we must recognize that if we adopt this position, we cannot go on to make use of the argument from design. This view of things presupposes the existence of God, and so cannot be used to prove the existence of God.

On the other hand, if we think the world is just the product of blind natural forces, we should not say that natural objects have been made *for* various purposes. We should say instead that such objects may be used for purposes. We contradict ourselves if we say that natural objects have been made for various purposes, but nobody and nothing made them.

A Final Design Argument

Before we conclude this consideration of teleological arguments, it may be worthwhile to mention another version. This version is based on such notions as "the harmony of nature," or "the interconnectedness of the universe." It is especially popular among people who understand and appreciate the beauty and subtlety of a delicately balanced ecological system.

If you contemplate some fairly large natural system, such as a tropical rain forest, or a vast African grassland, you may discover that the various plants and animals

---

[8]One minor problem with (1b) is that it suggests that eyes can be used for exactly *one* purpose. That seems to me to be wrong. I can think of lots of purposes for which eyes can be used. But let's ignore this point. It's not really important in the present context.

that live there relate to one another in some remarkable ways. One pretty obvious relationship is that of prey-to-predator. If people mind their own business, the number of prey animals will generally remain fairly constant, as will the number of predators. There will always be enough antelope to feed the lions, but never so many that they will die of starvation. Similarly, the number of carrion eaters will generally remain just about right. There will be sufficient vultures to clean up the remains of the animals that die.

More subtle relationships are brought to light by closer study. It may be found, for example, that a certain insect must lay its eggs in the fruit of a certain flower. Amazingly, the fruit is always at just the right stage of development when the insects are ready to lay their eggs. Furthermore, it may be found that the flower gives off a certain odor that is attractive to the insect, but which is ignored by every other creature in the forest.

There is no need to multiply examples. If you have ever watched a TV documentary on the ecology of a pond, or a jungle, or a grassland, you know what I'm talking about. Furthermore, in light of our earlier discussion of design arguments, you should be able to figure our what's coming—an argument for the existence of God based upon the apparent designedness of nature as a whole.

There is one respect in which this sort of argument seems to be more persuasive than Paley's argument about the eye. A critic of Paley's argument might insist that something less grand than God might be responsible for the intricate structure of our eyes. Maybe Oculus designed them. However, this sort of criticism seems less plausible when we consider the magnitude of the design job involved in the creation of the natural world as a whole. The design here is so magnificent, and so enormous, that only an infinitely powerful creator could have designed it. Oculus could not have done it. Furthermore, there seems to be a sort of unity, or interconnectedness among the parts, that rules out the notion that a plurality of Gods might have designed the components separately. The unity of nature demands a unity in designers. It could not have been done by any committee.

So we may formulate the argument in this way:

1 All the parts of the universe are arranged in such a way as to enable it to achieve its purpose.

2 If all the parts of the universe are arranged in such a way as to enable it to achieve its purpose, then exactly one thing designed the universe.

3 If exactly one thing designed the universe, then God exists.

4 Therefore, God exists.

The problem here, as should be obvious, is that there is no independent way to establish that the universe has any purpose. If you believe in God, you may think that God designed the universe as an arena in which people could freely seek their salvation. Of course, it would be begging the question to defend line (1) by appeal to any such consideration.

We might attempt to salvage the argument by modifying lines (1) and (2). Why not replace them by something more open to independent verification? What I have in mind is this:

1 All the parts of the natural world fit together so as to form a complex and beautiful whole.

2 If all the parts of the natural world fit together so as to form a complex and beautiful whole, then exactly one thing designed the natural world.

3 If exactly one thing designed the natural world, then God exists.

4 Therefore, God exists.

I guess I am a bit of a "lover of nature," and so I accept line (1). Nevertheless, I think this is a very weak argument. I also think that, by this time, you should be able to figure out why I'm not impressed by the argument. You should be able to identify the controversial premise, and you should be able to state a clear objection to it. You should also be able to determine for yourself whether the objection is a good one.

With this we conclude our discussion of traditional arguments for the existence of God. In Chapter 7 we will return to the *Meditations* to see how Descartes tried to establish his theistic conclusions.

CARTESIAN PHILOSOPHICAL THEOLOGY

DESCARTES' COSMOLOGICAL ARGUMENTS

Just about everybody, at one time or another, has reflected on the question whether God exists. Some of us face the question at a time of despair—perhaps when a friend or family member is suffering from a terrible disease. "How can there be a God," we ask, "if there is such pointless misery?" Others ask the question on happier occasions. For example, you might consider it when your first child is born. On this occasion, you might ask, "How can there be such a miracle as this if there is no God?"

As we saw above, Descartes raised the question in a somewhat different context. He was trying to achieve "maximal epistemic purification." He wanted to have the largest possible number of metaphysically certain beliefs, while having no meta-physically uncertain beliefs. He found, in the first place, that he could be metaphysi-cally certain of his own existence. He also seems to have decided that he could be metaphysically certain about his current "directly accessible" mental states. However, at least at the end of the *Second Meditation*, he felt that there were no other metaphysical certainties. Every other belief, no matter how obvious it might seem, was cast into doubt by the possibility of a deceptive God.

I think we can be a little more exact about the problem that Descartes faced. First of all, he had to determine whether or not there is a God; for if there is no God, then the causal chain leading up to Descartes consisted entirely of finite and imperfect substances such as his parents and grandparents—mere mortals. Since such imperfect causes might have imperfect effects, Descartes could never then be metaphysically certain of anything more. For all he could ever know, he might have defective epistemic faculties. Even when those faculties were used in the best way possible, they might produce errors.

113

Furthermore, even if Descartes can prove that there is a God, he still will not be out of the woods. For if that God should choose to deceive Descartes, he surely would be able to do so. An omnipotent being could easily see to it that Descartes makes lots of mistakes. So, assuming that he can establish the existence of God, Descartes next has to prove that God cannot be a deceiver. Until he has proved (a) that there is a God, and (b) that this God is no deceiver, Descartes cannot be metaphysically certain of anything beyond his own existence and current mental states. As Descartes himself puts it:

> in order to remove this doubt, I ought at the first opportunity to inquire if there is a God, and, if there is, whether or not he can be a deceiver. If I am ignorant of these matters, I do not think I can ever be certain of anything else.[1]

It is in this context that Descartes sets out, in the *Third Meditation*, to reflect on the questions of God's existence and nature.

An Argument to Be Rejected[2]

As we have seen, philosophers and theologians have made use of many different premises in their arguments for the existence of God. Some have appealed to the widespread belief in God. Others have pointed out that the Bible says that God exists. Still others have argued from the premise that there is design and purpose in nature.

It is important to understand why Descartes cannot make use of any such premise in the traditional way. In accordance with his fundamental epistemic principle, he has decided to suspend judgment with respect to everything that is less than perfectly certain. None of these premises is metaphysically certain for Descartes, and so it would appear that none of them can be used in the attempt to establish the existence of God. Descartes has to find premises that are metaphysically certain for him at the time in question. As we have seen, the only such premises are (a) the proposition that Descartes exists, and (b) various propositions about his current mental states.

I believe that as Descartes begins his discussion there is a certain argument in the background. This argument is never explicitly formulated, but it still exerts an influence on what Descartes says. In order to clarify what Descartes says in the passage,[3] it will be worthwhile to draw out this argument.

The argument in question is an argument for the existence of God, based on certain facts about what's going on in Descartes' mind. The fundamental premise here is that Descartes has an idea of God. Descartes apparently thought that, when he thinks of God, he can know with perfect certainty that he is thinking of God. This seems pretty reasonable, since the fact in question concerns the current contents of Descartes' mind. Thus, he may be entitled to make use of this claim as a premise without violating his epistemic principle.

---

[1] Cress, 24.
[2] Reading Assignment: the *Third Meditation*, Cress, 23–24.
[3] Cress, 24–26

But how does this provide the basis for an argument for the conclusion that God actually exists? Here's one way: we can suppose that our ideas are caused by the things they represent. For example, we can suppose that, if I have an idea of the Statue of Liberty, then it must have been caused, either directly or indirectly, by the statue itself. Perhaps I once saw the statue, or maybe I saw a drawing that was made by a person who saw the statue. In any case, the statue itself figures somehow in the causal history of my idea of the statue.

If we put these two premises together, we get a very simple cosmological argument for the existence of God. It goes like this:

A Bad Cosmological Argument

1 An idea of God exists.
2 Ideas are caused by the things they represent.
3 If God caused something, then God exists.
4 Therefore, God exists.

The first premise here is based directly on Descartes' mental experience. He has an idea of God, and he knows this with perfect certainty. Hence, such an idea exists. The second premise is a causal principle connecting ideas to their causes. If an idea represents some object, x, then that idea was caused by that object, x. Let's call this "CP1," for "Causal Principle Number One." Together with (1), this implies that the idea of God must have been caused by God. Line (3) now generates our conclusion. If God caused the idea of God, then God exists. The conclusion, (4), validly follows.

This is a miserable little argument, and Descartes rightly rejected it. He knew that the causal principle CP1, which appears here as (2), is false. Many ideas represent things that do not exist. For example, consider your idea of Santa Claus. Surely, you are not silly enough to think that, since you have the idea, there must really be a Santa Claus! Since Santa Claus does not exist, he surely isn't the cause of your idea of Santa Claus. You must have gotten the idea in some other way.

In order to explain what's wrong with CP1, Descartes distinguishes among three classes of ideas. He says, "Among these ideas, some seem to me to be innate, some seem to be derived from an external source, and some seem to be produced by me."[4] Taking these in reverse order, we can start with ideas "produced by me." These are sometimes called "factitious" (or manufactured) ideas. If a person creates an idea by putting together some old ideas that he already had, then the new idea is said to be factitious. Descartes suggests that the idea of a hippogriff is an example of this sort of idea. It is created by joining together the idea of a horse and the idea of a griffin—which itself was created by joining together the idea of an eagle and the idea of a lion. It should be obvious that at least some factitious ideas are not caused by the things they represent. Since there are no hippogriffs, the idea of a hippogriff cannot be caused by a hippogriff. Similarly for the idea of Santa Claus. The existence of factitious ideas such as these clearly refutes CP1, and so shows that this version of the cosmological argument fails.

[4]Cress, 25.

② ̄sense

② The second class consists of ideas that pop into Descartes' mind involuntarily. If your eyes are open, and you are outdoors, and you glance upwards, you might suddenly find yourself having a strong visual image, or idea, of the sun. Many of our ideas arise suddenly and without effort in this way. They seem to be imposed upon us from some outside source. Such ideas are to be classified as "adventitious." They arise suddenly, involuntarily, and seemingly from some object in the outside world.

Descartes recognizes that there is a natural inclination to suppose that adventitious ideas are caused by the things they represent. However, Descartes rejects this by pointing out that, in a dream, we often get adventitious ideas that presumably are not caused by the things they represent. For example, while dreaming, you might suddenly and involuntarily have the idea of some outlandish monster. This idea is adventitious, but there's no reason to suppose it is caused by a real monster. So CP1 also runs into trouble in connection with adventitious ideas.

② The first class consists of "innate" ideas. We mustn't think that we are born with all our innate ideas right at the forefront of consciousness. Some of them don't emerge for quite a while. What's distinctive about innate ideas is that they are not derived from sense experience (as adventitious ideas seem to be), and they are not manufactured by putting together other ideas already in the mind (as factitious ideas seem to be). An innate idea is one that "arises from the very nature" of the person who has the idea. Descartes suggests[5] that the ideas of "thing," "truth," and "thought" are innate.

Perhaps the Cartesian view was something like this: since you are a thing, and you can come to know that you are a thing merely by reflecting on your own nature, the idea of "thing" (or "entity") can arise in you independently of any sensory experience. Furthermore, this idea is not a compound of other ideas you already had. Hence, we can say that the idea of "thing" is innate. Many philosophers and psychologists have rejected the doctrine of innate ideas. They have insisted that the mind is, at conception, a "blank slate" (or *tabula rasa*). According to this view, if there were no sense experience, there would never be any ideas at all.[6]

Descartes does not discuss the question whether innate ideas must be caused by the things they represent. It is not clear to me what he would say about this. However, it doesn't matter very much here, since he has already produced plenty of counterexamples to the causal principle that appears in the bad cosmological argument. If he is to argue from premise (1) to the conclusion that God exists, he's going to have to do it in some other way, and he knows it.

A New Causal Principle

In order to understand the argument that Descartes does present, we need to sharpen up a concept we have already discussed—the concept of "grades of existence."

In Chapter 5, under "Necessary Existence," I mentioned that some philosophers accepted the idea that there are various grades of existence, or reality. I tried to

---

[5]Cress, 25.

[6]The classic statement of this so-called "empiricist" view about concept formation can be found in Book II, Chapter 1, of John Locke's *Essay Concerning Human Understanding*, first published in 1690.

explain this idea by some remarks about the varying degrees to which things may be "ontologically independent." When we speak of the degree of reality of a thing, we are speaking of the degree to which that thing is able to exist on its own. Hence, an event, such as a football game, has a very low degree of reality, since it cannot exist unless there are plenty of players, a field, and a ball, and unless these things are all properly related to one another. Similarly for a nation, corporation, or club. These things cannot exist unless their members exist, and are properly related to one another.

Some other things with low grades of reality would be smiles and shadows. These things cannot exist on their own. Perhaps that explains what's so humorous about the Cheshire Cat in *Alice in Wonderland*. The smile is supposed to remain after the cat disappears—but if smiles are ontologically dependent on faces, then no smile can exist once the relevant face if gone. Similarly for Peter Pan's shadow. You can't roll up a shadow and put it in the dresser drawer. It doesn't have enough reality for that. A shadow exists only if there is a light source, an opaque physical object, and a suitable surface, and these are properly lined up.

Let's use the technical term "mode" for all entities of this lowest category. All event-like things, such as games, walks, talks, and love affairs, are modes of the things that participate in them. They are "ways of being," and hence depend for their existence upon the things that exist in those ways. Smiles and shadows may belong in this category, too.

Inanimate substances seem to fall into a slightly higher category. A thing such as a brick is capable of existing pretty much on its own—so long as somebody creates it. But a brick cannot do very much for itself, and it cannot create anything else. So inanimate objects are "more real" than mere modes, but less real than living things.

Among living things, plants fall into the lowest class. Descartes would probably say that they are just "machines," only slightly superior to inanimate things. The next higher class consists of animals, followed by people and, in turn, by angels. The rankings, I suspect, have something to do with the extent to which these things are tangled up with their bodies. Descartes considered animals to be mindless living bodies of a special sort. People, according to him, are intimately mixed up with their bodies, but at least people have minds. Angels, perhaps, are bodiless spirits, or minds, and hence are "purer." Be this as it may, living things are apparently to be ranked in this way: plants at the bottom, then animals, then people, and then angels.

All of the preceding classes consist entirely of contingent existents—things that in fact exist, but might not have. The final class consists of all the necessarily existing substances. If there is a God, he goes in this highest category, since he has the highest possible degree of ontological independence, and everything else depends upon him. If there is no God, then this category is empty.

Table 7-1 lists some of the main ontological categories. For each, it gives examples of some of the things in the category. If it is not clear whether the things in question actually exist, a question mark has been inserted. Associated with each category is a number that represents the relative amount of ontological independence had by things in that category.

The numbers in the right hand column in the table indicate the "degree of reality" of things in the various categories. Thus, if you want to know the degree of reality of

TABLE 7-1

formal reality

Category	Examples	Reality rating
1 Infinite Substances	God(?)	infinite
2 Angels	Gabriel(?), Satan(?)	1,000,000
3 People	Descartes, Leibniz, you	1,000
4 Animals	My dog, my cat	100
5 Plants	The weeds in my garden	50
6 Inanimate Substances	My truck, this brick	10
7 Modes	My smile, your frown	1

ideas

your dog, you check the number to the right of category 4, "animals." You will find that the number is 100, indicating that you dog has a "reality rating" of 100—higher than plants, but lower than people. Descartes sometimes uses the expression "degree of perfection" or "amount of perfection" to refer to these numbers. Thus, the degree of perfection of a thing is the same as the degree of reality of that thing. It's the number in the column to the right of the name of the thing's category.[7]

Now we may be in a position to consider an important Cartesian metaphysical principle. First, let's see how Descartes phrases it. In an interesting (if somewhat puzzling) passage, he says:

> But it is evident by the light of nature that at the very least there must be as much in the total efficient cause as there is in the effect of that same cause. For, I ask, where can an effect get its reality unless it be from its cause? And how can the cause give that reality to the effect, unless the cause also has that reality? Hence it follows that something cannot come into existence from nothing, *nor even can what is more perfect, that is, that contains in itself more reality, come into existence from what contains less.*[8]

The general principle asserted in this passage can be formulated in a variety of ways. The basic idea, however, is that "the more perfect cannot be caused by the less perfect." If some object, e, has been caused by some other object, c, then the amount of perfection or reality in the cause, c, must be at least as great as that in the effect, e. Let's refer to this as "Descartes' Second Causal Principle," or "CP2." Rigorously formulated, it is:

CP2 If some effect, e, exists, then some cause, c, of e must exist, too, and c must have at least as high a degree of perfection as e.

Descartes argues for this by asking a rhetorical question: "How can the cause give that reality to the effect unless that cause also has that reality?" The point seems to be that if there were more reality in some effect than there were in its cause, then the extra perfection in the effect would have arisen out of nowhere. This is impossible,

---

[7]The numbers in the chart are, as should be obvious, merely intended to suggest relative rankings—except in the case of the first category. In the case of necessary beings, it is important that the degree of perfection be infinite.

[8]Cress, 27 (emphasis mine).

however, since "out of nothing, nothing comes." Therefore, according to Descartes, CP2 is true.

The introduction of CP2 suggests a new version of the causal argument, based upon the fact that there is an idea of God. Descartes points out that ideas can be ranked in terms of their perfection, too. And when we rank ideas in this way, the idea of God comes out on top. So we can argue for the existence of God in this way:

Another Bad Argument

   1 An infinitely perfect idea of God exists.
   2 If an infinitely perfect idea of God exists, then there must be some infinitely perfect being that caused that idea.
   3 Therefore, there is an infinitely perfect being.
   4 If there is an infinitely perfect being, then God exists.
   5 Therefore, God exists.

The first line here is just supposed to record the fact that there is an idea of God as infinitely perfect. We will discuss this again shortly. The second line is derived from CP2. If some effect is infinitely perfect, then its cause must be infinitely perfect, too. According to CP2, the cause cannot be any less perfect than the effect. Since the idea of God is infinitely perfect, there must be an infinitely perfect cause for this idea. (3) is a lemma. It follows from (1) and (2). Line (4) is derived from a slightly revised version of our concept of God. If we define God as "the infinitely perfect being," then line (4) can be viewed as being analytic. Clearly enough, line (5) validly follows from lines (3) and (4).

It should be clear that there is something terribly wrong with this argument. The problem, as I see it, is in line (1). There is an enormous difference between these two claims:

   1a There is an idea of an infinitely perfect God.
   1b There is an infinitely perfect idea of God.

If somebody has an idea of God according to which God is supposed to be infinitely perfect, then (1a) is true. However, that would not make (1b) true. In order for (1b) to be true, the idea itself would also have to be infinitely perfect. To say that an idea is infinitely perfect is to say that it (not the thing it represents) belongs in the very highest ontological category. But this is absurd. Ideas, no matter what they represent, all go into the category of modes. Every one of them has an extremely low degree of perfection. None of them is as perfect as God. Hence, (1b) cannot be true.

It is important here to recognize that there is no way to combine (1a) with CP2 so as to derive (3). If there is an idea of God, then, according to CP2, there must be a cause for that idea, and that cause must be at least as perfect as the idea is. But since the idea is only a mode, and has a reality rating of only one unit, we are only entitled to conclude that there must be a cause whose reality rating is at least one unit. Thus, there is simply no way to derive the conclusion that the cause must have an infinitely great reality rating. The upshot is that this argument is a washout.

Objective and Formal Reality *of ideas*

In order to understand Descartes' cosmological argument, we must come to grips with an important distinction. This is the distinction between "objective reality" and "formal reality." Descartes draws the distinction in this passage:

> Now, insofar as these ideas are merely modes of thought, I do not see any inequality among them; they all seem to proceed from me in the same way. But insofar as one idea represents one thing and another idea another thing, it is obvious that they are very different from one another. There is no question that those ideas that exhibit substances to me are something more and, as I phrase it, contain more objective reality in themselves than those which represent only modes or accidents. Again, the idea that enables me to understand a highest God...has more objective reality in it than those ideas through which finite substances are exhibited.[9]

I think that Descartes is suggesting that there are two different ways in which we can evaluate ideas. On the one hand, we can pay no attention to the thing that the idea represents, and simply consider the degree of reality of the idea itself. According to Descartes, ideas are just modes of thought. Since every idea is just a mode, it follows that every idea has the same degree of reality as every other idea. Every idea has a reality rating of one unit. When we evaluate ideas in this way, we are ranking them in terms of their "formal reality."

Ideas are like pictures and names in a certain respect. Each idea represents some object. The idea of my dog represents my dog. The idea of my truck represents my truck. The idea of God represents God. This provides the basis for another way of evaluating ideas. We can rank them in terms of the degree of reality of the objects they represent. When we evaluate ideas in this way, we are ranking them in terms of their "objective reality."

Let's consider some examples. We can start with my idea of my truck. Since this idea is an idea, it is a mode of my thought. Every mode has a reality rating of one. Hence, the formal reality of my idea of my truck = 1. However, since the idea represents my truck, its "object" (my truck) is an inanimate substance. A glance at Table 7-1 will reveal that my truck has a reality rating of 10, and hence the idea of my truck has an objective reality rating of 10.

Suppose I imagine the angel Gabriel. Then my idea of Gabriel has a formal reality of one (since it is just a mode of my thought, and all modes have formal reality = 1). But since this idea represents an angel, and angels have formal reality of 1,000,000, it follows that my idea has an objective reality of 1,000,000.

Finally, let us consider the idea of God. Like every other idea, this one has a formal reality of one. However, since it represents the object with infinite formal reality, this idea must have infinitely great objective reality. In this way, the idea of God turns out to be the most perfect of all ideas. Not "perfect" with respect to formal reality—all ideas are equal in formal reality—but perfect with respect to objective reality. No idea could have higher objective reality than the idea of God has.

[9]Cress, 26–27.

We can explain these new technical terms as follows:

FR The formal reality of an object is the number indicating the position of that object on the scale of ontological perfection.

OR The objective reality of an idea is the number indicating the position on the scale of ontological perfection of the object represented by that idea.

A New Causal Principle and an Argument

We are now in a position to understand the causal principle that Descartes uses in his cosmological argument. This principle is stated (though not too clearly) in the following passage:

> That this idea contains this or that objective reality rather than some other one results from the fact that the idea gets its objective reality from a cause in which there is at least as much formal reality as there is objective reality contained in the idea.[10]

As I understand it, the new causal principle is based on the view that every idea has a cause. The principle says that the cause must have at least as much formal reality as the idea has of objective reality. It is allegedly impossible for there to be an idea that has more objective reality than its cause has of formal reality. We can call this principle "CP3": "The cause of an idea must have at least as much formal reality as the idea itself has of objective reality."

Now it should be clear how the argument is to work. Since the idea of God has infinite objective reality, it must have been caused by something that has infinite formal reality. Only God has infinite formal reality. Hence, God must have caused the idea. If God caused the idea of God, then God exists. Hence, God exists.[11] We can formulate the argument as follows:

Descartes' Cosmological Argument

1 There is an idea of God, and it has infinite objective reality.
2 The cause of any idea must have at least as much formal reality as the idea has of objective reality.
3 Therefore, there is something with infinite formal reality.
4 If there is something with infinite formal reality, then God exists.
5 Therefore, God exists.

The first premise of this argument seems to me to be quite plausible. If I can form an idea of God (and I think I can) then there is such an idea. Since it represents an object that would have infinite formal reality if it existed, the idea itself has infinite objective reality. And that's what (1) says.

---

[10]Cress, 27–28.

[11]It must be admitted that the argument is only suggested by the text of the *Meditations*. To see it stated in all its glory, one would have to look into the *Replies* to the second set of objections, where Descartes presents the argument in "geometrical fashion." See HR II, 52–57.

Line (2) is just CP3. We have already discussed it and so its meaning should be clear.

(3) is a lemma. It is derived from lines (1) and (2). It seems to me that the inference here is valid. Line (4) is based on a new, but not terribly controversial definition of "God." We can think of God as the being with infinite formal reality. So if such a being exists, then God exists. Our final conclusion, (5), follows straightforwardly.

A Problem for Descartes' Argument

It seems to me that if there is a difficulty here, it is in line (2), or CP3. Many readers have been skeptical about this principle. "Why," we might ask, "can't an idea have more objective reality than its cause has of formal reality? Why, for example, can't my idea of God be caused by me, or by some books, or by my parents or religious teachers? Why must it have been caused by God himself?" It should be clear that if there is some way in which a person can create his own idea of God, without any help from God, then CP3 must be rejected and the argument as a whole will fail. Let's consider one way in which a person might construct his own idea of God.

First of all, a person might recognize that he himself is a substance. Thus, by inner reflection he might come to have the concept of "substance." Then, by noticing that he makes various mistakes, and fails at some of his projects, and sometimes sins, the person might come to see that he is limited and finite with respect to some important properties—such as power, knowledge, and virtue. Hence, he might come to have the concept of "limitation" or "finiteness" or "imperfection." We can assume that he also has the concept of negation. That is, he already understands "no," "un-," "in-," "im-," etc., which are used to express the absence, or lack of some feature (as, for example, in "unlucky," "insufficient," and "imperfect"). Finally, by putting together the concepts of negation, finiteness, and substance, he construct the concept of a non-finite substance, or God.

If a person can thus create his own concept of God, without any help from God, then CP3 must be rejected. For this would show that an idea with infinite objective reality can be created by a person—who has only 1000 units of formal reality. Descartes understood this point, and insisted that it would be impossible for anyone to create an idea of God in the manner suggested. His argument appears in this passage:

> the perception of the infinite somehow exists in me prior to the perception of the finite, that is, the perception of God exists prior to the perception of myself. Why would I know that I doubt and I desire, that is, that I lack something and that I am not wholly perfect, if there were no idea in me of a more perfect being by comparison with which I might acknowledge my defects?[12]

It appears, then, that Descartes wants to say that it is impossible for anyone to come to have the concept of "limited substance" unless he already has the concept of "unlimited substance." You can't recognize that you are less than omniscient, less than omnipotent, and less than omnibenevolent, unless you have already conceived

---

[12]Cress, 30.

of God, and entertained the concepts of omniscience, omnipotence, and omnibe-nevolence. Otherwise, with what are you comparing yourself when you judge yourself to be less than perfect?

I leave it to the reader to reflect upon and evaluate Descartes' reply to this objection. The time has come for us to move on.[13]

THE ONTOLOGICAL ARGUMENT

One of the most puzzling and controversial arguments for the existence of God was originally formulated by St. Anselm, who lived from 1033 to 1109, and served as the Archbishop of Canterbury from 1093. The argument appeared in Anselm's *Proslogion*. Anselm's concept of God is very much like the concept with which we have been working. He thought of God as "the being than which none greater can be conceived." In other words, the concept of God is the concept of an entity so perfect that it is impossible to conceive of anything more perfect than it.

Anselm distinguished between "existence in reality" and "existence in the understanding." If a thing actually exists, then it has existence in reality. My truck, for example, has existence in reality. If a thing is imaginary, and doesn't exist in reality, then it has only existence in the understanding. It would appear that Santa Claus has only this sort of reality. He's purely imaginary.

Anselm maintained that existence in reality is better than mere existence in the understanding. I have already mentioned an experiment that may seem to bear this out.[14] Ask yourself which is better: a five hundred dollar gold piece that exists in reality, or a five hundred dollar gold piece that exists only in the understanding. Given the choice, most people would take the real money, rather than the imaginary. Wouldn't you prefer the existent gold piece to the imaginary one? Doesn't this seem reasonable? If so, it would seem that existence in reality is better than mere existence in the understanding. So if two things are exactly alike in all other respects, but one of them exists in reality while the other exists just in the understanding, then the one that exists in reality is greater than the one that exists just in the understanding.

In the *Proslogion*, Anselm first pointed out that the atheist (or, as Anselm calls him, "the fool") has the concept of God. When the atheist hears the word "God," he understands what it means. Thus, the fool has to admit that God exists at least in the understanding. Anselm then argues as follows:

> And assuredly that, than which nothing greater can be conceived, cannot exist in the understanding alone. For, suppose it exists in the understanding alone: then it can be conceived to exist in reality; which is greater.
>
> Therefore, if that, than which nothing greater can be conceived, exists in the understanding alone, the very being, than which nothing greater can be conceived, is one, than which a greater being can be conceived. But obviously this is impossible. Hence, there is

---

[13] I should perhaps mention that Descartes repeats the argument, with some added complications, in the final few pages of the *Third Meditation*. A full review of all the main Cartesian arguments would require careful consideration of this argument, too. I have chosen to skip it since I think that all the really interesting metaphysical issues appear also in the first version of the argument, which I have discussed.

[14] See above, Chapter 5, under "Necessary Existence."

no doubt that there exists a being, than which nothing greater can be conceived, and it exists both in the understanding and in reality.[15]

As I understand it, Anselm's argument works in this way: we first introduce the hypothesis that God exists just in the understanding. Then we note that, if God exists only in the understanding, then we can conceive of a being greater than God. This would be a being just like God, but existing in reality. Hence, if God exists just in the understanding, we can conceive of a being greater than God. However, this is impossible, since God is by definition the being than which none greater can be conceived. Therefore, our original hypothesis must be false. God cannot exist just in the understanding. He must exist in reality, too.

Anselm's argument has been the focus of an enormous amount of controversy.[16] Some have maintained that it fails, while others have defended it. Although there can be little doubt but that it would be worth our while to study this argument in some detail, I think we may do better to consider the version of the argument that Descartes presented. For one thing, Descartes' formulation of the argument is considerably simpler than Anselm's. For another, I think that all the really interesting elements in Anselm's argument show up again in Descartes'.

The Cartesian Ontological Argument[17]

In order to find the Cartesian ontological argument, we must look ahead a few pages, into the seventh paragraph of the *Fifth Meditation*.[18] Descartes has been imagining a triangle. He apparently thinks that it would be possible to prove various things about this triangle, even if neither it nor any real triangle exists anywhere. You can do the same. Imagine a triangle. Now reflect on the sizes of the angles. If you are good at geometry, you will be able to see that the sum of the angles is 180 degrees. (Maybe it will be easier for you to see that the longest side will always be opposite the largest angle.) At any rate, you can prove certain things about a triangle, even if you completely put aside the question whether any triangular objects exist.

Next Descartes begins to reflect on his concept of God. He says:

> Certainly I discover within me an idea of God, that is, of a supremely perfect being, no less than the idea of some figure or number. And I understand clearly and distinctly that it pertains to his nature that he always exists, no less than whatever has been demonstrated about some figure or number also pertains to the nature of this figure or number. Thus, even if everything that I have meditated upon during these last few days were not true, I ought to be at least as certain of the existence of God as I have hitherto been about the truths of mathematics.[19]

---

[15]St. Anselm, *Proslogion*, Chapter II. The translation is by S.N. Deane, and it originally appeared in *Anselm's Basic Writings*, translated by S.N. Deane, with an introduction by Charles Hartshorne, LaSalle, Illinois: Open Court Publishing Company, 1962. It was reprinted in *The Ontological Argument*, edited by Alvin Plantinga, with an introduction by Richard Taylor, London: Macmillan and Company, 1968, page 4.

[16]For an excellent survey of of this literature, see Plantinga's anthology, *The Ontological Argument*, op. cit.

[17]Reading Assignment: the *Fifth Meditation*, Cress, 40–45.

[18]Cress, 42.

[19]Cress, 42.

The argument is not stated as clearly as wé might wish, but I think we can draw it out.[20] The first premise is hardly more than a definition. Instead of saying that God is, by definition, the supreme being, Descartes says that God is, by definition, "supremely perfect." This may be understood as meaning that God has all perfections. That will be our first premise.

The second premise (which is suppressed in the *Meditations*) merely points out that necessary existence is one of the perfections. The passage from Descartes suggests that he might have confused necessary existence with "omnitemporality," or "existence at all times," but it really doesn't matter very much, since the argument will work just as well either way.

It should be clear that if God has all perfections, and necessary existence is one of the perfections, then God has necessary existence. But to say that God has necessary existence is just to say that God exists necessarily. Hence, he exists. Here is the argument:

Descartes' Ontological Argument

1 God has all perfections.
2 Necessary existence is a perfection.
3 If God has necessary existence, then God exists.
4 Therefore, God exists.

Line (1) is supposed to follow immediately from a definition of "God." We can state the definition in a variety of ways, but here's the easiest:

D1 x is God = df. x is the being with all perfections.

The connection between premise (1) and D1 is supposed to be obvious. If "God" means "being with all perfections," then God must have all perfections.

The reasoning behind line (2) was presented in Chapter 5, and was reviewed a few paragraphs back. Existence is good in itself, and comes in various degrees. Hence the highest possible degree of existence is a perfection.

Line (3) seems to be analytic. To say that a thing has necessary existence is just to say that it exists necessarily. Obviously, if a thing exists necessarily, it exists. So there's no problem with (3).

The argument seems to be valid as formulated here. So if (1), (2) and (3) are true, then God exists.

An Objection to the Ontological Argument

The ontological argument has been attacked and criticized by atheists and theists alike ever since its first appearance. Some have objected to certain metaphysical presuppositions they see lurking behind premise (1). Others have claimed that the argument is not valid. Still others have insisted that you can't just "define something into existence."

---

[20] Especially so, if we take account of what Descartes says on this topic in the *Second Replies* where he formulates this argument in "geometrical fashion." See HR II, 57.

One of the most penetrating criticisms of the ontological argument was originally developed by a monk, Gaunilo of Marmoutier, who was a contemporary of Anselm. Gaunilo introduced a definition of "Lost Isle." Lost Isle is, by definition, the island with all the perfections appropriate to islands. Then, making use of an argument just like the ontological argument, Gaunilo purported to prove that Lost Isle must exist. But, of course, there is no such island. Since the arguments are so similar, and Gaunilo's argument leads to a false conclusion, there must be something wrong with both of them. This casts doubt on the ontological argument.

Gaunilo's objection was originally directed against Anselm's version of the ontological argument, but we can easily modify it so as to make it apply to Descartes' argument. Let's see how this can be done.

First we need to consider the features that serve to make an island good—the "insular perfections." These include: wide sandy beaches; warm, pleasant climate; good ferry service; pleasant accommodations; first-class, inexpensive restaurants; good fishing; etc. Furthermore, it would appear that existence is also an insular perfection. We can see this if we make use of a by-now familiar test: suppose you are given the choice of spending your holiday at either Island A or Island B. Suppose the Islands are alike in almost all respects. Each has wide sandy beaches, excellent hotels, and good fishing. The islands differ with respect to existence. Island A exists, while Island B is merely imaginary. Now, which island would you choose for your vacation? If you pick Island A, that seems to show that existence is an insular perfection. Let's suppose it is.

Next, we have to introduce a definition. This merely records our intention to use a certain expression in a certain way. It is:

D2 x is Lost Isle = df. x is the island with all of the insular perfections.

Now we can formulate our argument:

A Parody of the Ontological Argument

1 Lost Isle has all the insular perfections.
2 Existence is an insular perfection.
3 If Lost Isle has existence, then Lost Isle exists.
4 Therefore, Lost Isle exists.

A comparison of this argument with Descartes' ontological argument will reveal that each line of the parody argument is modeled upon the corresponding line of the ontological argument. Yet it is clear that there is something seriously wrong with the parody—the conclusion is simply false. There is no such place as Lost Isle. Therefore, there must be something wrong with the ontological argument, too.

It seems to me that the parody really does show that there is something wrong with the ontological argument. However, the precise nature of the difficulty remains unclear. Some would say that the trouble is in line (2). They would say that existence isn't a property at all. If this is right, then necessary existence isn't the highest degree of a *property* that is good to have. Hence, necessary existence isn't a perfection. This sort of criticism of the ontological argument was first raised by Gassendi, who wrote the fifth set of *Objections* to the *Meditations*.[21] It was later developed by Immanuel Kant in his *Critique of Pure Reason*.[22] Kant claimed that existence is no property. He also attempted to cast doubt on the idea that we can compare an existent gold coin with a nonexistent one.

Others have objected to line (1). They have admitted that we can define terms in any way we like, but they have denied that definitions can have such straightforward ontological consequences. Perhaps such critics would allow that our definition of "God" would generate this premise:

1a If God exists, then God has all perfections.

It should be clear that if (1a) is the strongest first premise we can use, then our conclusion will not be (4), but:

4a If God exists, then God exists.

Obviously, (4a) is a far less controversial conclusion. Even the most adamant atheist should be willing to accept it.

The analysis and evaluation of these criticisms would carry us deep into some very controversial areas of metaphysics and philosophical logic. I'm afraid that this is not the place to undertake such a project. For our purposes, it may be sufficient to understand the basic structure of the ontological argument, to understand the parody of the argument, and to recognize that there is probably something fishy here.

Conclusions Concerning Cartesian Philosophical Theology

We have now reviewed the most important of the arguments Descartes presented in his attempt to establish the existence of God. I think it must be acknowledged that none of these arguments is a total success. No clear-headed and careful atheist would be deeply shaken by any of them. Nevertheless, the arguments are subtle and ingenious, and surely deserve the most serious attention.

Although this may seem to involve a bit of self-deception, I want to suggest that we proceed as if we thought that Descartes had produced a good argument for the existence of God. If we do proceed on this assumption, we will be better able to appreciate some of the things Descartes says in later parts of the *Meditation*.

GOD AND KNOWLEDGE[23]

In order to understand what Descartes is up to in the *Fourth Meditation*, we must recall something about his purpose in trying to prove that God exists. For him, theology and epistemology are intimately connected. As we saw it, one of the most powerful sources of doubt is the possibility that he was created either by a deceptive God, or by something less powerful than God. In either case, it would be possible

---

[21] HR II, 186.
[22] The relevant passage can be found in Plantinga, *The Ontological Argument*, 57–64.
[23] Reading Assignment: the *Fourth Meditation*, Cress, 34–40.

that Descartes has seriously defective epistemic faculties. Even when used in the best way possible, these faculties might yield error.

In order to remove this source of doubt, Descartes feels that he has to prove (*a*) that God exists, and (*b*) that God is no deceiver. Once he has done this, he will have no further reason to doubt his clear and distinct perceptions, and so they will become metaphysically certain. He will then be permitted to believe in them, while adhering to hs epistemic principle, and will be on the road toward refilling his "basket of apples." He will be able to accept many beliefs, every one of which is metaphysically certain for him. Thus, he will be approaching maximal epistemic purification.

By the end of *Meditation Three*, Descartes thinks he has completed the first of these tasks. He has proved that God exists. Now he has to undertake the second. He must prove that God is no deceiver.

Descartes presents a very simple argument to establish this point. It appears at the end of *Meditation Three*, and is discussed further in *Meditation Four*. Here's the clearest statement of the argument:

> God, I say, that same being whose idea is in me: a being having all those perfections that I cannot comprehend, but in some way can touch with my thought, and a being subject to no defects. From these things it is sufficiently obvious that he cannot be a deceiver. For it is manifest by the light of nature that fraud and deception depend on some defect.[24]

The argument seems to be this:

The Honest God Argument

1 God has no defects.
2 If something is a deceiver, it has some defects.
3 Therefore, God is not a deceiver.

This little argument would be more convincing if it were not for the fact that people make plenty of mistakes. If God is not a deceiver, why does he allow us to make mistakes? Wouldn't it be better for him to make us in such a way that we never err? Surely, if God is omnipotent, he is powerful enough to make us error-free. Why hasn't he done this?

Descartes attempts to answer this objection by appeal to a theory about judgment. He explains that God has given us two faculties—a faculty of knowing and a faculty of choosing.[25] The faculty of knowing is a purely intellectual faculty. By means of it we can "perceive ideas."[26] I suspect that Descartes means to say that the faculty of knowing, or the intellect, is the power to entertain concepts and consider propositions. It is by means of this faculty that we can contemplate ideas and understand the meanings of sentences. In Descartes' view, there is no room for error here. When a person considers some concept or reflects upon some proposition, nothing goes wrong. He or she simply "sees" the concept or proposition, and makes no judgment about it.

[24]Cress, 34.
[25]Cress, 36.
[26]Cress, 36.

The faculty of choosing, or the will, is another matter entirely. According to Descartes, God has given us a good deal of freedom. Our faculty of choosing enables us to affirm or deny, to seek or to shun, a wide variety of objects. In fact, this faculty enables us to affirm or deny propositions that our intellect has not yet grasped. Thus, even though your intellect has not fully understood some hypothesis, your will might jump in and affirm that proposition. Here, then, is the source of error. Our free will allows us to make judgments about things before our intellects have sufficiently grasped those things.

Descartes explains the point quite nicely in this passage:

> From what source, therefore, do my errors arise? Solely from the fact that, because the will extends further than the intellect, I do not contain the will within the same boundaries; rather, I even extend it to things I do not understand. Because my will is indifferent to these latter things, it easily turns away from the true and the good; in this way I am deceived and commit sin.[27]

Descartes apparently thinks that he has shown that there is a supreme God, who has created him. He thinks that this God is not a deceiver—that would be contrary to his goodness. The errors that Descartes commits, he thinks, can be explained by appeal to the fact that God has given him a good deal of freedom. Sometimes he misuses this freedom and makes judgments about things he hasn't fully understood. Thus, the fact that people err is allegedly shown to be consistent with the claim that God is no deceiver.

The Principle of Clarity and Distinctness

Descartes is convinced that if he sticks to concepts that are fully understood, he will not err. So if he considers some proposition, and he sees the various concepts in it clearly and distinctly, and he sees that the concepts are related in such a way as to make the proposition true, then he can be absolutely certain that it in fact is true. For example, consider the proposition that all triangles have three sides. Suppose Descartes sees that the concept *triangle* is the same as the concept *closed, three-sided, plane figure*. Then he can see that the proposition simply must be true. In light of this, Descartes determines that whatever is clearly and distinctly perceived in this way, is true.

When Descartes speaks of "clear and distinct perception," he is not referring to any sort of *sense* perception. Rather, he is referring to a special way of grasping concepts and propositions. If you contemplate a concept, such as the concept *triangle*, and you "see" all the simple concepts out of which it is composed, and you "see" how the are put together to make the concept *triangle*, then you are clearly and distinctly perceiving the concept. If you contemplate a proposition, and you clearly and distinctly perceive every concept involved in that proposition, and you "see" how they are involved in the proposition, and you "see" that they are so related that the proposition simply must be true, then you are clearly and distinctly perceiving the proposition. Obviously, this is not a matter of sense perception. In Descartes' view, sense perception does not yield metaphysical certainty.

[27]Cress, 38.

If something clearly and distinctly perceived could be false, then we'd have to conclude that God permits a sort of deception that is inconsistent with divine goodness. Even when using the God-given faculty of knowing in the best possible way, it would lead to error. As we've seen, Descartes thinks this is impossible.

In all his further studies, then, Descartes thinks he can rely on the principle:

CD For any proposition, p, if I clearly and distinctly perceive that p is true, then p is true.

So, armed with this new principle, and with perfect confidence that God will not lead him astray, Descartes can now set out to discover many new metaphysical certainties. With effort, and a bit of luck, he may be able to construct a perfectly adequate scientific account of everything that interests him. Furthermore, if he is careful, he may do this in such a way as to ensure that every one of his beliefs is metaphysically certain. If he is successful, he will have achieved a very high grade of epistemic purification.

The Cartesian Circle

When the *Meditations* was first published, it was accompanied by a set of *Objections* and *Replies*. One set of *Objections* was written by Antoine Arnauld, a brilliant young theologian and philosopher. Arnauld pointed out a very serious problem with Descartes' argument. The problem has come to be known as "The Problem of the Cartesian Circle," but some people still refer to it as "Arnauld's Circle," since he was the first to notice the difficulty. The name isn't important, but the problem itself is.

At the end of his commentary on the argument for the existence of God, Arnauld makes the following remark:

> The only remaining scruple I have is an uncertainty as to how a circular reasoning is to be avoided in saying: the only secure reason we have for believing that what we clearly and distinctly perceive is true, is the fact that God exists.
> But we can be sure that God exists, only because we clearly and evidently perceive that; therefore prior to being certain that God exists, we should be certain that whatever we clearly and evidently perceive is true.[28]

Arnauld seems to be claiming (in a very polite way) that Descartes has argued in a circle. We can put Arnauld's point somewhat more clearly, if we consider two little arguments. The first argument purports to show that clear and distinct perceptions are true. It is as follows:

Argument A—The Divine Guarantee

1 God exists.
2 If God exists, then whatever I clearly and distinctly perceive is true.
3 Therefore, whatever I clearly and distinctly perceive is true.

The second argument is designed to establish the existence of God, and it makes use of the principle of clarity and distinctness. Here it is:

[28] HR II, 92.

Argument B—The Proof of God's Existence

1 Whatever I clearly and distinctly perceive is true.
2 I clearly and distinctly perceive that God exists.
3 Therefore, God exists.

It should be obvious that we cannot first make use of Argument A to establish the principle of clarity and distinctness, and then make use of Argument B to establish the existence of God. We cannot make use of Argument A unless we already know that God exists, and we apparently don't know that until we have made use of Argument B. However, we cannot first make use of Argument B to prove that God exists, and then go on to use A to establish the principle of clarity and distinctness. The problem here is that premise (1) of B cannot be certain for us until we have shown it to be true. To do that, we'd need to make use of Argument A. Thus, neither conclusion can be shown to be true until the other has been shown to be true. Clearly, such circular reasoning will get us nowhere.

I think Descartes is not guilty of so gross a violation of the principles of good reasoning. In fact, I think that a close study of the text will show that Descartes never made use of either of the arguments mentioned above. However, it does seem that Arnauld has a good point. Descartes does seem to be guilty of a somewhat more subtle fallacy. We can appreciate this apparent fallacy if we focus our attention on one of the premises in the Cartesian cosmological argument. The premise in question is based on the causal principle, CP3. It is:

2 The cause of any idea must have at least as much formal reality as the idea has of objective reality.

Now, here's the question: was (2) metaphysically certain for Descartes when he used it in his proof of the existence of God? Either it was, or it wasn't. If it wasn't metaphysically certain for Descartes at the time of its use, then it is hard to see how he could have made use of it in his attempt to prove the existence of God. After all, Descartes' epistemic principle requires that he suspend judgment on everything that's less than metaphysically certain. If (2) is less than metaphysically certain, then it has no business in the argument. Descartes shouldn't even be thinking of it. In any case, if (2) is uncertain, and it is an essential premise in the proof of the existence of God, then the conclusion ("God exists") cannot be made certain by that proof. It seems clear that if (2) was not metaphysically certain when used in the proof, the proof fails, and the rest of the Cartesian system is unsupported.

On the other hand, perhaps we should say that (2) was metaphysically certain at the time when it was used in the cosmological argument. In this case, the argument itself may be acceptable. However, this suggestion raises more questions than it answers. Now we have to ask *how* (2) could be certain at that time. For if the deceptive God hypothesis has not yet been ruled out, surely there are plenty of reasons to doubt (2). Couldn't God, or an evil demon, make (2) seem true when it's really false? Couldn't (2) seem true only because Descartes has defective epistemic faculties? Furthermore, if we suppose that (2) was certain at the time of the cosmological argument, then we have to ask ourselves something about the need for proving God's existence and veracity. Didn't Descartes say that until he has established the existence and veracity of God, he could be certain of nothing beyond his own existence and the present contents of his own mind?[29] If a complex metaphysical principle such as CP3 can be metaphysically certain even before God's existence and veracity have been established, then why does Descartes need to prove these things? He apparently can get on quite well without them.

Descartes' Reply

In his *Replies*, Descartes comments briefly on Arnauld's objection. Unfortunately, Descartes doesn't say very much, and what he does say is a bit unclear. First he claims that he has already drawn a distinction between (*a*) propositions that are currently being clearly and distinctly perceived, and (*b*) propositions that are not now being so perceived, but which we remember to have so perceived. He then goes on to answer Arnauld:

> For first, we are sure that God exists because we have attended to the proofs that established this fact; but afterwards it is enough for us to remember that we have perceived something clearly, in order to be sure that it is true; but this would not suffice, unless we knew that God existed and that he did not deceive us.[30]

Descartes apparently wants to claim that even before we have established the existence and veracity of God, our current clear and distinct perceptions are beyond doubt. Hence, we may make use of these perceptions as premises in the arguments that prove that God exists and is no deceiver. Then, once we know that God exists, we can be absolutely confident of the truth of propositions that were formerly perceived clearly and distinctly. So even if we are no longer seeing some proposition to be true, we can be metaphysically certain of it if we can recall that, at some time in the past, we did perceive it clearly and distinctly.

This provides the basis for answers to all the questions I mentioned earlier. How can Descartes make use of CP3 before he has proved that God exists? Easy. He just needs to perceive CP3 clearly and distinctly at the very time that he uses it in the argument. Merely recalling that he formerly perceived it would not be sufficient. Why does Descartes need to establish the existence and veracity of God if it is possible for him to be metaphysically certain of plenty of things before completing the proof? That's easy, too. He needs to establish the existence and veracity of God so that he can continue to be metaphysically certain of things *after* he has perceived them clearly and distinctly.

I think it is fair to say that this so-called "memory defense" is generally considered by scholars to be a failure. Descartes seems to have misrepresented his own position, and he seems to have underestimated the seriousness of Arnauld's criticism. Descartes suggests that the deceptive God hypothesis casts doubt only upon propositions that we *recall* having formerly perceived. But this is wrong. The deceptive God hypothesis casts doubt on present clear and distinct perceptions, too. If I have been created by a deceptive God, then even the things that I am now perceiving clearly and distinctly might be false. Surely, an omnipotent deceiver could see to it that I err in this way.

---

[29] Cress, 24.
[30] HR II, 115.

Furthermore, it is quite unrealistic to suppose that God would guarantee our memories in the way suggested. Descartes suggests that, once he has established the existence and veracity of God, he can be metaphysically certain of things he recalls to have clearly and distinctly perceived. But what if his memory is playing tricks on him? What if he recalls having clearly and distinctly perceived something, when in fact he did no such thing? Will God step in and see to it that the thing is true anyway? This seems absurd. Will God step in and see to it that Descartes' memory never errs in this way? This seems absurd, too. Thus it appears that Descartes' memory defense is not successful.

Another Reply

Before closing this chapter, I would like to suggest another way in which Arnauld's objection can be answered. I have to acknowledge that Descartes did not answer Arnauld in this way, and there is no clear evidence that he would have accepted the answer if he had known of it. Nevertheless, it seems to me that the proposal I shall make is consistent with Descartes' main ideas. Perhaps we can give this answer on his behalf.

First we must recall something about Descartes' procedure in the *First Meditation*. There, when he was attempting to clear his mind of everything less than metaphysically certain, he sought "powerful reasons for doubt." His view was that a thing is not doubtful unless there is some good reason for doubting it. That explains why he went to such trouble reviewing and evaluating all the skeptical arguments. Some of those reasons for doubt, it should be recalled, were rejected. They simply did not make Descartes' beliefs doubtful. Only the deceptive God hypothesis was accepted as a good enough reason for nearly universal doubt.

It seems to me that one of the things that helps to make the deceptive God hypothesis such a good source of metaphysical doubt is the fact that this hypothesis might be true. For all Descartes knew at the time, God really might be a deceiver. Of course, Descartes didn't believe that God was a deceiver, but he was then going just on faith. At the time, he did not have sufficient evidence to support his conviction.

Earlier[31] I distinguished between two grades of certainty. There is the sort of "supercertainty" that Descartes was seeking. We have been calling that "metaphysical certainty." There is also the ordinary, weaker sort of certainty that is involved in ordinary, run-of-the-mill knowledge. We called that "practical certainty." Everything that is metaphysically certain for a person at a time must also be practically certain for him then, but not vice versa. A thing can be practically certain, but still subject to some metaphysical doubts.

Before the proof of the existence and veracity of God, Descartes was not even practically certain that the deceptive God hypothesis is false. It was then a "practical possibility" for him. Later, after he had given his proofs, the deceptive God hypothesis was no longer a practical possibility. He was then practically certain that it was false. Maybe this is the crucial point.

---

[31] Chapter 2, under "Practical Certainty and Metaphysical Certainty."

Perhaps we should say that in order for one proposition to cast another into metaphysical doubt, it must be practically possible. More exactly:

MD If p casts q into metaphysical doubt for S at t, then p must be practically possible for S at t.

Once a source of doubt is no longer practically possible, it no longer serves to make other things metaphysically doubtful. At any rate, that's the suggestion.

If we assume that MD is true, we can make a proposal concerning the structure of a solution to the problem of the Cartesian circle. According to this proposal, before the proofs of the existence and veracity of God, the deceptive God hypothesis was a practical possibility. It cast metaphysical doubt on very many beliefs—just about everything other than "I exist" and directly accessible psychological facts. All such beliefs were metaphysically uncertain. Nevertheless, many beliefs remained practically certain. Among these is the all-important causal principle, CP3. Using that, and some other practically certain premises, Descartes proved the existence and veracity of God. Since the premises were only practically certain, the conclusion ("God exists and is no deceiver") was only practically certain. But that was sufficient to make the deceptive God hypothesis stop being practically possible. Therefore, it could no longer cast metaphysical doubt on Descartes' clear and distinct perceptions. Since nothing else cast doubt on such perceptions, the removal of this last source of doubt made them metaphysically certain. Hence, Descartes could accept these things once again, while not violating his epistemic principle.

This proposal faces some difficulties, too. One of these has to do with the epistemic status of CP3 and the other premises of Descartes' cosmological argument. According to the account I have suggested, each of these premises must be at least practically certain at the outset. However, it may seem that these principles don't even have that fairly modest degree of certainty. Really, they just seem to be false!

This objection seems to me to be quite reasonable. However, my proposal is intended as a proposal about the *structure* of Descartes' reasoning. My main interest is in showing that there is a pattern of reasoning that was available to him and which he could have used without arguing in a circle. Surely, Descartes thought that CP3 was practically certain at the time of its employment in the cosmological argument.

A second objection is a bit harder to answer. According to my proposal, only the deceptive God hypothesis cast doubt on Descartes' clear and distinct perceptions. Once this was eliminated as a source of doubt, nothing cast doubt on clear and distinct perceptions, and they became metaphysically certain. It can be seen, then, that on this proposal nothing other than the deceptive God hypothesis cast doubt on Descartes' clear and distinct perceptions. Yet this point has not been proved. Perhaps some other source of doubt has been overlooked. Maybe something else still taints them, after the deceptive God hypothesis has been removed. How can we be sure that all of these clear and distinct perceptions are really metaphysically certain?

This is a difficult question. Perhaps I should say that I have no way of proving that there are no other sources of doubt. Perhaps I should say that Descartes merely assumed that there are no other sources of doubt. If this assumption is correct, then the proposed solution is basically successful. Descartes has not proved that his clear and distinct perceptions are metaphysically certain, but at least some of them in fact are metaphysically certain. Isn't this enough?

I recognize that this proposed solution is complex. I also recognize that there is not much in the text to support it. I present it here partly because I think it might be adequate, at least as an account of the structure of a solution, and partly to try to make the problem clearer. I think it must be admitted that the problem of the Cartesian circle is not a simple one.

ATHEOLOGY

Our discussion of philosophical theology would be neither complete nor balanced unless it also contained some consideration of the most important arguments *against* the existence of God. All such arguments can be categorized as "atheological," and the study of such arguments can be called "philosophical atheology." We begin with the most famous of such arguments.

THE PROBLEM OF EVIL

In Chapter 7, under "God and Knowledge," I mentioned the Cartesian problem concerning God and error. That problem arises because it is hard to reconcile the existence of God with the fact that humans are prone to error. If we were created by an omnipotent, omniscient, and omnibenevolent deity, why didn't he make us infallible? As we saw, Descartes attempted to answer this question by claiming that our errors arise from our own misuse of our God-given freedom. God gave us this freedom, according to this view, because he saw that it would be better for us to be free and fallible than it would be for us to be infallible but unfree.

It seems to me that there is a great analogy between this so-called "problem of error" and another, rather more famous problem—the problem of evil. This latter problem is generally regarded as the most persistent and serious difficulty for theism. It can be formulated very simply indeed. There is evil. If there were a God, there would be no evil. Therefore, there is no God.

Before we turn to a consideration of some of the ways in which theists have attempted to rebut this argument, let's try to clarify the alleged connection between God and evil. Why should we suppose that the existence of evil is incompatible with the existence of God?

First we must recall certain facts about our concept of God. According to that concept, God is supposed to be omniscient, omnipotent and omnibenevolent. We have also agreed that if there is a God, then he created the world. Let's start with this last feature—creativity. In a remarkable passage, Leibniz presented a marvelous account of creation.

> The wisdom of God, not content with embracing all the possibles, penetrates them, compares them, weighs them one against the other, to estimate their degrees of perfection or imperfection, the strong and the weak, the good and the evil. It goes even beyond the finite combinations, it makes of them an infinity of infinites, that is to say, an infinity of possible sequences of the universe, each of which contains an infinity of creatures. By this means, the divine Wisdom distributes all the possibles it had already contemplated separately, into so many universal systems which it further compares the one with the other. The result of all these comparisons and deliberations is the choice of the best from among all these possible systems, which wisdom makes in order to satisfy goodness completely; and such is precisely the plan of the universe as it is.[1]

On this view, then, the creation of the world is to be understood as a sort of selection, or choice. God selected a certain one of the infinite supply of possible worlds, and chose that one for existence. Of all the possible worlds, that one is the only one that's actual. It is this world—the one we all actually live in.

It is extremely important to recognize that each possible world is historically "complete." That is, each world is perfectly determinate with respect to what goes on at every moment. For every moment of its history, there are certain facts such that, if that world is created, those very facts will obtain at just that moment. In light of this, I think we must also maintain that each possible world is determinate with respect to the amount of good and evil it contains. For each possible world, there is a certain amount of good that would exist if that world were created, and there is a certain amount of evil that would exist if that world were created. Thus, prior to creation, each possible world has a perfectly determinate potential value. It seems to follow from this that, of all these possible worlds, one must be best. It is the one whose potential value is greater than that of each other possible world.

I should point out that I am here skirting a rather deep and perplexing issue concerning the idea of a "best possible world." It might be said that, just as there is no highest number and no largest set, so there is no best possible world. Perhaps it is the case that for each possible world, no matter how good it is, there is one that is just a little better. If this is so, God would have a hard time choosing a world for creation. No matter which one he selects, he will realize that he could have done better by selecting another. How, then, does he manage to choose any world? I have no solution to this problem, but shall proceed here as if it had not arisen. Let's assume that there is a best possible world.

If there is an omniscient God, then he must know the value of every possible world. We mustn't suppose that God discovers the values of the world only *after* he has created one. There can be no surprises for an omniscient being. If there is an omniscient being, he must know, at every time, everything that's knowable at that

---

[1]G. W. Leibniz, *Theodicy*, edited and with an introduction by Austin Farrer, translated by E. M. Huggard, London: Routledge and Kegan Paul, 1951, pp. 267–268.

time. Thus, if there is an omniscient being, he must know the value of each world prior to the moment of creation. It seems to follow from this that, if there is an omniscient being, he must have known which world would be the best of all the possible worlds.

Omnibenevolence is another divine perfection. This may be understood as the property of always preferring the better to the worse.[2] So if there is a God, then there is a being who always prefers what's better to what's worse. Obviously, then, if there is an omnibenevolent being, he prefers the best of all possible worlds. That is, he would rather have that world exist than have any other world exist. To prefer any other world would be to prefer something that is less good than the best. If there is a God, he would never do this.

Finally, God is supposed to be omnipotent. He is supposed to be able to do anything metaphysically possible.[3] Since each of the worlds is indeed *possible*, each of them is such that an omnipotent being would be able to make it actual. Hence, the best of them is such that an omnipotent being would be able to make it actual. If some possible world is somehow "beyond God's power," so that he couldn't create it even if he wanted to, then it's hard to see how God can be truly omnipotent.

So we can conclude that an omniscient being would have to know which world is the best of all the possible worlds; an omnibenevolent being would have to prefer to create the best of all possible worlds; and an omnipotent being would be able to create the best of all possible worlds. It follows, then, that if there is a single entity that is at once omniscient, omnipotent, and omnibenevolent, then that being would know which is best, would prefer to create what's best, and would be able to do so. Hence, if there is such a being, and he created a world, then the world he created must actually be the best of all possible worlds. The actual world, then, must be the best of all possible worlds.

It is hard to see how any evil could exist in the best of all possible worlds. For surely, if you imagine a world with some evil in it, you can always imagine another world, very much like the first, but with that evil missing from it. And the world without the evil would apparently be better than the one with the evil. Thus it would seem to follow that in the best of all possible worlds, nothing evil would happen.

So now we can see a bit more clearly how God and evil are connected. God is supposed to be omniscient, omnipotent, omnibenevolent and creative. Hence, the world he created—this world—is supposed to be the best of all possible worlds. Hence, there should be no evil in this world. Unfortunately, there seems to be quite a lot of evil in the world. Murder, torture, war, injustice, and many other apparent evils can be found wherever we look. So how can there be a God?

Let's formulate the argument somewhat more clearly.

The Problem of Evil

1 If God exists, then there is an omniscient, omnipotent, omnibenevolent and creative being.

[2]See above, Chapter 5, under "Omnibenevolence."
[3]See above, Chapter 5, under "Omnipotence."

2 If there is an omniscient, omnipotent, omnibenevolent and creative being, then this is the best of all possible worlds.

3 If this is the best of all possible worlds, then there is no evil.

4 But there is evil.

5 Therefore, God does not exist.

In this form, the argument is quite straightforward. Line (1) is pretty directly derived from our concept of God. We think of God as the supreme being. Thus, he must have all perfections. Among the perfections are omniscience, omnipotence, and omnibenevolence. We have also seen that God is supposed to be creative. Every contingent thing is supposed to depend upon God. Hence, if God exists, there is an omniscient, omnipotent, omnibenevolent and creative being. That's what (1) says.

The reasoning behind line (2) is also quite simple. An omniscient being would know which world is best; an omnibenevolent being would prefer to create the best world; and an omnipotent being would be able to create it. So if there is such a being, this must be the best of all possible worlds.

How can the best of all possible worlds contain any evil? Presumably, if a world contains some evil, then there must be another world, like that one, except lacking that evil. The second world would have to be better than the first, since they differ only in that some evil is present in the former, but lacking in the latter. Hence, it is reasonable to conclude that the best world of all must contain no evil.

We can see for ourselves that this world does contain some evils. "Man's inhumanity to man" is an undeniable fact. If you doubt it, just purchase a copy of one of the more lurid newspapers, and read some of the crime articles. If you're still not convinced, go to the library and browse through some books on European history in the late 1930s and early 1940s. After that, you will agree that line (4) cannot reasonably be rejected.

Since the argument is clearly valid, it would seem that the theist must find some premise to reject. Otherwise, the conclusion is inescapable—there is no God.

THEISTIC REPLIES TO THE PROBLEM OF EVIL

Some theists respond to the problem of evil by making vague remarks about "God's mysterious ways." Often they suggest that it is somehow impertinent of us to ask why God permits so much evil. The idea, apparently, is that we should maintain our faith even when we can't find any rational explanation for certain facts.

In certain contexts, this sort of reply may be quite fitting. However, if we are engaged in philosophical theology, we must reject this appeal to faith. In the present context, we are committed to giving careful, rational consideration to arguments against the existence of God. We are attempting to determine whether, in the sense explained earlier, there is good reason to believe that there is no God. If, when all is said and done, we find that atheism is the more reasonable position, we may still retain our faith. In that case, we will have to acknowledge that our faith is not supported by reason.

The Free Will Defense

One of the most popular theistic replies to the problem of evil involves a sort of "passing of the buck." Some theists are willing to admit that there's plenty of evil in the world, but they insist that God is not to be blamed for it. It's not his fault. It's all *our* fault. All the evil in the world is caused, they say, by people.

Merely saying this, of course, hardly solves the problem. Why did God create people who would bring so much evil into the world? Why didn't he create better people? Surely, if God is omnipotent, he could have created a world without murderers and torturers. In order to give a fully satisfactory answer to the problem of evil, then, the theist must explain why God permits people to create so much trouble.

According to the free will defense, God allows us to cause evil, not because he can't stop us, but because he sees that freedom is a good thing.[4] Freedom is so good, on this view, that it is better for us to be free (even though we will often misuse our freedom) than it would be for us to be unfree (and forced to do good). Thus, even though there is plenty of evil in the world, this is still the best of all possible worlds. The best world in which we lack freedom is not as good as this world, in spite of the evils we have produced. Thus, paradoxical as it may seem, a world cannot be best unless it has some evil in it. If you remove that evil, you will make the world worse overall (because you will also have to remove an even greater good—freedom).

Thus, if we adopt the free will defense, we will reject line (3) of the argument. From the fact that this is the best of all possible worlds, we will say, it does not follow that this is a world devoid of evil. In order to be best, the world had to have free agents in it. And if there are free agents in the world, some of them are sure to create trouble. Thus, according to this approach, theism can be reconciled with the existence of evil in the world.

Critics of this approach often ask why God couldn't have created a race of people who would be free, but who would nevertheless avoid evil. If it is metaphysically possible for there to be a world full of such people, surely it would be better to create them than it would be to create free sinners such as us.

Even if this first question can be answered, the free will defense still faces serious difficulties. To see these, let us assume that in order to create free people, God had to pay the price of creating some who would sin. Now, by appeal to a certain relatively simple distinction, we can revise the problem of evil so that the free will defense will no longer apply. The distinction I have in mind is the distinction between evil produced by people, and evil produced in all other ways. Let's call the first sort of evil "human evil," and let's call the second sort of evil "natural evil."

The atheist now can acknowledge that the free will defense may provide an explanation for the existence of *human* evil, but he can go on to insist that it does not provide an explanation for the existence of *natural* evil. Surely, no theist is foolish enough to suppose that natural disasters such as hurricanes, tornadoes, floods, famines, and earthquakes are in some way due to human vice. Such evils cannot be ascribed to some person's misuse of his or her freedom. Surely, if there

---

[4]It should be clear that there is an important similarity between this answer to the problem of evil and Descartes' answer to the problem of error. See above, Chapter 7, under "God and Knowledge."

were a God, he could have created a world with free people, but without such natural evils. And just as surely, such a world would have been better than this one. Hence, the problem of evil remains. We can present it, in revised form, as follows:

The Problem of Evil—Revised Version

1 If God exists, then there is a being that is omniscient, omnipotent, omnibenevolent, and creative.

2 If there is a being that is omniscient, omnipotent, omnibenevolent, and creative, then this is the best of all possible worlds.

3 If this is the best of all possible worlds, then there is no natural evil.

4 But there is natural evil.

5 Therefore, God does not exist.

In this form, the argument is still valid. Lines (3) and (4) have been altered in light of the free will defense. If theists want to reject this argument, they will have to find some other way out. They can't blame people for *all* the evil in the world.

The Manichaean Defense

A second possible answer to the problem of evil is like the first in that it involves "passing the buck." However, this second answer does not require putting all the blame for evil on people. Rather, it posits the existence of a supernatural source of evil—some entity as powerful and intelligent as God, but unlike God in his preferences. Whereas God is supposed to be omnibenevolent, this being is supposed to be "omnimalevolent." He always prefers the worse to the better. If he had his way, this would be the worst of all possible worlds. Fortunately, he doesn't have his way. He has to contend with God. Since God is just as powerful as this bad deity, but God prefers good to evil, the result is that this is neither the best nor the worst of possible worlds. Rather, it is a sort of compromise between good and evil. Maybe we should call it the most mediocre of possible worlds.

This sort of dualistic approach was adopted by a religious group that flourished in the third and fourth centuries A.D. The founder of the religion was a Persian called "Mani," and his followers were called "Manichaeans." In light of this, the approach itself is now called "Manichaeism."

If we adopt the Manichaean defense, we will attack the argument at line (2). Even though God exists, and has the divine perfections, still this is not the best of all possible worlds. God was not able to create that world, since the evil deity would not permit it. Thus, God had to be satisfied with a compromise. He had to accept a world containing a lot of evil. We should be thankful, in any case, that God did as well as he did. If the evil deity had his way about it, we would find ourselves in a much worse world.

From the earliest days, Christian leaders recognized that Manichaeism is incompatible with the fundamental monotheism of their tradition. It was obvious to them that it is impossible to have a proper appreciation of God, and still believe that there is another deity as powerful as he is. Indeed, later dualistic doctrines were declared to be heretical, and one Pope even launched a crusade to wipe them out. Thus, as far as Christian doctrine is concerned, the Manichaean defense is unacceptable.

For our purposes here, of course, the fact that Manichaeism is a heresy is irrelevant. We have to evaluate it on its own merits. So the question for us is not the question whether Manichaeism is acceptable to the Church. Rather, it is the question whether it provides a satisfactory solution to the problem of evil. In my view, Manichaeism does not provide a solution to the problem of evil. Let me attempt to explain why.

We are working with a concept of God according to which "God" means the same as "supreme being." We have also assumed that a supreme being would have all the perfections, including omnipotence. If God is omnipotent, then God is able to bring about any metaphysically possible state of affairs. Thus, it should be clear that there cannot be another entity powerful enough to thwart God's will. For suppose there were such an entity. Then it would be possible for God to prefer some metaphysically possible state of affairs, but to be unable to bring it about (because the other entity won't let him do it). In that case, there is a certain state of affairs that is metaphysically possible, but which God cannot bring about. Hence, if there were an evil deity, God would not be omnipotent. Since God must be omnipotent, there cannot be such a deity.

So the problem with Manichaeism is not simply that it is a heresy. Rather, it is that it is internally incoherent. It posits the existence of God, and it also posits the existence of an evil deity. However, it is impossible for both of these entities to exist at the same time. Thus, Manichaeism is false, and the Manichaean defense is not acceptable.

Evil as a Privation

Some philosophers have suggested that we can solve the problem of evil if we come to a deeper understanding of the nature of evil. Evil, they say, is not a "positive thing." It is a "privation." Leibniz, who seems to have maintained this view, once said:

> God is not the cause of evil.... [T]he root of evil is in nothingness, that is, in the privation or limitation of creatures, which God in his grace remedies by the degree of perfection which it pleases him to bestow.[5]

Descartes also seems to have accepted this view. In the *Fourth Meditation*, he seems to say that God is not responsible for sin and errors, since these are merely privations. He goes on to say that

> a privation, in which alone the meaning of falsehood and sin is to be found, in no way needs the concurrence of God, for a privation is not a thing; and it is not related to God as its cause; rather, it ought to be called only a negation.[6]

So the suggestion seems to be that we can solve the problem of evil if we accept the doctrine that evil is a privation. But what can this mean, and how exactly does it bear on the problem?

---

[5] Parkinson, 40.
[6] Cress, 39.

In order to clarify the nature of a privation, let us contemplate holes. I have in mind the sort of hole that one finds in a doughnut, or in a piece of Swiss cheese. Let's concentrate on the hole in a doughnut. It is clear that there really is a hole there—it's not just an illusion, or a mistake. And yet the hole seems somewhat less real than the rest of the doughnut. We can bring out something of the oddity of the hole if we ask certain questions about it. If it is a physical object, then what is it made of? Where does it go when the doughnut has been eaten? Why doesn't it add to the weight of the doughnut? On the other hand, if it is not a physical object, then what sort of object is it, and how are we to explain the fact that we can see it, and measure it, and describe its shape?

There is a temptation to say that the doughnut hole is just the absence of doughnut from a certain volume of space. But this is pretty clearly wrong. Surely, there is a complete absence of doughnut from the space inside your skull. Nevertheless, you would not want to say that there is a doughnut hole there. So it is wrong to say that a doughnut hole exists in a place whenever there is an absence of doughnut in that place.

Perhaps it will be better to think of the hole as a *property* rather than as an *object*. The doughnut has the property of *being holed*. That is, it is a physical object, and there is a relatively empty volume of space surrounded by it. More exactly, there is a volume of space which does not contain any part of the doughnut, but which is surrounded by volumes of space that do contain parts of the doughnut. Furthermore, there is a sense in which we might have expected that space to have contained doughnut—after all, the spaces around it are all occupied by bits of doughnut.

If we think of it in this way, we can begin to develop some answers to the questions about the hole. When we say that a hole exists at a certain spot, all we mean is that the spot is the relatively empty spot surrounded by some holed object. Thus, the hole is not a physical object, and we can evade the question about the stuff out of which it is made. This gives us the answer to the question about where the hole goes when the doughnut is eaten. The hole stops existing, not because it has been eaten, but because there is no longer a holed object there. Furthermore, we can give sense to the notion that the hole can be seen. We explain this by saying that the doughnut can be seen, and when it is seen, we can see that it is holed. Furthermore, we can see the inner surface of the doughnut, and we can measure and diagram that surface. When we speak of measuring and diagramming a hole, all we mean is that we measure and diagram the inner surface of the holed object.

This little theory of holes provides an answer to a question about the creation of holes, too. Does the baker have to create the hole in addition to the doughnut? If not, who does create the hole? The answer, clearly enough, is that the hole is not an object, and does not have to be created. The baker merely needs to create the doughnut, and see to it that the doughnut is holed. If he does this, we can say, somewhat loosely, that the hole exists. However, strictly speaking, there is no such *object* as the hole. It's just that there is a holed doughnut.

I'm inclined to believe that a pseudo-entity such as the doughnut hole is a good example of a "privation." It is not a genuine object. We speak as if there were an object there, but all of our talk can be reformulated in terms of various properties of the objects that really are there.

When philosophers say that evil is a privation, they mean to suggest that evil isn't a genuine object. It's just that something is missing from something in a place where we might have expected it to be. Thus, blindness (which seems to be an evil) should not be thought of as an extra object somehow added to some people. Rather, we should think of it as the absence of vision in a place where we might have expected to find vision. Similarly for illness and death. These are not positive things, but just absences (of health and life) in places where it would be fitting for health and life to be.

If we take this approach, we may absolve God of any blame for the creation of evils. We may say that just as the baker does not have to create the holes in addition to the doughnuts, so God does not have to create the evils in addition to the various positive objects he creates. He just creates the genuine objects, and, as a result of the fact that these objects fail to have certain properties, the privations may be said to exist, too. However, since the privations are not genuine objects, they are not created by God.

Even if this approach to the problem of evil succeeds in solving some problem about the creation of evil, I think it does not solve the problem we have been considering. It gets us no closer to an understanding of the fundamental issue: if this is the best of all possible worlds, then why are there so many bad things going on?

If we insist on viewing evil as a privation, we still face the same question. Perhaps we should rephrase it. Perhaps we should ask: if this is the best of all possible worlds, then why are things so limited? Why is health missing from so many lives? Why is happiness absent from so many places where we might have expected it? Why are justice, beauty, and joy spread so thinly? Why didn't God create a world with fewer "holes" and more "doughnut"?

Necessary Evils

Perhaps the most promising reply to the problem of evil is one based on the concept of "necessary evil." When we speak here of necessary evils, we do not mean to suggest that there are some evils that absolutely must occur. This would imply, quite implausibly, that there are some evils that occur in every possible world. Rather, when we speak of necessary evils, we mean to suggest that if this is to be the best of all possible worlds, then there must be some evils in it.

In order to make this notion clearer, let's put ourselves into the position of a creator. Suppose we have to create a world, and suppose we have decided to create the best one we can. Imagine that we've found a possible world in which there is lots of happiness. It looks like the traditional image of heaven, with plenty of musical groups and a population that spends substantial amounts of time walking around in lovely gardens. Surveying this world, we may be a bit disappointed. Certain great goods seem to be missing. There is no courage, no compassion, no mercy, no charity. Surely, the world would be improved if an opportunity for the display of these great human virtues could be added. Suppose we set about to add them.

Let's image that we first try to add courage to the world. Since courage requires standing your ground in the face of evil, we find that we cannot add some courage to the world without also adding some evil. Some wrongdoers must be created, since without them there would be no opportunity for courage to be displayed. Thus we discover that the existence of some wrongdoers is a necessary evil. The world cannot be the best of worlds unless that evil is present in it.

Similarly, we will find that it is impossible for us to add compassion to the world without adding some evil. For compassion is a sympathetic appreciation of another person's sorrow. Unless there are sorrowful people, there cannot be any compassion. Thus, in the effort to make the world better by the addition of compassion, we have to add some sorrow, too. So a certain amount of sorrow seems to be a necessary evil.

Mercy is another good that cannot exist unless there is some evil. A judge shows mercy in forgiving someone for a crime. If the convict never committed the crime, then the judge is not being merciful in letting the convict off the hook. That would simply be justice. So in order to improve the world by the addition of mercy, we need to add a few criminals and a few crimes. Hence, crime seems to be another necessary evil.

Finally, we can consider charity. To be charitable, one must give something of value to another person who is in need of that thing. In a world without need, there can be no charity. Thus, in order to make the world better by the inclusion of charitable persons, we will need to add a few needy people, too. Hence, the existence of such needy persons seems to be another necessary evil.

We have already seen that freedom may be another thing that contributes to the value of a world. In order for a world to be the best of all possible worlds, it may need to have free people in it. Yet if there are free people, some of them are sure to do evil. In light of this, two more sorts of evil may be necessary. The first of these is the evil done freely by people. The second sort of evil is the evil those people suffer as punishment for their sins. Surely, the world would be worse if wrongdoers were never punished. In that case, justice would be missing. So, in order to make the world as good as it can possibly be, we must add the evil entailed by just punishment for free evil acts.

Now we can see how the necessary evils reply works. We deny line (3) of the problem of evil. There is a God, we insist, and he did create the best of all possible worlds. However, some goods cannot exist unless they are accompanied by certain evils. Thus, in order to create the best of all possible worlds, God simply had to create a world containing some evils. A world utterly lacking in these evils could not contain certain important goods, and so could not be as good as this world.

This sort of reply to the problem of evil is often ascribed to Leibniz. In his *Theodicy*, he did insist that this is the best of all possible worlds. Furthermore, he acknowledged that there is evil in this world. His position, apparently, was indeed that all of that evil is necessary evil. In the following passage, he seems to be making just this point:

> Thus, if the smallest evil that comes to pass in the world were missing in it, it would no longer be this world; which, with nothing omitted and all allowance made, was found the best by the Creator who chose it.[7]

---

[7]Leibniz, *Theodicy*, op. cit., 128–129. Leibniz discusses this point further in the *Summary of the Controversy*, in the passage concerning the first objection. op. cit., 377–378.

Many people find this approach incredible. After reviewing some of the horrors and atrocities in human history, and some of the enormous disasters in natural history, they have concluded that there is far more evil here than is needed in order to make this the best of all possible worlds. Surely God could have made do with just a little less famine, and just a little less war, and just a little less cruelty. Much of the evil, these people insist, is utterly unnecessary. It is not required in order to bring about some greater good.

On this basis, we may formulate a final version of the problem of evil. It is this:

The Problem of Evil—Second Revised Version

1 If God exists, then there is a being that is omniscient, omnipotent, omnibenevolent, and creative.

2 If there is a being that is omniscient, omnipotent, omnibenevolent and creative, then this is the best of all possible worlds.

3 If this is the best of all possible worlds, then there is no unnecessary evil.

4 But there is unnecessary evil.

5 Therefore, God does not exist.

It seems to me that this is the most powerful version of the problem of evil. As I see it, there is no simple reply here, as there was with each of the earlier versions. If a theist is to reject this argument, he or she must find some way to reject line (4). In his *Theodicy*, Leibniz attempted to explain how this can be done. He defended the idea that all evil is necessary evil. However, not all readers of the *Theodicy* have been convinced. Perhaps the most famous attack on Leibniz' view was written by Voltaire (1694–1778). In his devastatingly satiric book, *Candide*, he ridiculed the Leibnizian position. The ludicrous character Dr. Pangloss is widely assumed to be a grotesque mockery of Leibniz. After suffering through earthquakes, plagues, insane wars, religious intolerance, and every sort of misery, Dr. Pangloss calmly insists that "all is for the best in the best of all possible worlds." Anyone inclined to believe in God must come to grips with this problem. How can the existence of so much apparently unnecessary evil be reconciled with the existence of an omnipotent, omniscient, and omnibenevolent creator?

SOME PROBLEMS WITH OMNIPOTENCE

The concept of divine omnipotence has been the focus of a fair amount of puzzlement. It has seemed to many philosophers that there is something incoherent in the idea that God might be omnipotent. In one form, the difficulty goes as follows. There are many little tasks that some people can accomplish quite easily. For example, some people can wiggle their ears. This shows that ear-wiggling is a possible task. However, God cannot do this (since he has no body). Since there are possible tasks which God cannot perform, God is evidently not omnipotent.

A moment's reflection will enable us to formulate a large list of tasks that are, for one reason or another, beyond God's power, but which are not beyond the power of some ordinary human being. For example, consider any task that requires a body, such as combing your hair, or brushing your teeth, or scratching your nose. You can do such things, but God cannot. Other tasks seem to involve the ability to err. For example, you can make an honest typographical error while writing a term paper. God cannot do that. Does this show that God is less than omnipotent?

I think we can deal with these puzzles rather straightforwardly. First, we must reflect upon the "tasks" we have been discussing. It may seem that the task I do when I wiggle my ears is somewhat different from the task we ask of God when we ask him to wiggle his ears. My task seems possible, but his task seems impossible. Thus, it is not clear that it is the same task.

It will be useful to introduce some technical locutions here. Let us agree that every task may be understood as the bringing about of some state of affairs. Thus, when I wiggle my ears, I bring about the state of affairs of *Fred's ears wiggling*. When I brush my teeth, I bring about the state of affairs of *Fred's teeth being brushed*. I think we can see that it will be possible to describe any task in this "state of affairs" terminology.

We gain certain advantages if we adopt the proposed locutions. For one thing, we have a clear way of explaining what's meant by "same task." In one sense, we can say that two different people perform the same task if they bring about the same state of affairs. So if I bring about *there being wood in the woodshed* and Bill brings about *there being wood in the woodshed*, then we have performed the same task. However, if I bring about *there being wood in Fred's woodshed*, and Bill brings about *there being wood in Bill's woodshed*, then Bill and I have preformed different tasks.

Furthermore, we now have a very simple way of deciding whether a given task is genuinely possible. We can say that a task is possible provided that it is the bringing about of a metaphysically possible state of affairs. A state of affairs is metaphysically possible, you may recall, just in case it occurs in some possible world.

Now we must consider the tasks that God allegedly cannot perform. He cannot wiggle his ears. What state of affairs is it that he cannot bring about? Presumably, God cannot bring about the state of affairs of *God's ears wiggling*. Now, however, we can see that this inability does not detract from God's omnipotence. If we assume that God is essentially incorporeal, then we must conclude that the state of affairs of *God's ears wiggling* occurs in no possible world—it is metaphysically impossible. This is because God doesn't have ears in any possible world.[8] Omnipotence is the ability to do everything that is metaphysically possible. The inability to do the impossible is irrelevant.

Similar considerations should resolve the puzzle about the honest typographical errors. God cannot bring about *God correcting an honest typographical error made by God*. But this is consistent with his omnipotence, since it is impossible for God to make an honest error. On the other hand, God would surely have no trouble

---

[8] If you assume that God is corporeal, and has ears, you will undoubtedly also assume that he can wiggle them. Thus, you will have to consider some other, more interesting version of the puzzle. I assume that God is essentially incorporeal, and so I'm satisfied with this version of the puzzle and with this solution.

bringing about *someone making an honest typographical error, and then correcting it*. He'd just have to be sure that the person who makes, and then corrects the error is someone who is not essentially omniscient.

I think the same sort of maneuver will resolve the other puzzles mentioned above. In each case we have to be quite clear about the identity of the task. We must ask ourselves just what state of affairs God supposedly cannot bring about. Then we must carefully consider whether the state of affairs really is possible. If it is an impossible state of affairs, then it's no wonder God can't bring it about. And it's no argument against his omnipotence, either.

The Paradox of the Stone

Let's now turn to a somewhat more complicated atheistic puzzle concerning omnipotence—the paradox of the stone. This puzzle is usually stated in the form of a short question: "Can God create a stone so heavy that he can't lift it?" Although some people apparently can understand the puzzle as soon as they have seen the question, we will have to try to spell it out, and put it into the form of an argument.

There are only two possible answers to the question about the creation of the too-heavy stone. Either we say that God can create such a stone, or we say that he cannot. Either answer leads to trouble. Suppose, first, that we say that he *can* create such a stone. Then it seems that it is possible for such a stone to exist. However, if there is a stone so heavy that God can't lift it, then there is something that he cannot do. He can't lift the stone. In this case, God would not be omnipotent.

On the other hand, suppose we say that God can*not* create the stone. Then it seems that there is something else that he cannot do, namely, he cannot create a certain stone. In this case, we are driven again to the conclusion that God is not omnipotent. Thus, no matter whether he can or cannot create the too-heavy stone, God cannot be omnipotent. Since God cannot exist without being omnipotent, there is no way to avoid the conclusion that God does not exist.

In order to make discussion easier, let's lay out the details of the argument. Although it can be formulated in a variety of ways, this one seems to me to be easiest to handle:

The Paradox of the Stone

1 Either God can create a stone so heavy he can't lift it, or he cannot create a stone so heavy he can't lift it.

2 If God can create a stone so heavy he can't lift it, then there is something that God cannot do. (He cannot lift the stone.)

3 If God cannot create a stone so heavy he can't lift it, then there is something that God cannot do. (He cannot create the stone.)

4 Therefore, there is something that God cannot do.

5 If there is something that God cannot do, then God is not omnipotent.

6 If God is not omnipotent, then God does not exist.

7 Therefore, God does not exist.

In this form, the argument is logically valid. Furthermore, each premise can be given a plausible defense. Line (1) just says that either God can or cannot create a too-heavy stone. If there is a God, then he either has this power or not. hence, any theist has to accept line (1).

Line (2) draws out a certain consequence of the first alternative. If it is possible for God to create a too-heavy stone, then it is possible for there to be such a stone. In that case, there is a possible task that God cannot perform. He cannot lift the stone. Hence we have line (2).

Line (3) draws out a consequence of the second alternative. If God cannot create the too-heavy stone, then there is another possible task that seems to be beyond his power. He seems to be unable to create a certain stone. Thus we can see that whether he can create the too-heavy stone or not, there is something beyond the power of God. This is recorded in line (4), which is just a lemma.

If there is a possible task that God cannot perform, then God is not omnipotent. This is supposed to follow directly from the definition of omnipotence. In order to be omnipotent, a thing has to be able to do anything metaphysically possible. So we have (5).

We have defined "God" in such a way that nothing could count as God unless it had all the divine perfections. It has traditionally been assumed that omnipotence is one of these perfections. Hence, if God exists, he is omnipotent. Turned around, this means that if God is not omnipotent, then God does not exist. Now we can derive our atheistic conclusion: there is no God.

There are several possible ways in which a theist may attempt to deal with the puzzle. One fairly popular approach requires tinkering with the definition of omnipotence. The hope is that it will turn out that there is some new definition of omnipotence that will permit us to say that God is omnipotent, even though we admit either that he cannot create the too-heavy stone, or that he cannot lift it.

My own view, however, is that we must insist that the puzzle be put into proper order before we attempt to solve it. As it stands, the argument is not adequately formulated. We can see this if we recall our official definition of omnipotence.[9] We have not defined omnipotence as the ability to do absolutely everything. Rather, we have defined it as the ability to bring about any metaphysically possible state of affairs. Thus, in order to show that God is not omnipotent, we need to establish that there is some metaphysically possible state of affairs that he cannot bring about. This will require relatively trivial changes in lines (2), (3), (4), and (5).

A further problem has to do with the notion of "lifting." Strictly speaking, I would say that God (if he exists) cannot lift anything. The problem, once again, has to do with corporeality. As I see it, God is incorporeal, and ordinary lifting requires some sort of physical interaction with the lifted object. Perhaps it would be better to put the question in terms of God's ability to "see to the lifting" of the stone, or his ability to "arrange things so that the stone is lifted." Let us understand "lift" in a suitably extended sense so that it makes sense to speak of God's lifting of various things.

---

[9]See above, Chapter 5, under "Omnipotence."

When altered in these ways, the argument looks something like this:

The Paradox of the Stone—Tidied Up Version

1 Either God can create a stone so heavy he can't lift it, or he cannot create a stone so heavy he can't lift it.

2 If God can create a stone so heavy he can't lift it, then there is a metaphysically possible state of affairs that God cannot bring about. (Specifically, he can't bring about *God lifting a stone so heavy that God can't lift it.*)

3 If God cannot create a stone so heavy he can't lift it, then there is a metaphysically possible state of affairs that God cannot bring about. (Specifically, he can't bring about *God creating a stone so heavy that God can't lift it.*)

4 Therefore, there is a metaphysically possible state of affairs that God cannot bring about.

5 If there is a metaphysically possible state of affairs that God cannot bring about, then God is not omnipotent.

6 If God is not omnipotent, then God does not exist.

7 Therefore, God does not exist.

Now I think the theist's reply should be more obvious. He can deny lines (2) and (3). According to line (2), *God lifting a stone so heavy that God can't lift it* is a metaphysically possible state of affairs that God can't bring about. But it is clear that this state of affairs is not metaphysically possible. It is as impossible as *Fred splitting a log that Fred cannot split* or *Bill chopping down a tree that Bill cannot chop down.* These are all impossible, and no one should be blamed for being unable to bring them about.

Line (3) says that if God cannot create the too-heavy stone, then there is a metaphysically possible state of affairs he can't bring about. But the state of affairs mentioned in the parentheses in (3) is pretty clearly *not* a metaphysically possible one. There is no possible world in which *God creating a stone too heavy for God to lift* occurs. Every possible stone, no matter how heavy, is such that God can arrange for it to be lifted. Thus, the fact that God cannot bring about the state of affairs of *God creating a stone too heavy for God to lift* does not entail that there is something metaphysically possible that God cannot bring about.

My conclusion then, is that the theist has a satisfactory answer to the paradox of the stone. I have to admit that the answer is rather complicated, and that some readers may fail to be convinced. Perhaps, if you find my answer unsatisfactory, you will develop a better one of your own.

A PROBLEM ABOUT GOD AND FREEDOM

Here is a sort of scientific experiment: hold up your right hand a few inches in front of your face. Point your index finger straight up into the air, while holding the rest of your fingers in a relaxed, loose fist. Without moving your index finger, consider the possibility of moving it to the right, and then consider the possibility of moving it to the left. Now count to three, and at the count of three, move it either to the left or to the right, but not both. I think you will find that even if you in fact moved it to the right, you could have moved it to the left. Unless there is something special about your case, nothing *forced* you to move your finger in the way you did. Whichever way you moved it, you could have moved it the other way. The experiment thus shows that you have a certain amount of freedom.

Some philosophers and theologians have suggested that this freedom is a sort of gift from God. They have maintained that God made us free because he recognized that freedom is a good thing, and so preferred to create a world in which people have some freedom. However, there is a line of reasoning that purports to show that God and freedom are incompatible. If we have any freedom, there is no God. Let us now turn to this puzzling argument.

The first premise of the argument follows from our analysis of the concept of God, together with the empirical fact that you moved your finger as you did when you performed the experiment. Let's suppose you moved it to the left at the count of three. (You may substitute "right" for "left" if you in fact moved your finger to the right.) If God exists, then he has always been omniscient. Every moment of time is such that God knows, at that time, everything that is then true. Since you in fact did move your finger to the left at the count of three, it has been true for thousands of years that you would move your finger to the left at the count of three. Thus, if there is a God, he has known for thousands of years that you would move your finger to the left at the count of three. So the first premise is

1 If God exists, then he has known for thousands of years that you would move your finger to the left at the count of three.

It is reasonable to maintain that we have a certain amount of choice with respect to the future. Where your own actions are concerned, you seem to be able to determine whether you will perform an action or whether you will refrain. At least a part of the future is, in this sense, "up to us," or not yet entirely "fixed." The past, on the other hand, seems to be fixed and unalterable. What's done cannot be undone. If a thing has already happened, then we cannot go back and see to it that that very thing did not happen. At best, we can resolve that similar things will not happen in the future.

If there is a God, and he has known for thousands of years that you would move your finger to the left when undertaking our experiment, then this fact about God's knowledge seems to be fixed and unalterable. Apparently, nothing you could have done today could have changed the fact that God has had this bit for knowledge for all these many years. Thus, we have our second premise:

2 If God has known for thousands of years that you would move your finger to the left at the count of three, then it is unalterable that God has known for thousands of years that you would move your finger to the left at the count of three.

Now it should be clear how the argument proceeds. If God's past knowledge is unalterable, then you could not have done anything other than what you in fact did. For God has known all along that you would do precisely that. Thus, you *had* to move your finger to the left. Doing anything different would be inconsistent with the fact that it was an unchangeable fact that God had known for thousands of years that you would move to the left at that moment. This gives us premise (3):

3 If it is unalterable that God has known for thousands of years that you would move your finger to the left at the count of three, then you couldn't have done otherwise than move your finger to the left at the count of three.

A moment ago, when you performed the experiment with your finger, you agreed (I hope) that you could have moved your finger in the other way. Thus, even if you in fact moved your finger to the left at the count of three, you could have done otherwise. You could have moved it to the right. Indeed, you could have messed up the experiment by refusing to move it, or by wiggling it both ways. Surely, you have at least this trivial bit of freedom! Thus, we have our final premise:

4 You could have done otherwise than move your finger to the left at the count of three.

If these four premises are true, then we may validly derive the atheistic conclusion:

5 Therefore, God does not exist.

So the fundamentals of this line of reasoning are pretty easy to understand. If there is a God, then he has known, since the creation of the universe, everything that would happen. Since the past is unalterable, the fact that God knew all these things is currently unalterable. But if the fact that God knew all these things is unalterable, then the things themselves are also unalterable—nothing we can do today can be incompatible with the knowledge God had thousands of years ago. Thus, if there is a God, we have no freedom. Conversely, if we have some freedom, then there is no God.

Critics of this argument have attacked it in several different ways. Some have suggested that line (1) is false. They have claimed that, until you make up your mind about how your finger is going to move, there simply is no "fact of the matter." It is not yet true that you will move it to the left. The statement that you will move it to the left starts being true when it becomes a "settled fact." While it is not yet decided, this statement is neither true nor false. Since a thing cannot be known unless it is true, God did not know that you would move to the left until you determined that you would move to the left.

If we attack the argument in this way, we give up "the Law of the Excluded Middle." This "Law" is the principle that every proposition is either true or false—there is no third (or middle) possibility. It would be convenient to be able to retain the law, and so it would be preferable to find some other way of attacking the argument.

Others have rejected line (1), but for entirely different reasons. They have suggested that God does not exist in space and time. As Leibniz said, God is an "extramundane necessary being"—a necessary being that does not exist *in* our world. If God does not exist in time, then he did not exist thousands of years ago, and he does not exist today, and he will not exist next Thursday. On the view in question, however, God nevertheless does exist. He exists at a time outside of our earthly temporal scheme. He exists at "eternity," a time that is neither before nor after nor simultaneous with any time with which we are familiar. Thus, God did not know anything thousands of years ago, since he did not exist thousands of years ago. Indeed, since God did not exist at any time in the past, he did not know anything at any time in the past.

This approach has its problems. For one thing, it seems incredible that there should be a time that is neither earlier than, nor later than, nor simultaneous with the present. To say that God exists only at this odd time is to say that he never has existed in the past, and he never will exist in the future, and he does not exist now. This surely seems to imply that he is simply nonexistent! Furthermore, if God does not exist now, what's the point of praying to him now? He cannot hear your prayers now, and he doesn't even know now that you exist! Going still further, even if we grant that there is such a time as eternity, it seems that what happens then is just as unalterable as what happens in the past. How can you have it in your power today to determine whether God knows, at eternity, that you move your finger to the right, or whether he knows, at eternity, that you move your finger to the left?

Others have attacked line (2). They have pointed out that certain aspects of the past are still open to alteration. For example, suppose a friend predicted yesterday that you would neglect to study tomorrow for a certain exam. Suppose you now have your choice of studying or not. It seems that you now also have the power to see to it that your friend's prediction was true when he made it, and you now have it in your power to see to it that your friend's prediction was false when he made it. Maybe something like this is true of God's knowledge. Perhaps you can now see to it that God knew, thousands of years ago, that you would move to the left, and you can now see to it that God knew, thousands of years ago, that you would move to the right. All you have to do, on this view, is decide how to wiggle your finger!

A theist could maintain that line (4) is false. In fact, he could say, no human action could have been different from the way it is. Perhaps the theist will insist that our feeling that there are alternative possibilities is fueled entirely by our ignorance. When we say that we could have done something that we in fact did not do, all we mean is that we didn't know in advance whether we were going to do it or not. Since it in fact was not done, it was impossible for it to be done. The feeling that you could have moved your finger the other way was entirely misleading. If you moved your finger to the right, then, the fatalist will say, it was necessary for you to have done so, and you simply could not have done otherwise.

This fatalistic approach is not very popular nowadays. It is in direct conflict with the well-entrenched notion that people are sometimes free to choose their actions. Many philosophers have insisted that morality would be impossible in a fatalistic world. If no one ever could have done anything different from whatever he or she in fact did, and if no one ever has any genuine alternatives, or choices, then what point can there be in saying that someone *should* do something, or *should not* have done what he or she in fact did? No matter what we do, we would inevitably have a perfectly good excuse—"I had no choice. I couldn't have done otherwise."

These reflections on God and freedom lead naturally to a much larger issue concerning God and possibility. Since it is unlikely that we will be able to solve the puzzle about freedom and divine foreknowledge here, let us turn briefly to that larger issue.

A DEEPER PROBLEM ABOUT POSSIBILITY

Possibility, necessity, and impossibility form a close-knit group of important and familiar concepts. According to a long-standing philosophical tradition, these concepts are all definable in terms of possible worlds. The concept of a possible world may be elucidated as follows. Start with the total history of the real world. Now imagine some change in this history. Now imagine all the other changes that would be required in order to accommodate that initial change into an internally coherent story. The result is the history of some other possible world. So long as such a history is internally consistent and complete, it may be taken to be the history of a possible world. In some possible worlds, there are no people. In others, there are people, but there are no plants. In yet others, there is no earth—we all live on Mars or Jupiter. Clearly, some possible worlds are quite weird and different from the real world. All that's required is that each such world be internally consistent and complete. Now, making use of this concept, we can go on to explain possibility, necessity, and impossibility.

To say that a state of affairs is *possible* is to say that it happens in some possible world; to say that it is *necessary* is to say that it happens in all possible worlds; and to say that it is *impossible* is to say that it happens in no possible world. When defined in these ways, these terms are said to express *metaphysical* necessity, possibility, and impossibility.

A closely related concept is the concept of truth. To say that a state of affairs is *true* is to say that it happens in this (the actual) possible world. As a matter of convenience here, let us agree to use the name "Alpha" as a proper name for the actual world—the only world that actually exists.

If we assume that Alpha is just one of many possible worlds, and that it differs from all the rest in that it is the only one that's actual, or which occurs, then these definitions give us the basis for a variety of very general principles concerning the logical connections among necessity, possibility, impossibility, and truth. For example, we can see that what's necessary must be true—for if a thing happens in every possible world, then it must happen in Alpha. Equally, we can see that what's true must be possible, for if a thing happens in Alpha, then it must happen in some possible world (since Alpha is one of the possible worlds). Furthermore, what's necessary must be possible, since what happens in all possible worlds must happen in some possible world. On the other hand, we can see that what's true need not be necessary, since something that happens in Alpha might fail to happen in another world. Equally, not everything that's possible is true. Some things happen in some possible worlds, but not in Alpha.

In spite of the popularity and apparent usefulness of this view concerning necessity, possibility, impossibility, and truth, it does not rest comfortably with the notion that there is an omnibenevolent God. Let us attempt to see why.

First let's focus on some state of affairs that is not actual, but which seems to be possible. To locate such a state of affairs, you may repeat the experiment I described in the last section. Put your hand a few inches in front of your face, and stick your index finger up into the air. Now count to three, and at the count of three move your finger either to your right, or to your left, but not both. If you in fact moved your finger to the right, then I think you will agree that you could have moved it to the left. Similarly, if you moved it to the left, I think you will agree that you could have moved it to the right. Thus, whichever way you in fact moved your finger, it was possible for you to have moved it in the other way. This experiment thus seems to show that certain nonactual states of affairs are possible. More specifically, it seems to show that the state of affairs of *your moving your finger the other way* is possible but nonactual. I think you can easily identify an enormous number of other states of affairs relevantly like this one. These are things that in fact do not happen, but which could have happened. In other words, these are things that happen in other possible worlds, but not in Alpha.

The example just cited involves a human action—presumably the result of a free human choice, or decision. But the realm of possibility extends beyond the realm of human freedom. Consider any ordinary matter of fact, such as that it takes the earth about 365 days to go around the sun. Surely, the solar system could have been arranged in such a way that it would take 366 days for the earth to go around the sun. For example, the rotation of the earth around its axis could have been just a bit faster, so that it would complete 366 complete rotations before returning to its starting place in orbit. Equally, the earth's orbit could have been just a bit further out from the sun, so that, while rotating at the same speed, it would take longer to complete one revolution. Thus, a year would be 366 days long.

In light of considerations such as these, it seems reasonable to suppose that very many empirical facts are merely contingent. Each of them could have been otherwise. Things could have been different from what they are. In other words, worlds other than Alpha are possible. Each other possible world is such that it would have existed. If God had so chosen, some other world would have been actual. If some other world had been actual, things would have been different from what they in fact are.

Now let's ask ourselves whether God really could have created any of these other possible worlds. Could God have made one of them actual instead of Alpha? The answer, amazingly enough, seems to be that he could not have done so. The argument is simple. Since Alpha is the best of all the possible worlds, each other world is less good than Alpha. If God had created any other world, he would be guilty of either (*a*) preferring to create an imperfect world, or (*b*) being ignorant of the fact that he was creating an imperfect world, or (*c*) being incapable of creating the best possible world. But since God is essentially omnibenevolent, he cannot prefer to create an imperfect world. Since he is essentially omniscient, he cannot be ignorant of the fact that Alpha is the best world. Since he is essentially omnipotent, he cannot be incapable of creating Alpha. Thus, God could not have created any other possible world.

We can see, then, that when it comes to a choice of worlds, God has no freedom. Since omniscience, omnipotence, omnibenevolence, and creativity are parts of his essential nature, he cannot alter these features of his personality. And given that he has these features, he must create the best of all possible worlds. Since Alpha is the best of all possible worlds, God simply must create Alpha, and he cannot create any other world. God's essential omnibenevolence seems to rob him of freedom.

In light of this, we can see that no other world could have existed. God could not have created any world other than Alpha. No world can exist without being created by God. Thus, none of these worlds is truly *possible*. The only world that's genuinely possible is this world, Alpha.

The consequences of these considerations are truly bizarre. If Alpha is the only possible world, then what happens here is necessary, and what fails to happen here is impossible. So if you moved your finger to the right when you performed the experiment mentioned a few paragraphs back, then it was metaphysically necessary for you to move it to the right then, and metaphysically impossible for you to move it in any other way. Clearly, then, every action of yours is metaphysically necessary. Everything you fail to do is something that was metaphysically impossible for you to do. Thus, you are as unfree in your actions as God is in his. None of us ever could have done anything other than what we in fact did.

Furthermore, if Alpha is the only possible world, we can prove a number of shocking general principles: what's true is necessary, because what happens in Alpha happens in every possible world. Going even beyond this, what's *possible* is necessary, since what happens in any possible world happens in all of them. What's false is impossible, since what fails to happen here fails to happen anywhere. Clearly, then, our concepts of metaphysical necessity, possibility, and impossibility would be in a shambles if it could be shown that Alpha is the only possible world.

Let us attempt to display the reasoning here in a somewhat more systematic form:

The Paradox of God and Possibility

1 If God exists, then he is essentially omniscient, omnipotent, omnibenevolent, and creative.

2 If God is essentially omniscient, omnipotent, omnibenevolent, and creative, then he cannot create any world other than Alpha.

3 If God cannot create any world other than Alpha, then Alpha is the only possible world.

4 If Alpha is the only possible world, then everything that fails to happen is metaphysically impossible.

5 But some things that fail to happen are metaphysically possible.

6 Therefore, God does not exist.

Let us briefly review the premises here. Line (1) follows straightforwardly from our concept of God. God is, by nature and essentially, omniscient, omnipotent, omnibenevolent, and creative. Thus, if God exists, he simply must have these perfections. They enter into the very definition of "God." Line (2) can be defended easily: since Alpha is the best of all possible worlds, each other world is somehow imperfect. For each other world, God must know it to be imperfect (because he's omniscient), must prefer Alpha to it (because he's omnibenevolent), and must be able to create Alpha instead of it (because he's omnipotent). Hence, he cannot create the other world. Line (3) also seems to be true. Since Alpha must be created, and there cannot be two worlds, no other world can be created. If no other world can be created, no other world can exist. Thus, Alpha is the only possible world.

According to the standard definition of metaphysical impossibility, what's impossible in this sense is what happens in no possible world. If Alpha is the only possible world, then what doesn't happen here, doesn't happen anywhere. Thus, what doesn't happen here is metaphysically impossible. This establishes line (4).

Line (5) is based upon ordinary experience, as well as upon experiments such as the one involving the movement of your finger. Surely you could have moved your finger in some direction other than the one in which you in fact moved it. Thus, your moving it in some other direction is a thing that failed to happen here, but which is nevertheless possible. It is something that didn't happen, but which could have happened. It would be absurd to suppose that there are no such things. Thus, line (5) seems to be true. Only the most extreme of fatalists could accept the notion that what in fact happens is absolutely necessary, and what fails to happen is absolutely impossible.

The argument thus seems to show that there is a conflict between the notion that there is an essentially omnibenevolent God and the notion that things could have been different from the way they are. What replies are available to the theist?

One theistic reply involves the rejection of line (2). According to this approach, God was free to create any of the infinite number of different possible worlds. The choice of Alpha was not imposed upon him. Prior to his decision to choose Alpha, no world was any better than any other. He chose Alpha, and so Alpha is best. However, if he had chosen some other world, that other world would have been best. It is not the case that God chose Alpha because it was the best. Rather, Alpha is best because God chose it. On this view, then, God's preferences *determine* the values of the worlds, rather than vice versa. This view about God's freedom is sometimes called "theistic voluntarism."

This approach has been subjected to criticism. Leibniz pointed out that theistic voluntarism conflicts with the principle of sufficient reason. If Alpha was neither better nor worse than each of an infinite supply of other possible worlds, then why did God choose Alpha? Did he simply flip a coin? Did he pick it at random? If so, then, when he chose Alpha, he did not have any good reason for doing so. This seems to conflict with the Leibnizian principle that "nothing happens without some sufficient reason for its being so rather than otherwise."

Leibniz also claimed that theistic voluntarism "destroys all the love of God and all his glory."[10] Leibniz went on to suggest that we would have no reason to revere and respect God unless his choice of worlds was somehow founded upon their objective values. What sort of moral authority can we attribute to God if we suppose that he selected this world simply at random? Were it not for a happy accident, he could just as easily have created a world crammed full of utterly meaningless pain and suffering and ugliness. What possible sense can be made of the notion that, if he had created such a world, it would have been the best of all possible worlds?

A second reply to the paradox would be based upon an extreme form of fatalism. According to this view, everything that happens is metaphysically necessary. Not only human actions, but seeming contingent facts, such as the fact that a year is 365 days long, are taken to be as necessary as the fact that $2+2=4$. Anything that does not happen is utterly impossible. If this is correct, then line (5) of the argument is

---

[10]*Leibniz: Basic Writings*, translated by George R. Montgomery, La Salle, Illinois: Open Court Publishing Company, 1962, p. 5. The passage occurs in the second article of the *Discourse on Metaphysics*, unfortunately not included in Parkinson.

false. We have already considered some of the difficulties involved in ordinary fatalism. This extreme form of fatalism has all those difficulties. Furthermore, it conflicts with some well-founded intuitions about the logic of possibility. Does it seem credible that whatever is possible is necessary? Personally, I find it incredible, and so I reject this extreme fatalism.

Other replies to the paradox of God and possibility can be constructed, but I shall not discuss them here. To do so would carry us too far into territory not discussed by Descartes in the *Meditations*. My main purpose here has been to give a brief account of some of the most serious and puzzling arguments that have been raised against the existence of God, and to outline some of the most plausible lines of rebuttal open to theists. Any person who wants to expose his or her faith to the test of reason will eventually have to grapple in earnest with these and other atheological arguments.

The time has now come for us to leave philosophical theology altogether, and turn to the third main topic of the *Meditations*. That topic is philosophical anthropology—the philosophical study of the nature of persons.

PART THREE

PHILOSOPHICAL ANTHROPOLOGY

As we have seen, the Cartesian project begins in epistemology. In Part One of this book, we followed Descartes' lead, and reviewed his skeptical arguments and his discovery of the first certainty in the Cogito. The second main stage of the Cartesian project is in philosophical theology. As we saw, Descartes felt that he could not significantly extend the realm of certainty unless he could be sure that God exists and is no deceiver. We studied the arguments on these questions in Part Two. Once he was confident that he had proved that God does exist, and is no deceiver, Descartes turned to the third major topic of his *Meditations*. This, of course, is philosophical anthropology.

The fundamental question of philosophical anthropology may be put in this way: what is the nature of persons? Since it is very easy to confuse this question with another question, I want to spend a little time explaining what's meant by "nature" here.

Sometimes, when philosophers inquire into "human nature," or (as they used to put it) "the nature of man," they are really asking a question in psychology. They want to understand the most fundamental human drives or motives. They want to know what "makes us tick" psychologically. An answer to this question might be framed in terms of "economic determinism," or perhaps by appeal to the concepts of ego, id, and superego. Someone interested in this question might want to know, for example, whether all human motivation is essentially selfish, or whether there might be some truly altruistic drive. However interesting and important such speculations may be, this is not the question we must consider here, and these answers are not relevant to our question.

In the present context, when we raise the question about the nature of persons, we are interested in the *metaphysical* nature of persons. More exactly, we are

159

interested in the *ontology* of persons. Is a person just a physical object, or does each person also have a non-physical part—a "mind"? If each person does have a non-physical mind, how is this mind related to the person's body? These are some of the fundamental questions of philosophical anthropology.

Part Three of this book is devoted to these issues. In Chapter 9, I give a more detailed account of the metaphysical question about persons, and I present and explain one of the most popular answers—materialism. According to materialism, each person is just his or her body. There are no minds. Materialism has been subjected to a wide variety of objections. I present and evaluate several traditional objections, and then go on to consider some of Descartes' arguments against materialism.

In Chapter 10, we investigate Descartes' own views concerning the nature of persons. According to this view, now known as "Cartesian Dualism," each person is a compound substance composed of a physical body and a nonphysical mind. Furthermore, the mind and body are alleged to enter into two-way causal interaction. I describe some alleged advantages of this conception of persons, and I present and evaluate some of the main arguments against it. I also mention some alternative conceptions of persons.

In the final chapter of the book, we return to the epistemological problem with which we started. Now that Descartes has proved (to his satisfaction, if not to ours) that there is a non-deceptive God, and Descartes has come to a conclusion about his own nature, he can attempt to discover the limits of human knowledge. What can we know about the external world? Descartes' answer is discussed and evaluated.

Finally, I conclude by considering the nature and importance of Descartes' achievement.

Let us turn, then, to the first issue we must take up in this Part—what do we mean when we ask about "the nature of persons"?

PHILOSOPHICAL ANTHROPOLOGY

PHILOSOPHICAL ANTHROPOLOGY

The fundamental question of philosophical anthropology is the question "what is the nature of persons?" When we ask, in this context, about the nature of persons, we are not asking a question about the *psychological* nature of persons. Rather, we are asking about the *metaphysical* nature of persons. More exactly, we are asking about the ontology of persons. Now, however, the question itself may be a bit obscure. In order to explain this question about the ontology of persons, I will have to digress for a moment. I will have to explain what an "ontological system" is.

Ontological Systems

Suppose you are asked to produce a list of all the main sorts of things that there are. Suppose, further, that you are asked to see to it that your list is constructed in such a way that nothing is left out. Of course, we can't ask you to produce a list in which every object in the universe is listed. Rather, we want a list in which *kinds* of objects are listed, and we want it done in such a way that, for every object in the universe, some kind that it is of is listed. Thus, if you include some very general kinds, such as " physical objects," you will be able to include vast numbers of individual items even though there are relatively few kinds on your list.

If your list is complete in the way just indicated, we will say that it is "exhaustive." Every item in the universe will be such that there is some kind on your list such that the item is of that kind. Nothing will be left out.

Furthermore, you may want to construct your list in such a way that none of the listed categories overlaps another. No object in the universe will be a member of two of the kinds. In this case, your list will be "exclusive."

161

This project is very much like one of the fundamental projects of biology. Some biologists spend their time attempting to construct classifications, or "taxonomies," of living things. They try to construct these classifications in such a way that every animal will fall into exactly one species. If the taxonomist succeeds, he will produce an exhaustive and exclusive list of species. Of course, there is more to taxonomy than this. The taxonomist also attempts to construct a suitable hierarchy of races, subspecies, species, families, genera, orders, etc. Each of these projects has its analogue in ontology. The main difference is that instead of classifying just animals, the ontologist attempts to classify *everything*.

I suspect that just about everyone would include "physical objects" in a list of ontological categories. Just about everyone believes that there are plenty of physical objects. If you do include "physical objects," then an enormous number of items will be taken care of at one fell swoop. All the stars and planets, all the mountains and seas, all the rocks and bricks and grains of sand, all the atoms and molecules and cells, and all the pieces of furniture in the world will thereby be included indirectly on our list—for each of these is a physical object.

Perhaps some people would want to stop at this point. Maybe they think that there are no more items, and so the list is already exhaustive. I'm sure that that would be a mistake. For in addition to all the physical objects that there are in the world, there are the various properties that these objects have. For example, some of these objects are wooden, and others are stone, and others are metal. So there are such properties as the property of *being made of wood* and the property of *being made of stone*, and the property of *being made of metal*. Indeed, it is reasonable to suppose that each physical object has an enormous number of properties—perhaps a limitless supply. Hence there are probably at least as many properties as there are physical objects.

Thus, it appears that our list is growing larger. Instead of having just one item on it, it now has two. It looks like this:

1 Physical objects
2 Properties

One of the things that we notice about physical objects and their properties is this—things change. A thing might have a property at one time, and then fail to have it at a later time. For example, my old truck used to have a dull rusty finish, and now it is shiny and blue. So it formerly had the property of being dull, but now it lacks that property. This rather mundane fact about physical objects and their properties is really quite important, ontologically. We can see why if we attempt to explain, in a general way, what's involved in change.

As I see it, a thing changes just in case there is some property that it has at one time, but lacks at another time. Clearly then, if changes occur, there must be *times*. We can say, rather loosely I must admit, that if there were no times, the world would be a very dull place indeed. Nothing could change. Nothing could even stay the same! If there were no times, nothing could happen at all. Fortunately, there are times. So we have to recognize the existence of another ontological category—the category of times.

As soon as we recognize that there are times, we also recognize that there are places. Indeed, times and places are alike in certain structural respects. Just as there are instants of time that "take up" no time, so there are points of space that take up no space. Just as there are stretches, or intervals of time, so there are stretches, or volumes of space. And just as there is a grand, all-encompassing stretch of time (sometimes called TIME), so there seems to be a grand, all-encompassing volume of space (sometimes called SPACE).

Now our list looks like this:

1 Physical objects
2 Properties
3 Times
4 Places

I mentioned a moment ago that my truck formerly was dull, but now is shiny. It has changed. It was painted. Some philosophers would say that this indicates that a certain event—the painting of my truck—has occurred. I am inclined to agree. I think that there are events, and that the painting of my truck is a good example. Reflection on our list will reveal, I believe, that events are not yet included. Although events generally involve physical objects in one way or another, no event is itself a physical object. Although events also involve properties, no event is itself a property. Nor are events to be identified with times or places, even though each event occurs at some time and at some place. Thus, we must add events to our list of kinds of things in the world.

I think we will recognize yet another main sort of entity if we reflect on certain facts about agreement and disagreement. My wife and I agree that I own a truck. We disagree on the question whether it would be better if I owned two trucks. So there are some things that we both believe, and there are other things that I believe, but she disbelieves. This raises an ontological question: what, exactly, are these things that we agree and disagree about? What is the ontological status of the thing that I believe when what I believe is that I own a truck? Surely, when I believe this, there is *something* that I'm believing. So what is it?

Although there is considerable disagreement on this point, I accept the idea that there are propositions, or states of affairs. As I see it, when I believe something, and my wife rejects it, the entity about which we disagree is a proposition. Propositions serve as the objects of the propositional attitudes. If you believe that something is the case, or fear that something might be the case, or hope that something will be the case, or wonder whether something is the case, or have evidence that something is the case, then that thing is a proposition. Such things as belief, hope, fear, and wonderment, when they take propositions as their "objects," are said to be propositional attitudes.

Propositions are also thought to serve as the meanings of declarative sentences. Consider the sentence, "There is a truck in the garage." As I see it, that sentence expresses the proposition that there is a truck in the garage. A person understands such a sentence only if he or she knows what proposition it expresses. Two declarative sentences mean the same only if they express the same proposition.

My truck is shiny. That's a fact. But what sort of thing is a fact? Surely no fact is a physical object, or a property, or a time or place. Perhaps some will say that facts are just events. The fact that my truck is shiny, they will say, is nothing other than the event which consists in its being shiny. My own view is different. I think that facts are true propositions. So far as I know, there is no common expression in English for false propositions. Sometimes people call these "false facts," but that seems incoherent to me. They are also sometimes referred to as "errors," but that seems wrong, too. An error occurs only if someone mistakenly believes a false proposition. Whatever we choose to call them, we should recognize that if there are propositions, half of them are true (these are the facts), and half of them are false.

In any case, our list now looks like this:

1 Physical Objects
2 Properties
3 Times
4 Places
5 Events
6 Propositions

If you think about the tires on my truck, you will recognize another sort of entity. When I first got my truck, the tires were in terrible condition. So I had to buy a new set of tires. That set of tires is still on the truck. Consider that set. Although each member of the set is a physical object, the set itself is not a physical object. It is hard to say exactly why that set of tires is not a physical object, but the explanation probably would have something to do with the fact that the set would continue to exist no matter how widely the tires were scattered. If you separated the tires by thousands of miles, that set of tires would still exist. However, if you split apart a physical object, and separate the parts by thousands of miles, it becomes doubtful whether that very physical object still exists. So it seems unlikely that the set of tires is itself a physical object.

In any case, it is clear that at least some sets are not physical objects. For there are plenty of sets that do not have any physical objects as members. There's no inclination to suppose that any such set is a physical object. Consider, for example, the set of properties that you have. That set has, as members, only properties. None of them is a physical object. Other sets have events as members—consider the set of the five most exciting events you ever participated in. Other sets are "mixed bags," such as the set consisting of my truck, its color, the date on which I bought it, and the event which was my purchasing of it. That set contains a physical object, a property, a time and an event.

So we can add one more category to our list:

7 Sets

If this list were adequate, it would be both exhaustive and exclusive. Everything that exists would fit into some category or other, and nothing would fit into more than one category. In this case, we could say that our list provides the basis for an "ontological system." To complete the ontological system, we'd have to say more about each category. For each category, we'd have to explain what general feature is present in all and only the things belonging in that category. For example, we'd have to say what it is that makes something be a physical object. What is it about my truck, for instance, that makes it a physical object rather than an event? Needless to say, such questions as these can be pretty abstract and pretty deep.

Now we may be able to return to our question about the nature of persons. I said that the question is best understood as a question about the ontology of persons. How do people fit into our ontological system? Are they somehow already included in the categories mentioned above? If so, do all people go into the same category, or are some in one category, and others in other categories? If people do not go into the categories already mentioned, then what categories must we add in order to include them? Such questions as these, as I see it, must be answered if we are to answer the question, "what is the nature of persons?"

MATERIALISM

One of the simplest and most popular views concerning the nature of persons is generally known as "materialism" (or "physicalism"). It is the view that people are physical objects. More exactly, it is the view that each person is his or her body.

In order to understand materialism properly, we have to consider not only what materialists affirm, but also what they deny. Most importantly, they deny that people have minds, or souls, or spirits. This does not mean that materialists have to claim that people are unconscious, or that they have no psychological properties. Materialists maintain that each person is a purely physical object. Every part of a person is a physical part. It is not the case that, in addition to the physical parts, there is also a nonphysical, mental part that does the thinking. If a person's brain is in proper working order, then the person will be able to think, even though he or she has no mind.

In order to state the main thesis of materialism clearly, we have to introduce a few technical terms. The first of these is "mind." When, in the present context, we speak of a mind, we mean to be speaking of a nonphysical substance capable of thought. Minds, if there are any, are not physical objects. They are not made of atoms or molecules. They have no mass. They are not "extended"—that is, they take up no space. Materialists maintain that there are no minds.

A second technical term is "mental property." Any property that entails consciousness is a mental property. So, for example, consider the property of *feeling happy*. If you have this property, then you must be conscious. Hence, the property of *feeling happy* is a mental property. Some other mental properties would be: the property of *believing that it will rain*; the property of *hoping that it will be clear*; the property of *intending to get your umbrella*; the property of *fearing that the picnic will be ruined*. Perceptual properties are also mental. For example, the property of *seeming to see lightning* and the property of *seeming to hear thunder* are mental. If you have either of them, then you must be conscious.

So here is our official definition of "mental property":

D1 F is a mental property = df. Necessarily, if something, x, has F at a time, t, then x is conscious at t.

We can use the term "physical property" to indicate such properties as the property of *being made of steel*, and the property of *weighing almost two tons*. These properties can be had only by physical objects. If something is made of steel, it must be a physical object. Weights, heights, densities, colors, chemical structures, etc. are all physical properties.

We can define this technical terms as follows:

> **D2** F is a physical property = df. Necessarily, if something, x, has F at some time, t, then x is a physical object at t.

In addition to mental and physical properties, there are some "neutral" properties, such as the property of *being located in North America*. Many physical objects have this property, but it is not a physical property. Nonphysical objects can have it, too. For example, a certain shadow (not a physical object) might be located in North America. Equally, if there are minds, many of them are located in North America, and none of them is a physical object. So the property of *being located in North America* is not a physical property. It should be obvious that it is not a mental property, either. My truck is located in North America, but it is not conscious.

The fundamental materialist creed in philosophical anthropology—the central point upon which materialists are agreed—is that people are their bodies. In other words, each person is taken to be strictly identical to his or her body. Since the body is a physical object, the person is seen as being a purely physical object. Every part of a person is a physical object. According to materialists, it is not the case that, in addition to all the physical parts, there is also a mental part, the mind. Materialists deny that there are immaterial minds, or spirits, or souls.

One of the attractions of materialism is its ontological simplicity. It does not require any additions to our list of ontological categories. People are viewed as being members of a category (physical objects) that we are going to need anyway. Thus, materialism permits us to maintain that every individual substance in the universe is a physical object.

Varieties of Materialism

While materialists agree on the fundamental principle that each person is identical to his or her body, and they agree that there are no minds, they nevertheless disagree on a number of important questions. Some of these questions have to do with the status of mental properties. We can arrange several varieties of materialism in a sort of hierarchy, depending upon the relative amount of independence they ascribe to mental properties.

A materialist might maintain that people have mental as well as physical properties. This, of course, is taken by the materialist to imply that *bodies* have mental properties. If your body (especially your brain) is in good working order, it will be able to think. It will have such properties as the property of *seeming to see blue* and *seeming to feel cold as if it were in the toes*. Furthermore, a materialist might maintain that at least some of the mental properties that a given body has are utterly independent of the physical properties that it has. No amount of information concerning the physical properties of the body would enable us to predict or explain its mental properties. Thus, a person's mental life would be, at least in part, causally independent of his or her physical life. We can call this view "anomalism," or "anomalous materialism," because it implies that at least some of the mental properties of a body are not related in any lawlike way to its physical properties. ("Nomos" is Greek for "law.")

A more popular form of materialism would assign less independence to the mental properties. According to this view, a person's mental properties are fully determined by his or her physical properties. Thus, a person's mental life is causally dependent upon his or her physical life. If we knew enough about the physical properties of a person's brain and nervous system, and we knew all the relevant psychophysical laws, we could predict and explain the mental properties of that person on the basis of his or her physical properties.

An example may make this point clearer. Suppose we focus on some interesting mental property—the property of *seeming to feel a tingling sensation in the fingertips* may be a good example. A person may have this property, and may be annoyed by it. Suppose he or she wants to get rid of it. Neurophysiologists may then search for the physical basis of this mental property. That is, they may try to discover the physical properties of the brain and nervous system that are causing this tingling sensation. They may assume that there simply must be some physical property associated with this mental property, and they may assume that the physical property, whatever it may turn out to be, is the cause of the mental property. The neurophysiologist's project is to discover that physical property. If the physical property can be found, it may be possible to remove it, either by administering drugs, or by performing surgery, or by some other means. Once the physical property has been removed, the mental property will no longer have its basis, and will go away.

We can call this position "moderate materialism." Materialists in this tradition accept the view that it is impossible for a person to have a mental property, M, unless he or she also has some physical property, P, such that P is causally sufficient for M. If P is causally sufficient for M, then a person couldn't have P without also having M. According to moderate materialism, then, a person is just his or her body. There are no minds. A living body can have mental as well as physical properties, but the mental properties of the body are causally determined by the physical properties of that body.

This view about persons is materialistic in two ways. In the first place, it is materialistic because it implies that each person is a purely physical object. So it is materialistic concerning the ontology of persons. In this respect, it is like anomalous materialism. Furthermore, however, this view maintains that a person's mental properties are causally dependent upon his or her physical properties. Thus, the physical (or material) properties of a person are causally sufficient for his or her mental properties. We have here a sort of "causal primacy of the material," and this suggests a second way in which moderate materialism is materialistic.

A somewhat more extreme form of materialism has been the subject of considerable interest in recent years. Philosophers in this camp do not maintain merely that a person's mental properties are *caused by* his or her physical properties. Rather, they maintain that each mental property is *identical to* some physical property. That is, for each mental property, M, there is some physical property, P, such that M is identical to P. If this is right, then the mental properties are just a certain subset of the physical properties. This view can be called "the psychophysical property identity theory," or "the identity theory."

If we accept the identity theory, we will give a slightly different account of the example concerning the tingling sensation. Instead of saying that the neurophysiologist is looking for the physical property that causes the mental property of *seeming to feel a tingling sensation in the fingertips*, we will say that the neurophysiologist is looking for the physical property that *is* the property of *seeming to feel a tingling sensation in the fingertips*. On this view, every mental property is identical to some physical property. Thus, the mental properties, while real enough, are just physical properties of a special sort.

This view is even more materialistic than the preceding one, for on this view people are taken to be material objects, and their mental properties are taken to be a subset of their material, or physical properties. Thus, while the identity theorist acknowledges that there are some mental properties, he or she does not admit that they form an independent ontological category. They are included in the category of physical properties.

An even more extreme form of materialism should perhaps be mentioned. This one, generally known as "eliminative materialism," is the view that nothing has any mental properties. According to this approach, a person is a purely physical object, and none of his or her properties is a mental property. Some eliminative materialists go so far as to say that there are no mental properties. If this is right, then, of course, it would follow that nothing has any mental properties.

Eliminative materialism, like other forms of materialism, denies "substance dualism." That is, eliminative materialists maintain that all substances are of the same fundamental sort—they are all physical objects. There are no minds. But eliminative materialism denies "property dualism," too. Unlike other materialists, eliminative materialists maintain that nothing has any mental properties, perhaps because the category of mental properties is taken to be empty. The doctrine of the primacy of the material has here reached a rather extreme form.

There are many other forms of materialism. Some of these are subvarieties of versions mentioned here. Others would not fit very neatly into any of my categories. Nevertheless, it seems to me that most of the well-known materialistic positions can somehow be fitted into the scheme I have sketched.

For present purposes, it may be best to focus on a sort of generalized materialism. Let's take materialism to consist of three main tenets:

(a) Each person is identical to his or her body, so each person is a physical object;
(b) There are no minds; and
(c) Living human bodies can have mental as well as physical properties.

Let's not include any doctrine concerning the relation between mental and physical properties. In this way, our generalized materialism will be neutral as between anomalism, moderate materialism, and the identity theory. (Of course, it will not be consistent with eliminative materialism.) Hereafter, when I speak of materialism, I mean to be speaking of this generalized version of the materialist view.

PROBLEMS FOR MATERIALISM

Some people object to materialism because they find it to be somehow degrading. It seems to them to make people less "noble," less "sublime." Such critics apparently believe that, if people had no minds, they would just be complex living machines—hardly worthy of love and respect. As I see it, such attitudes are quite irrational. If people perform grand and noble acts, then they are worthy of love and respect, whether they have minds or not. To my way of thinking, our conclusions about the ontology of persons should in no way affect our sense of the grandeur or nobility of persons. The crucial question here, then, is whether materialism can be shown to be *false*—not whether it is an *offensive* doctrine. So let us turn to some attempted refutations.

The Argument from Ordinary Language

One of the most persistent objections to materialism is based on the fact that materialism seems to be incompatible with some well-entrenched ordinary ways of thinking and speaking about people. Some apparently uncontroversial everyday statements seem to entail the existence of minds. Of course, if there are minds, then materialism cannot be true. Let us consider this objection.

Here are some sentences:

A She had a strong mind, but a weak body.
B He changed his mind.
C Her body was motionless, but her mind was racing.
D He has a warped mind.

Notice that the word "mind" occurs in each of these sentences. Furthermore, in each case, the word "mind" occurs in such a way as to make it appear that the sentence could not be true unless there were minds. Consider sentence (A), for example. How can she have a strong mind if there are no minds? Surely, if she has a strong one, there must be some minds. Similarly, it would seem that he must have a mind if he is to change it. Thus, (B) seems to entail that there are minds. So, in each case it appears that if the sentence is to be true, there must be some minds.

Of course, if there are minds, then materialism is false; for materialism, as we have formulated it, entails that there are no minds. That is one of its central tenets. So that doctrine cannot be true if there are minds. Therefore, ordinary ways of speaking and thinking about people seem to show that materialism is not true.

This argument, which we can call "The Ordinary-Language Argument," can be formulated as follows:

1 Sentences such as (A), (B), (C) and (D) are often true.
2 If sentences such as (A), (B), (C) and (D) are often true, then there are minds.
3 If there are minds, then materialism is false.
4 Therefore, materialism is false.

The first premise of this argument seems to me to be beyond reproach. No materialist could plausibly maintain that sentences such as the ones illustrated are never true. Furthermore, it seems equally obvious that there's no getting around (3).

As we have formulated the materialist doctrine, it does entail that there are no minds. So if there are some, it is false. Finally, the argument is valid.

In spite of these strengths, the argument is not very persuasive. No sensible materialist would be moved by it. The weak premise here is (2). From the fact that the illustrated sentences are true, the materialist can maintain, it does not follow that there are minds. Take sentence (A), for example. The materialist can insist that when we say that she has a strong mind, we don't mean to imply that she literally has a mind. All we mean to say is that she is very intelligent. So we can rewrite the sentence in this way:

A′ She was very intelligent, but was physically weak.

(A′) has the same meaning as (A), but (A′) expresses that meaning more literally, while (A) expresses it in a misleading, idiomatic form. Notice that the expression "strong mind" does not appear in (A′). So a materialist can claim that (A) is "ontologically misleading." It suggests that there are minds. But the fact that (A′) means the same as (A), and contains no reference to minds, shows that what's really expressed by the sentence can be true even though there are no minds.

It is important to understand this reply properly. I'm not saying that materialists have to reject sentences such as (A), (B), (C), and (D). They can say that such sentences are perfectly acceptable and often true. But they must insist that these sentences are ontologically misleading. In virtue of containing some idiomatic expressions, they suggest that there are minds. When rewritten, so as to express their meanings more literally, these sentences become more "perspicuous"—that is, their ontological implications become clearer. Let us attempt to rewrite each of these sentences in such a way as to get rid of the controversial word "mind." I would propose the following:

(A′) She was very intelligent, but was physically weak.
(B′) He formerly believe something which he subsequently rejected.
(C′) She was thinking fast but her body was motionless.
(D′) He has bizarre opinions.

If each of these paraphrases is a more literal expression of what's expressed more idiomatically by the original sentence to which it corresponds, then we can see that what that original sentence expresses might be true, even if there are no minds. In that case, we can safely reject line (2) of the ordinary-language argument. To make that argument work, we'd need to find some incontrovertably true sentence of ordinary language which (a) seems to entail the existence of minds, and (b) cannot be replaced by a more literal equivalent that has no such implication. It's not clear to me that there is any such sentence. So it seems that, if we are to find a good objection to materialism, we'll have to look elsewhere. Ordinary language won't do the trick.

The Argument from Psychic Phenomena

Some philosophers seem to think that there is a certain sort of scientific evidence that establishes the existence of minds. If they are right, then materialism isn't true. The evidence comes from a field of study nowadays called "parapsychology," and it has to do with a variety of rather strange and puzzling phenomena. One such phenomenon is alleged to occur in some cases in which a person is teetering on the edge of death. In one case, a woman was hospitalized with inoperable bleeding ulcers. One day, while in the intensive care unit, she suddenly began to feel as if she were rising up out of her body. It seemed to her that she could look down and see her hospital bed, with her body in it. She could see all the medical equipment in the room in exquisite detail. She also began to feel happy and secure. She felt no pain. It seemed to her that she was being ushered into some magnificently peaceful place. However, because of her love for her husband and children, she chose to return to her body and to continue to live. She then felt herself re-entering her body. The woman eventually recovered from her illness. This experience apparently had an enormous impact on the woman, and changed her attitude toward life and death.[1]

Cases such as the one just described are called "near death experiences," or "NDEs." There is evidence that suggests that such experiences are pretty common. Millions of people have reported them, and the reports are quite consistent.

One of the components of the phenomenon just described sometimes occurs by itself. That part is the "out of body experience." There are apparently a variety of circumstances in which a person can seem to himself to be observing the world from some perspective other than that of his body. A person who takes certain types of drugs may seem to himself to have left his body. He may report that he has entered the body of some bird, and that he can see the earth passing by below him as the bird flies through the air. Another name for this phenomenon is "astral projection."

Another odd psychological phenomenon has been reported. Sometimes a young person will inexplicably report having memories of a past life in some distant land. For example, a youngster born in the United States might claim to have clear memories of a small town in Italy. She might be able to draw a map of the town, and she might be able to give detailed and accurate descriptions of the people and objects that were there three hundred years earlier. Furthermore, it might be the case that no one can provide a straightforward explanation for her apparent memories. No one recalls telling her stories about the town, and there are no books or pictures available to the youngster from which she might have learned about it. The phenomenon is alleged to be explainable in only one way—reincarnation. It is maintained that the soul currently in the body of the little girl formerly was in the body of some other person who actually lived in Italy. That other person observed the town and its inhabitants. When that other person died, these memories were not "erased" from her soul. Now the soul is in the body of the American youngster, and she has memories from her "former life."

Psychic phenomena such as astral projection and reincarnation seem to require souls. How can a person's soul go up out of his body, and observe the world from some unusual perspective unless he actually has a soul? How can a soul that formerly inhabited the body of someone in Italy hundreds of years ago now inhabit the body of someone in America unless there actually is a soul in each of these bodies? Thus, the evidence in favor of the psychic phenomena seems to support the

---

[1]This case is described in some detail in "Brush With Death Changes Life," by Judy Foreman, *The Boston Globe*, May 2, 1983.

conclusion that there are souls. If there are souls, then materialism is false. So there is scientific evidence that apparently shows that materialism is false.

The argument, then, is this:

The Argument from Psychic Phenomena

1 Psychic phenomena occur.
2 If psychic phenomena occur, then there are minds.
3 If there are minds, then materialism is false.
4 Therefore, materialism is false.

Although this is a fairly popular argument against materialism, I do not think that materialists need to be very concerned about it. It really doesn't refute their view. To see why, we need to understand a distinction between two different ways in which we can look at the psychic phenomena. On the one hand, we can view them as purely psychological experiences. Taken in this way, astral projection is nothing more than a certain way of feeling. A person is undergoing astral projection in this first way if he feels as if he is rising up out of his body, and viewing the world from some extrabodily perspective. When understood in this way, astral projection does not necessarily involve souls at all. It might be the case that the psychological experience of astral projection is always misleading. Surely it is conceivable that people might feel as if they were observing the world from some point outside of their bodies, even though they were not really doing so. Let's use the term "weak astral projection" to refer to this purely psychological experience.

In a similar way, we can use the term "weak reincarnation" to refer to the purely psychological component in reincarnation. So a person will be said to undergo weak reincarnation if she seems to recall a former life in another body. Clearly enough, weak reincarnation might occur even if there are no souls. It would be something like a delusion, or a hallucination. It would be a sort of false memory experience.

Some people think that when a person feels as if he is observing the world from an extrabodily perspective, he feels that way because he in fact is observing the world from such a perspective. That is, some people think that astral projection is more than a purely psychological experience. It is also "substantial." In order for it to occur, the person's soul, or mind, must actually leave the body, and have perceptual experiences elsewhere. Let us say that such a phenomenon, if it occurs, would be a case of "strong astral projection." Another strong psychic phenomenon would be strong reincarnation. This would occur only if some soul in fact did inhabit one body at one period of history, and then later came to inhabit another body.

I think it should be clear how this distinction between strong and weak psychic phenomena will help us to deal with the argument. Now we can maintain that the argument suffers from the fallacy of equivocation. The term "psychic phenomena," which appears twice in the argument, is ambiguous. If we understand it as meaning "strong psychic phenomena" in both occurrences, then the argument as a whole looks like this:

1 Strong psychic phenomena occur.
2 If strong psychic phenomena occur, then there are minds.
3 If there are minds, then materialism is false.
4 Therefore, materialism is false.

If interpreted in this way, line (2) is quite correct, but there's no conclusive evidence to support line (1). We know that weak psychic phenomena occur, but there is very little direct evidence to support the view that strong psychic phenomena occur. Perhaps the feelings of astral projection are nothing more than confused and misleading experiences that occur when the brain is subjected to certain unusual stresses—such as those it suffers when under anaesthesia, or while under the influence of psychoactive drugs. So the materialist can reject line (1), if understood in the strong way.

On the other hand, if we take "psychic phenomena" to mean "weak psychic phenomena," then the argument looks like this:

1 Weak psychic phenomena occur.
2 If weak psychic phenomena occur, then there are minds.
3 If there are minds, then materialism is false.
4 Therefore, materialism is false.

When formulated in this way, line (1) seems to be true, but line (2) becomes doubtful. The materialist can reject it. The fact that people have these unusual experiences does not entail that they have minds. As we have seen, these experiences may be explained by appeal to a variety of physiological factors. There is no need to appeal to minds here.

Furthermore, I think it is important to see that the assumption that there are minds really doesn't go very far toward explaining these psychic phenomena anyway. Since the mind has neither eyes nor ears, how could it have perceptual experiences outside of the body? Since the mind, when separated from the body, has no brain, how does it store its memories? Thus, it appears that there is no good reason to suppose that the existence of minds would help in any significant way to explain weak psychic phenomena. It is far more likely that such experiences are explainable strictly on the basis of neurological factors.

Finally, if we make use of the weak interpretation in line (1) and the strong interpretation in line (2), then both lines will be true, but the argument will no longer be valid. Hence, in no case have we got a refutation of materialism. As interesting and queer as the psychic phenomena may be, they seem to have no conclusive bearing on the question whether there are minds. Hence, they cut no ice with respect to materialism.

The Argument from Death

Another rather common phenomenon is alleged to cut considerable ice with respect to materialism. That phenomenon is death. Certain metaphysical features of death strongly suggest that people cannot be their bodies. If people are not their bodies, then, of course, materialism is false. We now turn to a consideration of this topic.

When a person dies, we say that he is "gone," "no longer with us," "departed." We say that such a person has "passed away." This strongly suggests that when a person dies, he ceases to exist. The same suggestion is present in the procedures we employ when taking a census. If we are asked to count the people in some community, we count only living people, not corpses in the graveyards. This suggests that those corpses are not people. The people who formerly inhabited those bodies are evidently gone. They do not exist any longer. They are "dead and gone."

Another relevant fact here is that we speak of the body of a deceased person as his "remains." The body, then, seems to be what remains after the person has gone away, or has gone out of existence. Of course, in some cases, the body goes out of existence at the moment of death, too. For example, if a person is at ground zero when a large nuclear device goes off, his body will cease to exist just when he ceases to exist. However, in typical cases, the body continues to exist for quite a while after the person stops existing. Some mummies, for example, last for thousands of years.

Let's consider the case of Abraham Lincoln. He died in April 1865. Subsequently, his body was put on a train which traveled around the country. People came down to the railroad stations to view the corpse. President Lincoln was gone, but his body was there for all to see. So there seems to be an important difference between the person, Abraham Lincoln, and his body. His body existed in May of 1865, but he didn't.

Let us say that something, x, is "discernible from" something, y, if there is some property that x has and y lacks. That is, things are discernible if there is some difference in quality or attribute between them. The difference does not have to be obvious, or even noticeable. It just has to be there. If so, the things are discernible, in this special sense. And let us say that something, x, is "diverse from" something, y, if x and y are not the same thing. So if x and y are two different things, then x is diverse from y. A fundamental principle of metaphysics states that if things are discernible, then they are diverse. In other words, if there is some property that x has and y lacks, then x is diverse from y. This principle is sometimes called "the Principle of the Diversity of Discernibles." I think it is true. If x is the very same object as y, how can x be different from y? Surely, nothing can differ from itself.

Since Lincoln's body had the property of *existing in May, 1865*, and Lincoln himself did not have that property, they were two different things. This is a fairly straightforward application of the principle of the diversity of discernibles. Thus, no matter how intimately connected Lincoln and his body were during the period of Lincoln's life, he and his body could not have been the same thing. After all, they apparently had different histories. One lasted longer than the other.

If what we have said about Lincoln and his body is correct, then materialism is false. For materialism entails that each person is identical to his or her body. If Lincoln was diverse from his body, then the materialist conception of persons is wrong. This one counterexample would be sufficient to refute the general theory. Of course, if Lincoln was diverse from his body, then undoubtedly everyone else is diverse from his or her body, too. Lincoln was special in many ways, but he was not ontologically special. If he was diverse from his body, then I am diverse from mine, and you are diverse from yours. For all its simplicity, materialism would then be wrong.

Let us consider the argument.

The Argument from Death

1 Abraham Lincoln ceased to exist at the moment of his death.
2 Lincoln's body did not cease to exist at the moment of his death.
3 If (1) and (2) are true, then Lincoln was diverse from his body.
4 If Lincoln was diverse from his body, then materialism is false.
5 Therefore, materialism is false.

The materialists' reply to this argument should be obvious. They will insist that line (1) is false. They will say that Lincoln did not cease to exist on the day of his assassination. In their view, he just ceased to *live* on that day. According to the materialists' conception of persons, the very same thing may be a living person on one day, and a dead corpse on the next.

Of course, if a materialist does want to reject line (1) of the argument, he will have to say something about the evidence that supports it. Why don't we count corpses when we take a census? Why do we speak of a corpse as the "remains" of a former person? Why do we say that a dead person is "no longer with us"?

I think that a clear-headed materialist will have no trouble answering these questions. A census, he will say, is a count of the number of persons living in some community. Since dead people don't *live* there, it would be wrong to count them. However, the materialist could say, those dead people are there. They still exist— at least until they "return to the dust"—and so we could count them if we wanted. The linguistic data are no more troubling. Much of our ordinary language concerning death does indeed suggest a dualistic conception of persons. Perhaps this is a result of the fact that our language developed in cultures dominated by religions that endorsed dualism. The fact that our common idioms suggest dualism, of course, does not constitute evidence that dualism is true. It only shows that, at some time in the past, our ancestors may have believed in dualism. Maybe they were wrong.

Some people find this view outrageous. "How can you say that some cold, dead, rotting carcass is a person? A person must be able to think, and to reason. Such things are not persons. They are just corpses!" Such questions as these seem to be based on a misunderstanding of the materialist view. The materialist does not have to maintain that a rotting corpse is still a person. The materialist can say that the rotting corpse is the very same thing as something that formerly was a person. This thing was a person in the past. Then it could think and reason. When it died, it lost the ability to think, and perhaps it even ceased to be a person. However, it continued to exist. So the corpse (which is now not a person) formerly was a person. When it was a person it could think. Now it can't think, and it isn't a person. So the materialist can agree with the view that if anything is a person at some time, then it can think and reason at that time. (Speaking strictly for myself here, I would insist that there is nothing absurd in the view that there really are dead people. These are people, but they are quite incapable of any mental operations. Why not?)

In any case, I think we have to conclude that the argument from death is inconclusive. It does not refute materialism. Although it is valid as formulated here, it contains a controversial premise that materialists can easily reject.

CARTESIAN OBJECTIONS TO MATERIALISM

Descartes rejected materialism. He maintained that no person is just his or her body. On Descartes' view, there's more to a person than that. There is also a mind. Since Descartes had some interesting things to say concerning materialism, let us consider his objections.

The Argument from Doubt

In the *Second Meditation*, right after the Cogito, Descartes raises the question about the nature of persons. Of course, since he is certain of the existence of just one person (himself), he puts the question in a somewhat peculiar way. He says, "I know that I exist; I ask now who is this 'I' whom I know."[2] In this passage, he makes some remarks that some have taken to contain an argument against materialism. He says:

> Now, I am a true thing, and truly existing; but what kind of thing? I have said it already: a thing that thinks.
>
> What then? I will set my imagination going to see if I am not something more. I am not that connection of members which is called the human body. Neither am I some subtle air infused into these members, not a wind, not a fire, not a vapor, not a breath—nothing that I imagine to myself, for I have supposed all these to be nothing. The assertion stands; the fact still remains that I am something.[3]

In this passage, Descartes denies the fundamental thesis of materialism. He says that he is not "this connection of members which is called the human body." That's just a grand way of saying that he is not his body. if he is not his body, then materialism is false—for materialism entails that each person is identical to his or her body. So what is Descartes' reason for thinking that he is not his body?

The heart of the argument seems to be this: at one and the same moment Descartes can (*a*) suppose that his body does not exist, and (*b*) remain certain that he himself exists. It's not entirely clear how this would show that he is diverse from his body. However, by making just a slight alteration to the text, we can develop a remarkably puzzling argument. Let's suppose that what Descartes really meant to claim is that at one and the same moment he can (*a*) be certain that he himself exists, and (*b*) fail to be certain that his body exists. From this it would seem to follow that he and his body differ with respect to a rather unusual property. He himself has the property of *being a thing of whose existence Descartes is certain*. However, it appears that his body does not have that property. His body is a thing of whose existence Descartes is not certain. By appeal to the principle of the diversity of discernibles, we can conclude that he is diverse from his body. Therefore, materialism must be false.

Let us formulate the essentials of this argument in a neat and tidy way. It is generally called "The Argument from Doubt" for reasons that will emerge shortly.

The Argument from Doubt

1 I am certain that I exist.
2 I am not certain that my body exists.

[2]Cress, 19.
[3]Cress, 19.

3 If (1) and (2) are true, then I am diverse from my body.
4 If I am diverse from my body, then materialism is false.
5 Therefore, materialism is false.

Now let us review the reasoning that stands behind each premise.

Premise (1) is based quite directly on the Cogito. Each of us can be certain of his or her own existence. I am certain that I exist, and you can be certain that you exist.

Premise (2) is based on the sort of skeptical considerations that Descartes introduced in the *First Meditation*. Perhaps he is only dreaming that he has a body; perhaps God has some good reason to deceive him on this topic; perhaps there is an evil demon who delights in fooling a bodiless Descartes into thinking that he has a body. Each of these is an extremely implausible hypothesis. Hence, it generates only metaphysical doubt. In any case, Descartes is not metaphysically certain of the existence of his own body. So, if we understand line (2) in this way, it seems to be true.

Line (3) is based on the principle of the diversity of discernibles. If I and my body differ with respect to the property of *being a thing of whose existence I am certain*, then I and my body must be diverse. Lines (1) and (2) seem to entail that I and my body do differ in this way. So line (3) seems to be in order. Line (4) is an immediate consequence of our formulation of materialism. Finally, the argument is valid as stated here.

In Chapter 7, under "The Cartesian Circle," I mentioned that one of Descartes' contemporaries, Antoine Arnauld, wrote a collection of objections, which was published with an early edition of the *Meditations*. Arnauld pointed out the problem of the Cartesian Circle. In his essay, Arnauld also commented on the passage currently under consideration. However, his formulation of the argument is slightly different from ours. As he saw it, the argument has to do with what one can doubt. I can doubt the existence of my body. I can't doubt my own existence. Therefore, my body is diverse from me.[4]

I think it should be clear that Arnauld's version of the argument is formally just like ours. Furthermore, it should be clear that it is a good argument if and only if our version is good. In any case, I suspect that we nowadays refer to this argument as "The Argument from Doubt" largely because Arnauld thought it should be formulated in terms of what we can doubt, rather than in terms of what we can be certain about. Be this as it may, the time has come to evaluate the argument.

A Problem for the Argument from Doubt

Nowadays, almost everyone who has given it careful thought agrees that the argument from doubt is unsuccessful. People disagree about the source of the trouble. I think that reflection on another argument will make it clear that something is wrong with the argument from doubt. This other argument is supposed to have the same form as the argument from doubt, and its premises are supposed to be just as plausible. But we know that its conclusion is false.

[4]HR II, 80.

According to the legend, Oedipus one day met a stranger on the highway. At the time, Oedipus was under the mistaken impression that his father was dead. Oedipus and the stranger got into a fight, and Oedipus killed the stranger. As it happened, the stranger really was Oedipus' father, and so when Oedipus killed the stranger, he unwittingly killed his own father, and thereby fulfilled an ancient prophecy. This story has given rise to many literary and psychological speculations, and Oedipus has given his name to a complex of drives and motivations. My present interest in the case is logical, not literary or psychological. I'm interested in the story of Oedipus because it provides the basis for a neat parody of the argument from doubt. It goes as follows:

The Oedipal Argument from Doubt

1 Oedipus was certain that the stranger existed.

2 Oedipus was not certain that his father existed.

3 If Oedipus was certain that the stranger existed, but was not certain that his father existed, then the stranger was diverse from Oedipus' father.

4 Therefore, the stranger was diverse from Oedipus' father.

Inspection will reveal that the premises of this argument are relevantly like the first three premises of the argument from doubt. Furthermore, the premises of the Oedipal argument are just as plausible as the premises of the Cartesian argument (if we assume, of course, that we have reason to think that the Oedipus legend is based on fact). However, we know that the conclusion of the Oedipal argument is false. According to the myth, the stranger was Oedipus' father. Thus, there is clearly something wrong with the Oedipal argument. This strongly suggests that there is something wrong with Descartes' argument, too.

Some people might say that the problem has to do with the principle of the diversity of discernibles. Perhaps the principle is not universally applicable. Maybe something can differ from itself with respect to such properties as *being a thing of whose existence I am certain*. My own view is different. I think there is such a property as *being a thing of whose existence I am certain*, and I think that nothing can both have and fail to have that property at the same time. However, I do not think that lines (1) and (2) of the argument from doubt together entail both that I have that property, and that my body lacks it. More particularly, I am inclined to think that there is an important difference between saying:

2a I am not certain that my body exists.

and saying:

2b My body lacks the property of *being a thing of whose existence I am certain*.

It might turn out that my body is identical to something of whose existence I am certain (me, for example) but, failing to know the identity, I might fail to be certain that my body exists. Hence, (2a) could be true even if (2b) were false. And it is (2b) that's needed to make the argument go through. In light of this problem, I am inclined to think that we must understand (2) as (2a)—so as to assure its truth—but that if we do, we can easily reject line (3). Although it is valid as formulated here, it seems to me that the argument from doubt is not sound.

It is important to notice that Descartes himself rejected the argument from doubt, too. In the passage immediately following the one quoted above, he says:

> But perhaps it is the case that, nevertheless, these very things which I take to be nothing (because I am ignorant of them) in reality do not differ from that self which I know? This I do not know. I shall not quarrel about it right now; I can make a judgment only regarding things which are known to me. I know that I exist; I ask now who is this "I" whom I know.[5]

The Argument from Divisibility

In the *Synopsis*, in the paragraph concerning the *Sixth Meditation*, Descartes says, "I prove that the mind is really distinct from the body (although I show that the mind is so closely joined to the body, that it forms one thing with the body)"[6] Let's look into the *Sixth Meditation*, then, to see how Descartes tries to prove this crucial point. If he does show that "the mind is really distinct from the body," he will have gone a long way toward refuting materialism. So what's his argument?

Although there is also another passage that we'll have to consider later on, I am fairly confident that the "proof" to which Descartes alludes is contained in the following passage:

> there is a great difference between a mind and a body, because the body, by its very nature, is something divisible, whereas the mind is plainly indivisible. Obviously, when I consider the mind, that is, myself insofar as I am only a thing that thinks, I cannot distinguish any parts in me; rather, I take myself to be one complete thing. Although the whole mind seems to be united to the whole body, nevertheless, were a foot or an arm or any other bodily part amputated, I know that nothing would be taken away from the mind; nor can the faculties of willing, sensing, understanding, and so on be called its "parts," because it is one and the same mind that wills, senses, and understands. On the other hand, no corporeal or extended thing can be thought by me that I did not easily in thought divide into parts; in this way I know that it is divisible. If I did not yet know it from any other source, this consideration alone would suffice to teach me that the mind is wholly different from the body.[7]

On one interpretation, Descartes' argument here seems to be the following:

The Argument from Divisibility—Version A

1 My body is divisible.
2 I am not divisible.
3 If my body is divisible, but I am not divisible, then I am diverse from my body.
4 Therefore, I am diverse from my body.

When we say that something is "divisible," we don't mean that it is *physically possible* to divide it. All we mean is that it is conceivable that it be divided. Descartes

---

[5]Cress, 19.
[6]Cress, 10.
[7]Cress, 53–54.

seems to have thought that every extended thing is divisible, in this sense. Anything that is extended takes up some space. Pick a point in the middle. You can conceive of the stuff to the left of the point being separated from the stuff to the right. Hence the object is divisible. Even an extraordinarily hard, extraordinarily tiny diamond is divisible, in this sense. Clearly, a human body is also divisible. If you amputate a finger, or clip a fingernail, you have divided it. So line (1) seems true.

Descartes seems to defend line (2) by pointing out that when a part is removed from the body, the person remains intact. He is still a whole person, even though his body is no longer a whole body. The principle of the diversity of discernibles would yield the result, then, that the person is diverse from his body. If this conclusion were reached, we would have a refutation of materialism.

It should be pretty clear, however, that there's something terribly wrong with this version of the argument. Line (2) is utterly indefensible. Even on Descartes' own dualistic conception of persons, it would be false. Suppose Descartes is right about the nature of persons. Suppose you are a compound of body and soul. Clearly, then, one of your major components is divisible, and so you are divisible. Thus, Descartes could not have meant to affirm (2). (Needless to say, no materialist would accept the idea that people are indivisible. On their view, a person is just a human body. Since the body is divisible, so is the person.)

A closer look at the text may suggest that the problem here is a problem with my interpretation, rather than a problem with Descartes' argument. For it may appear that Descartes was not trying to show that *he* was diverse from his body. Rather, Descartes was trying to show that *his mind* was diverse from his body. If we understand the argument in this way, we'll have to make a number of alterations:

The Argument from Divisibility—Version B

1 My body is divisible.
2 My mind is indivisible.
3 If my body is divisible, but my mind is indivisible, then my body is diverse from my mind.
4 Therefore, my body is diverse from my mind.

Descartes say things that tend to support line (2) of this version of the argument. He maintains, quite correctly, that a person's psychological capacities may remain perfectly intact even if an arm has been amputated. He also seems to defend (2) by insisting that the various mental "faculties" do not reside in different parts of the mind. Each faculty is a faculty of the mind as a whole. You will, sense, and understand with one and the same mind—not with different components of the mind.

In some ways, this is a more successful argument. On the Cartesian conception, the mind is different from the body in just the way specified. The body is an extended physical substance, and the mind is an unextended, nonphysical substance. So the former is divisible, and the latter is indivisible. However, it is quite unlikely that any materialist would be troubled by this "proof," since no materialist would see any reason to accept line (2). Since it has not yet been shown that there are any minds, there is no reason to agree that minds are indivisible. As we have seen, materialists deny that there are minds. The upshot is that Descartes' "Division Argument" seems to be a failure. It seems to presuppose that there are minds—but this is a point that must be proven. So let us consider the other passage from the *Sixth Meditation* that's relevant here.

The Argument from Conception

Descartes says:

> First, because I know that all the things that I clearly and distinctly understand can be made by God exactly as I understand them, it is enough that I can clearly and distinctly understand one thing without the other in order for me to be certain that the one thing is different from the other, because at least God can establish them separately.[8]

Descartes concludes the passage (which surely must be studied carefully and in its entirety) by saying that "it is therfore certain that I am truly distinct from my body, and that I can exist without it."[9]

The fundamental premise of this argument seems to be that Descartes can clearly and distinctly conceive of himself existing apart from his body. From the fact that he can conceive of these things existing apart from each other, it allegedly follows that it is possible for them to exist apart from each other. If they can exist apart from each other, then they are two different things—even if, as things in fact stand, they are very closely connected.

We can reconstruct this argument in a variety of different ways. I want to consider one way that seems to me to be especially interesting. I have to admit that it takes certain liberties with the text. In any case, on the interpretation in question, we view Descartes as pointing out that he himself has a certain feature that his body seems to lack. That feature is the property of *being such that it is possible to conceive of it existing without Descartes' body*. If Descartes can imagine himself existing in some other body, or perhaps existing without any body at all, then he himself has this property. He is such that it is possible to conceive of him existing without Descartes' body. However, it seems obvious that Descartes' body cannot exist without Descartes' body! If Descartes' body exists at some place and time, then Descartes' body exists at that very same place and time. Nothing can exist without itself. Thus, Descartes seems to differ from his body with respect to this rather odd property. The principle of the diversity of discernibles then entails that Descartes and his body are diverse, and so materialism is refuted.

Let us look more closely at the argument.

The Argument from Conception

1 I am such that it is possible to conceive of me existing apart from my body.

2 My body is not such that it is possible to conceive of it existing apart from my body.

[8]Cress, 49.
[9]Cress, 49.

3 If (1) and (2), then I am diverse from my body.
4 If I am diverse from my body, then materialism is false.
5 Therefore, materialism is false.

This is a fairly subtle argument, and so it may be necessary to contemplate lines (1) and (2) rather carefully. Line (1) says that I am such that it is possible to conceive of me existing apart from my body. To see why this is true, I must first focus my attention upon myself. I must think of me. Then I must consider whether this thing, me, could exist without the body that it in fact has. Can I conceive of a situation in which I exist without my body? Perhaps I think of an afterlife in heaven. I imagine myself as a member of the heavenly choir. Of course, I must be careful to avoid imagining myself having some thin, watered-down version of this body. I have to image myself existing without this body. It seems to me that I can do it. Thus, line (1) seems to be true. It appears that I have the property of *being such that I can conceive of it existing without my body*.

Next I must focus my attention on my body. I must think of it. And I must ask myself whether I can conceive of it existing apart from my body. Can I image a situation in which my body exists totally apart from my body? That surely seems impossible. My body evidently lacks the property of *being such that I can conceive of it existing without my body*. Hence, line (2) is true, too.

Line (3) is based upon the principle of the diversity of discernibles, and seems to me to be beyond reproach. Thus the argument as a whole looks pretty persuasive.

So far as I can see, the materialist has two reasonably plausible lines of defense against the argument from conception. He can reject either (1) or (2). Let us consider what can be said in opposition to these premises.

The first possible reply consists in the denial of (1). The materialist can say that no one can conceive of himself existing without his body. Since I am my body, I no more can think of myself existing without my body than I can think of my body existing without my body. Actually, the materialist will insist, when I try to conceive of myself existing without my body, I only succeed in conceiving of myself with a profoundly changed body. Whereas my body now in fact weighs 165 pounds, and is fairly solid, I imagine it to weigh only a few ounces, and to be semitransparent. I think of it as being something like a ghost, or a shadowy, angelic cloud.

In order for line (1) to be true, I must be able to do better than this. It's not enough to be able to think of myself existing in some different form. Surely, it is possible for my body to exist in a different form, too. What's necessary is that I conceive of myself existing without this body. It is not entirely clear that it can be done. A materialist will say it's impossible. Descartes though he could do it. I leave it to the curious reader to decide who is right.

The second possible reply requires the rejection of (2). The materialist may want to admit that a person with a very powerful imagination might be able to conceive of himself existing without his body. But, the materialist will go on, when he does this, he is conceiving of his body existing without his body. This may seem to be a contradiction, but deeper reflection will show that it is not. Consider the current President of the United States. Surely you can conceive of him existing in a situation in which the United States has no president. Imagine, for example, that we change our form of government so that we have a queen, instead of a president. If you do conceive of the person who in fact is the president, but you conceive of him existing in a situation in which there is no president, then you are conceiving of the president existing without the president. More precisely, the president is such that you are conceiving of him existing without there being any such person as the President of the United States.

The materialist may insist that something like this is also true with respect to your body. If you have a fertile imagination, and can conceive of yourself existing without there being any such thing as your body, then you can conceive of your body existing without there being any such thing as your body. Thus, line (2) may be rejected. My body does have the property of being such that I can conceive of it existing without my body. At any rate, so a materialist might insist.

For my own part, I have to admit that I just don't know what to say about the argument from conception. Sometimes it looks pretty secure, and then again at other times I'm inclined to reject it. So I conclude that it just isn't clear that Descartes has produced a good argument against materialism. Be this as it may, we must now turn to a consideration of Descartes' own theory about the nature of persons—Cartesian dualism. That is the topic of the next chapter.

CHAPTER 10

CARTESIAN DUALISM

CARTESIAN DUALISM[1]

Dualism is often said to be the view that each person has both a mind and a body. However, if we formulate our dualism in this way, it will fail to constitute an answer to the fundamental question of philosophical anthropology. That question is the question about the nature of persons. If, in an attempt to give an answer to this question, we merely say that a person is something that has both a mind and a body, we will have given no answer at all. For this proposed answer says nothing about the nature of the person. What sort of entity is it that has both a mind and a body? Is it a mind? Is it a body? Is it something else? Surely, it's possible for just about any sort of entity to have both a mind and body, and so it's not enough merely to tell us that a person is a thing that has both a mind and body.

Descartes was a dualist. He thought that for each person there is both a mind and a body. He thought that the mind is primarily responsible for the psychological properties, and that the body is primarily responsible for the physical properties. These things are pretty clear. Unfortunately, when we try to go beyond these rather sketchy remarks, we run into disputed territory. Scholars disagree about the details of Cartesian dualism. The texts are ambiguous and sometimes conflicting. Thus, we have to be cautious here. We must recognize that if we ascribe any single, straight-forward, coherent view in philosophical anthropology to Descartes, we will be oversimplifying (at best). In any case, I think it is clear that he did have at least one interesting answer to the question, "What is a person?"

In the *Synopsis,* Descartes states some of the main conclusions of the *Sixth Meditation.* Speaking of his accomplishments there, he says:

[1] Reading Assignment: the *Sixth Meditation,* Cress, 45–56.

I prove that the mind is really distinct from the body (although I show that the mind is so closely joined to the body, that it forms one thing with the body).[2]

In the *Sixth Meditation* itself, Descartes presents this view in greater detail. In a famous but often misunderstood passage, Descartes says:

I am present to my body not merely in the way a seaman is present to his ship, but . . . I am tightly joined and, so to speak mingled together with it, so much so that I make up one single thing with it. For otherwise, when the body is wounded, I, who am nothing but a thing that thinks, would not then sense the pain. Rather, I would perceive the wound by means of the pure intellect, just as a seaman perceives by means of sight whether anything in the ship is broken.[3]

The preceding passages suggest that Descartes' view might be that a person is a mind that is mingled with a body. But on the next, Descartes says " . . . I am composed of a body and a mind."[4] This suggests that his view was that a person is a compound thing composed of a mind and a body, rather than just a mental thing that happens to be lodged in a body.

Although both views can be found in Cartesian texts, I am inclined to think that the "compound substance" view better represents Descartes' considered opinion concerning the nature of persons. At any rate, that is the view I shall call "Cartesian Dualism." Let's consider its principal tenets.

Persons

The first component of Cartesian dualism is the doctrine that each person is a "compound substance" composed of two other "substances"—a mind and a body. This means that a person is not identical to his mind, and is not identical to his body. Rather, the person is a compound thing of which the mind and body are parts. So your mind is just a part of you. Obviously, the mind is an important part. Without it, you wouldn't be a person. But equally, you wouldn't be a person without your other main part—your body.

When Descartes says that these things are "substances," he makes use of a technical term of great antiquity. It is notoriously hard to say exactly what "substance" means. Generally, when a philosopher says that some ontological category contains all the substances, he intends to convey the idea that the things in that category are the most fundamental, from the ontological perspective. Perhaps the idea is that such things exist "in their own right," whereas entities in other categories must depend upon the substances for their existence.

Aristotle, who is generally credited with introducing the concept of substance into philosophy, suggested that substances are the entities upon which everything else depends for existence.[5] So, if a thing is not a substance, it would be impossible for it to exist entirely alone. This conception is problematic, for it is hard to see how substances could differ from non-substances in this respect. Surely, not even a substance could exist without having some properties. Thus, if any substance exists,

[2]Cress, 10.
[3]Cress, 50.
[4]Cress, 51.
[5]Aristotle, *Categories,* Chapter 5.

some properties must exist, too. Aristotle also suggested that a substance is a thing that has properties, but which is not a property of anything else.[6] So if the mind is a substance, then it's not a quality, feature, or attribute of any other thing. In this case, it is wrong to say that the mind is "the power of thought," or "the ability to reason," or "consciousness." Each of these seems to be a property. Perhaps the mind *has* these properties. But, since it is a substance, it cannot *be* any of them.

Since the mind and the body are substances, they are capable of relatively independent existence. Neither of them is something that can exist entirely alone, since each must have properties if it is to exist. Furthermore, Descartes thought that neither could exist without God. But each is independent of other contingent substances. The body could exist even if no other substance (aside from its parts and God) existed. Similarly for the mind. This implies that the body could exist without the mind, and that the mind could exist without the body. If someone dies, and his body rots away, then his mind does exist without his body. At any rate, Descartes seems to have maintained this view. Furthermore, after death, the body exists separately from the mind.

So, on the proposed interpretation of Descartes, each person is alleged to be a compound substance composed of two basic substantial parts. In order to have a clear conception of the compound, we need to have a clear conception of the components, and of the way in which they are combined. Let's start by considering what Descartes said about the nature of the mind.

Minds

Descartes maintained that each mind is essentially thoughtful and unextended. When we say that a mind is "essentially" thoughtful, we mean that it *must* think. Indeed, Descartes went so far as to suggest that each mind must think at every moment of its existence.

> ...thought is an attribute that really does belong to me. This alone cannot be detached from me. I am; I exist; this is certain. But for how long? For as long as I think. Because perhaps it could also come to pass that if I should cease from all thinking I would then utterly cease to exist.[7]

Descartes' concept of thinking is somewhat broader than our own. We tend to conceive of thinking as being primarily a matter of reasoning, or calculating, or pondering. But Descartes included quite a few other mental operations. In one place he gave a list of some main sorts of thinking. A thing that thinks is a thing that "doubts, understands, affirms, denies, wills, refuses, and which also imagines and senses."[8] It appears, then, that just about any mental operation is to be considered a form of thinking. So even if you're asleep and dreaming, you are still thinking, according to this conception of thought. Dreaming, after all, is a mental operation.

It is extremely important to avoid confusing the mind with the brain. The brain is a physical object. It takes up most of the space inside the skull. In an average adult

[6] Ibid.
[7] Cress, 18–19.
[8] Cress, 19.

human being, the brain weighs about 49 ounces. It is made of cells, which in turn are made of molecules and atoms. The mind is utterly unlike this. It is not a physical object. It does not take up any space at all. It has no weight. It is not made of cells or molecules or atoms. It has no physical parts at all. Making use of a technical term, we can say that the mind is "unextended"—it takes up no space.

Even though the mind takes up no space, still it may be *located* at a certain spot in space. Some people apparently find it hard to understand how an unextended object can have a location. But the idea is really quite familiar. Consider a point such as the midway point between New York and Los Angeles. Since that is just a point, it takes up no space, yet it surely has a location. An even more obvious case can be constructed, if you like. Draw a circle on a blackboard. That circle has a center. The center is an unextended point, but it has a location. Thus, there is nothing incomprehensible about the notion that an unextended object might have a location in space.

Descartes seems to have maintained two incompatible views about the location of the mind. According to one of these views, each person's mind is somehow spread throughout his or her body. This view is suggested in the passage about the seaman and his ship. The idea there is that the mind is "mingled together" with the body. In the division argument, Descartes says that "the whole mind seems to be united to the whole body...."[9] This also suggests that the mind is located at every point within the body. I must confess that I cannot understand how an unextended object can be present at several points simultaneously.

The other view about the location of the mind is clearly stated in some other writings, but is only suggested in the *Meditations*.[10] It is the view that a person's mind is located in a small organ at the center of the brain. This organ, the pineal gland, was formerly thought to play an important role in correlating the inputs of the various senses, and so Descartes refers to it as "the part in which the 'common sense' is said to be found."[11] This view seems to be presupposed in the passage in which Descartes explains how the nerves act upon the mind.[12] According to Descartes, the nerves are like "cords" which can be pulled and stretched. Each cord terminates at the pineal gland, and each has its characteristic motions. Somehow, when a cord is pulled, the motion is transmitted to the pineal gland, and from there to the mind, where perception takes place. We will discuss this view a bit later, when we consider mind–body interaction. My point in mentioning this here is just to bring out the fact that according to the second Cartesian view, the mind is located within the pineal gland.

Bodies

Descartes maintains a concept of the body that is a sort of "mirror image" of his concept of the mind. Whereas a mind is essentially thoughtful and unextended, a

[9]Cress, 53.
[10]See especially *The Passions of the Soul,* Part I, Articles 31–37; HR I, 345–349.
[11]Cress, 54.
[12]Ibid.

body is essentially extended and thoughtless. The property of extension is necessary to each body. If a body should lose the property of being extended—if it should cease to take up any space—it would cease to exist. Indeed, anything that is a body is such that it couldn't have existed without taking up space. Descartes also seems to have maintained that each of the other properties that any body has entails extension. Height, weight, color, density, physical structure, etc. seem to conform to this view. If a thing has any of these properties, it must be extended. (Some other properties of bodies seem not to conform to this thesis. A body could have the property of *being located in North America,* but this property does not entail extension.)

Since bodies are alleged to be thoughtless, no brain can think. No matter how well organized your brain may be, and no matter how much interesting electrical activity is taking place there, your brain cannot be conscious. At least, that seems to have been Descartes' view. This implies an answer to the modern question about whether or not machines can think. I suspect that Descartes would say that no computer, no matter how complex, can think. Even if we built a computer that could simulate every bit of behavior of some person, that computer would not be conscious. (However, if there were a mind in the computer, that mind would be conscious.)[13]

Mind–Body Interaction

We have already seen that, according to Descartes, there is no essential connection between a person's mind and his body. Either could exist without the other. However, in the ordinary case of a living person, the mind and body are very intimately associated. Descartes describes this association by appeal to some pretty vague terminology. In one passage that I have already quoted, he says that mind and body are "tightly joined and, so to speak, mingled together." We need to examine this association more closely.

In an interesting passage in the *Sixth Meditation,* Descartes describes what happens when a person perceives something. He gives the example of a person who feels a pain in his foot. According to Descartes, there are nerves "scattered throughout the foot."[14] Each of these is like a cord, and is extended up through the leg, spine, and neck, and ultimately reaches the pineal gland in the brain. If the person injures his foot, a motion is induced in some of the nerves there. The motion travels up the cord, and finally affects the pineal gland, which then moves, too. Perhaps it vibrates in a certain way. "This motion has been constituted by nature so as to affect the mind with a feeling of pain, as if it existed in the foot."[15] So the person then has a "pain-in-the-foot" sort of feeling. This is a form of consciousness, and occurs in the mind.

We can see, then, that there is a purely causal connection between certain bodily events and certain mental events. A certain sort of event in the body (the irritation of some nerves in the foot) leads to a certain sort of event in the mind (a feeling of pain

---

[13]For Descartes' discussion of this point, see HR I, 115–116.
[14]Cress, 54.
[15]Ibid.

in the foot). Descartes maintains that the person could have been constructed in such a way that that same bodily event might have caused some other mental event, or perhaps no mental event at all. However, God made us in the way he did because he recognized that it would be most useful for us to know in the way we do when something is wrong with our feet or other parts of our bodies.

Descartes also maintained that events occurring in the mind can cause events to occur in the body. Suppose, for example, that you have been thinking about a certain friend. You have been wondering whether you should call her. Finally, you decide to do it. You perform an act of "volition"—you will to dial the telephone. This volition is a mental event, and it occurs in the mind. When it happens, it causes some sort of motion in the pineal gland—perhaps another special sort of vibration. This motion is communicated along the nerves down to the fingers, where it makes some muscles contract. Then the finger moves in the way it must in order for the telephone to be dialed. So in typical cases of voluntary action, a mental event causes a bodily event.

The final component of Cartesian dualism is, therefore, the "interactionist" hypothesis. This is the view that a person's mind and body enter into two-way causal interaction. Events occurring in the mind cause events in the body, and events occurring in the body cause events in the mind. Volitions and actions are instances of the first sort of connection, and nerve stimulations and perceptions are instances of the second.

Now let us attempt to summarize the main tenets of Cartesian dualism. As I see it, there are five:

1 Each person is a compound substance composed of two substantial parts—a mind and a body.
2 The mind and the body are capable of independent existence. In typical cases, they do exist apart after death.
3 The mind is essentially thoughtful and unextended.
4 The body is essentially extended and thoughtless.
5 Mind and body enter into two-way causal interaction.

Ontological Implications of Cartesian Dualism

It should be obvious that no Cartesian dualist would be able to make do with the simple ontological scheme presented earlier.[16] That scheme makes no provision for minds. So, if we want to accept Cartesian dualism, we will have to enrich our ontology.

As I see it, the most important change in our ontological scheme is the admission of minds. We must say that, in addition to physical objects, there are also unextended thinking substances, or minds. But another change will be needed, too. To see why, let us consider our somewhat enlarged ontological scheme. It looks like this:

1 Physical Objects
2 Minds

[16]See above, Chapter 9, under "Ontological Systems."

3 Properties
4 Times
5 Places
6 Events
7 Propositions
8 Sets

A moment's reflection will reveal a most serious problem. There is no category here into which we can put people! As we have understood it, Descartes' view is that a person is neither a body nor a mind. Hence, people do not belong in either the first or second of the listed categories. In order to accommodate them, we will have to make things a bit more complex. We need to recognize a distinction between substances that are ontologically uniform and ones that are ontologically mixed. A substance is ontologically uniform if all of its parts, if any, are in the same category that it is in. Thus, a mind would be ontologically uniform since it has no parts. A body would be ontologically uniform since it is a physical object, and every one of its parts is also a physical object. A person, however, would be ontologically mixed, since some of its parts are physical objects, and one of its parts is a mind.

The following revised ontological scheme reflects this conception of substances:

1 Substances
   A Ontologically uniform substances
     i Minds
     ii Bodies
   B Ontologically mixed substances
2 Properties
3 Times
4 Places
5 Events
6 Propositions
7 Sets

Further distinctions are, of course, still possible. We could distinguish psychological from physical properties. We could make a similar distinction among events. We could distinguish among various sorts of times and places. However, our interest in ontology is derived from a prior interest in the nature of persons. Thus, this scheme may be adequate for our purposes. We have now identified a category (ontologically mixed substances) into which we can place persons, and we have said enough about it to suggest the ontological impact of Cartesian dualism. If we accept this view of persons, we will have to enlarge and complicate our ontological scheme.

ADVANTAGES OF CARTESIAN DUALISM

Sometimes we are moved to accept a philosophical theory because we have encountered a persuasive argument for it. Perhaps it has been shown that the theory follows from some obvious facts that we simply cannot deny. In other cases, we are led to accept a theory because it seems to be our only reasonable choice. Perhaps we have been convinced that every likely alternative is, for one reason or another, unacceptable. So we are driven to accept the remaining choice.

We are apparently not driven to accept Cartesian dualism for either of these reasons. There is no knock-down proof that shows that it is true. Nor have we seen any knock down proof that materialism is false. Every argument against materialism can be rebutted. Thus, if we decide to accept Cartesian dualism, we'll have to do so for some other reason.

Sometimes we are moved to accept a philosophical theory because it promises certain advantages—its acceptance, it seems, will make our intellectual lives easier or simpler. Many philosophers apparently have decided to adopt Cartesian dualism for this sort of reason. They have concluded that this conception of the person is intellectually advantageous. They feel that accepting this theory will help them to solve other philosophical problems about people. Let us consider some of the alleged advantages of Cartesian Dualism.

Ordinary Language

One alleged advantage has to do with some sentences we have already discussed in connection with materialism. These, of course, are the ordinary-language sentences that make use of the word "mind."[17] For example, there was this sentence:

A She had a strong mind, but a weak body.

We saw that a materialist cannot admit that (A) might express a literal truth. The materialist has to claim that (A) is, at best, an idiomatic expression of something that does not entail the existence of minds. So, for example, a materialist might say that what's expressed by (A) is more literally expressed by:

A′ She was very intelligent, but she was physically weak.

Similarly, the materialist will have to provide some sort of paraphrase for every apparently true sentence of ordinary language that seems to imply the existence of minds.

It's here that we can see the first apparent advantage of Cartesian dualism. The dualist does not have to provide paraphrases of sentences like (A). He can insist that such sentences are perfectly in order as they stand. Since he believes that there actually are minds, he can take (A) as a literal truth. He recognizes that (A) entails that she has a mind, but since he (unlike the materialist) thinks she in fact does have a mind, this is no source of trouble for the dualist.

It might appear that this would be a significant advantage for the dualist, but some further reflection will show that it is at best of marginal value. To see the trouble, consider again this sentence:

B He changed his mind.

We saw earlier that the materialist would have to treat (B) as an idiomatic expression of something that would be better expressed in such words as these:

[17]See above, Chapter 9, under "The Argument from Ordinary Language."

B′ There's something he formerly believed, but which he now rejects.

The alleged advantage of dualism is that it allows us to take these sentences literally, but surely no sensible dualist would want to take (B) literally. No dualist would hold that when someone changes his mind, he literally removes his old mind, and puts some new mind into its place! So even the dualist will have to provide a paraphrase such as (B′) for an idiomatic expression such as (B). Thus, we shouldn't think that accepting Cartesian dualism will get us out of the paraphrasing business altogether. We'll still have to do a fair amount of it. (If you were a dualist, would you be entirely happy with the sentence "I have half a mind to quit this job"?)

Furthermore, many of the paraphrases are so simple and obvious that it's really no trouble for the materialist to provide them when they are needed. Hence, it doesn't seem that the first alleged advantage is any major triumph for dualism.

Psychic Phenomena

A second alleged advantage of dualism has to do with the psychic phenomena we discussed earlier.[18] We found that a materialist will be forced to say that the so-called strong psychic phenomena simply cannot occur. He has to claim that, at most, the *weak* versions of the psychic phenomena may occur. However, some people who have studied these matters are convinced that certain of the strong psychic phenomena do occur from time to time. Wouldn't it be better to accept a theory of personhood that allowed for this possibility of strong psychic phenomena? Isn't that a point in favor of dualism?

It is important to understand this claim properly. I am not saying that Cartesian dualism is to be preferred because (*a*) strong psychic phenomena actually occur, and (*b*) Cartesian dualism is the only theory about persons that is consistent with this fact. If both of these points were true, we'd have a knockdown argument in favor of Cartesian dualism. Rather, what I'm saying is much weaker. It is that Cartesian dualism allows for the possibility of these strong psychic phenomena, and, for all we know, such phenomena might happen. Materialism, on the other hand, implies that they never happen. Thus, if we want to play it safe, and adopt a view of persons that is at least consistent with the hypothesis that strong psychic phenomena occur, we are better off accepting Cartesian dualism.

Some people will undoubtedly view this as a very trivial advantage for dualism. For example, if you are antecedently skeptical about strong psychic phenomena, you probably won't take this to be an advantage at all. However, if you already believe in astral projection or reincarnation, you may think that dualism is indeed to be preferred.

The Meaning of Life

A third alleged advantage of Cartesian dualism is connected with a very perplexing question about the meaning of life. We must be very careful here, since there are at

---

[18]In Chapter 9, under the "Argument from Psychic Phenomena."

least two very perplexing questions about the meaning of life. The first of these is the question about the purpose, significance, or importance of life. Sometimes, when in a gloomy mood, we may be inclined to suspect that our lives have no purpose, and we may express our view by saying that life has no meaning. If we wanted to consider this point, we might ask "what is the meaning of life?" It is obvious that this question about the meaning of life is a very difficult and troubling one. Fortunately, this is not the question about the meaning of life that I want to discuss.

The question I want to discuss may more properly be said to be the question about the meaning of "alive." The question is this: what do we mean when we say that something is alive? How are we to analyze the concept of life? Can we define "alive"?

Someone might maintain that there is a special fluid that is present in all and only living things. We can call this fluid "the vital spirit." Then we can say that to be alive is to have the vital spirit within you. But this seems to be a pretty bad analysis of the concept of life—there is no evidence that there is any such fluid.

Some philosophers have maintained that a thing is alive just in case it can engage in a certain collection of activities. For example, if it can nourish itself and grow, if it can reproduce, if it can get itself into motion without any help from any outside agent, then the thing is alive—or so some have suggested. This approach is problematic, too. For one thing, some living things cannot reproduce themselves (mules, for example), and others have no ability to get themselves into motion (most plants, for example). For another thing, it appears that a sufficiently careful engineer could produce a robot that would be able to "nourish" itself and grow. Perhaps it would eat nuts and bolts, and attach these to itself so as to become larger. Thus this second approach has its problems too.

Here's where Cartesian dualism may seem to help. Many philosophers have thought that the dualistic conception of persons provides the basis for the simplest and most plausible account of the meaning of "alive." Why not just say that life and death are to be understood as the arrival and departure of the soul? Why not say that a body is alive just so long as there is a soul, or mind, in it? If you are a dualist, this may seem to you to be the obvious answer to our question. If the dualistic answer is simple and plausible, then that gives us a further reason to adopt dualism.

Unfortunately, things are not quite so simple. In order to see what goes wrong here, let us formulate this dualistic proposal about life in a clear and tidy definition:

D1   x is alive = df. There is a soul in x.

This definition may seem to yield the correct results in standard cases. For example, I am alive, and (according to the dualistic conception) there is a soul in me. This rock is not alive—and there surely is no reason to suppose there is a soul in it. So in these two cases, D1 seems to yield the correct results. But it is quite easy to think of cases in which D1 yields absurd results. Suppose a man (we can call him "Jonah") is swallowed by a whale. Suppose the whale gets indigestion, and dies, leaving Jonah still alive inside the whale's belly. According to the dualist conception, there is a soul inside Jonah. Since Jonah is inside the whale, it seems to follow that there is a soul (Jonah's) inside the whale. If D1 were correct, it would follow that the whale is alive—but it is dead.

Similar reflections show that D1 implies that airplanes, cars, houses, and packing crates are all alive whenever they are occupied by living people—if we assume, of course, that people have souls when they are alive. Hence, D1 does not represent any suitable version of the dualistic conception of life.

We might suppose that the source of the trouble here is easily identified. In D1, we merely require the presence of a soul in an object in order for the object to be alive. Clearly, however, it takes more than that. The soul must be properly related to the body. But what is this "proper relation"? According to the fifth tenet of Cartesian dualism, souls interact causally with bodies. Perhaps this provides a clue. Maybe we can say that a body is alive not just when there is a soul in it, but when there is a soul in it that interacts causally with it. Then we can say that Jonah is alive because his soul interacts causally with his body, whereas the whale is dead, because no soul interacts causally with it. So the new proposal is this:

D2 x is alive = df. There is a soul in x, and that soul interacts causally with x.

A moment's reflection will reveal, unfortunately, that D2 is no better than D1. Assuming that there is a soul in Jonah, and that this soul interacts causally with Jonah's body, we can see that D2 yields the result that Jonah's body is alive. But it also yields the incorrect result that the whale's body is alive. If we assume that there is a soul in Jonah's body, and that this soul interacts causally with Jonah's body, we must also conclude that this soul interacts causally with the whale's body. For, in the first place, certain events occurring in the body of the whale will have causal effects in Jonah's mind. Suppose, for example, that the whale's body is rotting, and that Jonah smells it. Then *the rotting of the whale's flesh* is an event in the whale's body, and the *smelling* is an event in Jonah's mind. So we have a causal influence going from the whale's body to Jonah's mind. In the other direction, suppose that Jonah wants to get out, and decides to knock on the whale's ribs, hoping that someone will hear the noise and free him. Then *Jonah's deciding to knock* is a mental event occurring in Jonah's mind, and it leads to a physical event in the whale's body. This is a causal relation between Jonah's mind and the whale's body. Hence, there is two-way causal interaction between Jonah's mind and whale's body. D2 incorrectly implies that the whale is alive. So D2 must be rejected.

The problem with D2 is that it says that a thing is alive if it enters into any sort of causal interaction with a mind. As we have just seen, this won't do. If there are souls in living things, and those souls interact causally with those things, then nonliving things can enter into certain sorts of causal interaction with souls, too. However, it may still seem that the basic idea behind D2 is correct. We will need to be more careful to specify the exact nature of the causal connection.

While Jonah is alive, his soul enters into an especially intimate sort of causal connection with his body. As Descartes said, the mind is not just lodged in the body as a pilot is in his ship. Rather the mind is "intertwined with" and "commingled with" the body in such a way as to form a single living person. Let us say that when a mind is related to a body in this way, then the mind "animates" the body. Jonah's mind animated Jonah's body, but did not animate the whale's body. Now we can modify our analysis of life:

D3 x is alive = df. There is a soul in x that animates x.

I think you will find that it is impossible to produce a counterexample to D3. For my part, I cannot think of any clear case in which we'd all agree that a certain thing is alive, but in which we'd also agree that it is not animated by a soul. Similarly in the other direction.

Nevertheless, I think D3 is virtually worthless. One problem here is that D3 makes use of a technical term—"animates." This term has not been defined. I see two main possibilities. On the one hand, we might try to define "animates." Perhaps we would come up with something like this:

D4 x animates y = df. x is in y in such a way as to make y alive.

Obviously, the use of D4 in this context makes the whole project hopelessly circular. We attempt to define "alive" in terms of "animates," and then we attempt to define "animates" in terms of "alive."

On the other hand, we might choose to treat "animates" as an undefined "primitive"—an expression whose meaning is so clear and simple that it neither needs nor can have a definition. The problem in this case is that many people will claim that they simply do not understand what "animates" is supposed to mean. Just what is that intimate relation that holds between a living person's soul and his body? If you think about it, I believe you will find that it is hard to explain animation in any way other than the way suggested by D4. For present purposes, however, D4 isn't much help.

A second problem for D4 should be mentioned. People aren't the only living things. There are plenty of "lower" animals, and lots of plants. If D4 is correct, it follows that each of these organisms has a soul, too. I suppose someone could say that there is a soul for each worm and each cactus plant, but that seems a pretty far-fetched idea. There is simply no reason to suppose that there is an unextended thinking substance inside such things. Does a cactus think? Furthermore, it seems to me that many parts of living things are living, too. For example, unless you have a very severe case of gangrene, most of the cells in your body are alive. Shall we assume that there is a special soul for each of them?

My conclusion here is that Cartesian dualism does not help in the attempt to explain the meaning of "alive." So far as I can tell, this is simply no advantage at all for the dualist.

Personal Identity

Another alleged advantage of Cartesian Dualism can only be understood if we first understand the problem of personal identity. Perhaps we can best understand this problem if we consider an example. Suppose I go up to the attic, and there find an old photo album. In the album, let us imagine, I find an old, faded photograph showing a cute, chubby baby. The baby looks to be about three or four months old. It has a toothless grin, and only a few wisps of fair hair. On the back of the photograph there is an inscription in my mother's handwriting. It says, "Fred—aged four months." So it appears that the baby in the picture is me.

Let's suppose I find another photograph, this one showing a boy of about ten years. He is much bigger than the baby of the first picture, but much smaller than I am now. His hair is much darker and thicker than that of the baby, but his beard is much lighter than mine is today. On the back of this second photograph, I find another inscription in my mother's handwriting. It says, "Fred—aged ten years." So this too is a picture of me.

If one were to focus exclusively on my current body, and the bodies shown in the two photographs, one could easily reach the conclusion that these are three different bodies. The body of the baby was pink and round and chubby. It had light hair and no beard. The body of the ten-year-old was much taller and thinner, and it had dark hair. My current body is taller and heavier, I have a darker beard, and I'm now wearing glasses. In virtue of all these differences, it may seem that the body I have today is not the same one I had when I was ten, and neither of these is the one I had when I was an infant. Let's suppose that this is the case. Let's suppose that when a person's body changes sufficiently, it turns into a new body. Now we may be able to pose the question about personal identity.

If these are all different bodies, why is it correct to say that the photos are both photos of me? What is it that makes the baby in the first picture "the same person as" the youth in the second picture? What makes that person be me? Why don't we say instead that they are two other people?

It is very important to understand that I am not raising an epistemological question here. I am not wondering how we tell that a photograph shows me at age ten, or how we tell that a certain youth is the same person as a certain old man. These questions are questions about knowledge, and are answered in familiar, nonphilosophical ways. We can tell that the baby in the picture is me because my name appears on the back, because my sister can remember the day the picture was taken, because there is an amusing resemblance between the baby in the picture and my older daughter, etc. We can tell that the youth in the second picture is also me in similar ways. These are empirical questions of personal identity, and they boil down to one: given a person, x, and a person, y, how can we tell whether x and y are the same person? It does not seem to me that this question is one that calls for a philosophical answer. The question here is not a matter for us, as philosophers, to try to answer. It's a matter for a detective agency, or the police department.

The philosophical question is different. It is the question: what makes the baby in the first picture be the same person as the youth in the second picture? And what makes that person be the same person as me? Why are they one person, and not three?

Some philosophers have suggested that certain psychological facts provide the basis for personal identity. They have said things that imply that what makes me the same person as the ten-year-old is that I now remember various things that ten-year-old in fact did. Memories tie me to him. He, in turn, is tied to the infant in a similar way by memory. Since the ten-year-old remembers things in fact done by the infant, they are one person. Thus, we might say that a person is really just a sequence of living human bodies, such that each body in the sequence remembers things done by earlier bodies in the sequence.

This approach has seemed to some philosophers to be seriously flawed. They have described cases in which a person could not recall anything that happened to him previously. For example, consider someone who has just taken a sharp blow to the head, and who now has amnesia. The body before us now cannot remember anything done by anybody yesterday—yet we all recognize this body as the body of a person who existed yesterday. So the memory approach needs to be refined.

Recent developments in genetics suggest another answer to our question about personal identity. Every cell within the body of a living person contains genetic material ultimately derived from that person's parents. This genetic material is an enormously complex twisted ribbon of molecules, and it is responsible for all the inherited characteristics that the person has. Throughout a person's life, the precise nature of this material never changes. Perhaps this provides the basis for a solution to the puzzle about personal identity. Perhaps we can say that all the various bodies of a single person are tied together by virtue of the fact that they share the same microgenetic structure. So the general hypothesis is that person A is the same as person B in the event that the microgenetic structure of the cells in A's body is the same as the microgenetic structure of the cells in B's body.

This hypothesis seems to me to go wrong in the case of identical twins. If A and B are identical twins, then they are microgenetically alike, but they are nevertheless two different people. Furthermore, if the time comes when people can be cloned, we will find that there can be dozens of people who are absolutely indiscernible on the microgenetic level. Clearly, however, no one would want to say that all these clones would be the same person.

Another approach here is based upon a modified version of Cartesian dualism. Why not say, roughly, that all the different bodies of a given person are tied together by the fact that each of them is animated by the same soul? Why not say that sameness of persons is to be explained by sameness of souls? In our example about the baby pictures, we can say that the baby in the picture is me because the soul that animated that babyish body is the same soul as the one that animates my body now, and which also animated the body of the ten-year-old in the other picture. That's why each of them is me.

Sharp-eyed readers will have noticed that this proposal calls for a certain slight modification of our earlier Cartesian doctrine about persons. Earlier, we said that the Cartesian view was that a person is a compound substance composed of a body and a mind, or soul. On the present view, however, a person doesn't have just one body—each person has different bodies at different times. On the present view, then, a person is thought of as a sequence of mind-body compounds, tied together by the fact that the same mind shows up in every one of the compounds.

In order to state this properly, let us introduce the concept of the "person-stage." We can say that a person-stage is a compound substance consisting of a body and a mind, in which the mind animates the body. Such a compound lasts only so long as both components last, and continue to stand in the relation of animation. Thus, if we think that each person has a new body each day (because of change of cells, or atoms) then we will have to say that there is a new person-stage each day. Then we can go on to say that person-stages are "of the same person" provided that they share the same mind. More exactly, the proposal is this:

> **P1** Person-stage x is part of the same person as person-stage y if and only if the soul animating x = the soul animating y.

Now we have to introduce our needed modification of the Cartesian conception of the person. Instead of saying that a person is a compound of mind and body, we will need to say that a person is a sequence of such compounds. More precisely, the idea is that a person is a sequence of mind-body compounds consisting of all and only those compounds having the same mind as some member. So I am the sequence of all those mind-body compounds having the same mind that animates my body now, and you are the sequence of all the mind-body compounds having the same mind as the one that animates your body now.

There can be no doubt but that this does provide an answer to the question about personal identity. It gives us a precise statement of necessary and sufficient conditions for something being part of the same person as something else. Some may feel, nevertheless, that it provides a particularly empty and useless answer, since it would ordinarily be impossible to tell whether the mind animating this body today is the same as, or different from, the mind that animated that body yesterday. So far as I can see, there just wouldn't be any direct way to figure that out.

However, if someone were attracted to this proposal concerning personal identity, that would give him further reason to accept Cartesian dualism. The whole answer, as should be obvious, is based upon a fundamentally Cartesian conception. That is, it is based upon the idea that a person isn't just a body, but is some sort of compound thing made out of body (or a sequence of bodies) and a soul.

"Life after Death"

A final alleged advantage of dualism should perhaps be mentioned. Some people are attracted to the notion that there may be an "afterlife." Generally, those who accept this view accept it on the basis of some religious considerations. Perhaps they believe that when we die, some part of us goes to some other realm, there to suffer the rewards or punishments for our behavior here on earth.

It is pretty clear that our bodies do not normally go straight to any other realm at the moment of death. If a person dies in his sleep, his body normally remains right where it was in the bed. Thus, if something departs, it must be the mind or soul of the person, and not any physical part.

Once again, I am not proposing an argument for the existence of the soul based upon the premise that we survive in an afterlife. The evidence for the afterlife is far too weak to support the conclusion. Rather, I am making the much weaker point that (*a*) some people think that it is possible that we survive in an afterlife, and (*b*) if dualism were true, then this indeed might be a possibility. On the other hand, it is hard to see how survival could be possible if any form of materialism were true. (I suppose that someone *could* maintain that some thin, ghostly, but nevertheless physical object leaves the body, and goes to heaven or hell, but a more typical position is that what goes to heaven or hell is nonphysical.)

For my own part, I am not inclined to believe in the afterlife, and so I do not view this as any advantage for dualism. Perhaps, sometime in the future, I will discover that I am wrong about this. If that should happen, I hope that I make my discovery in heaven, and not in the other place.

PROBLEMS FOR CARTESIAN DUALISM

Many people find Cartesian Dualism quite unattractive. Perhaps some are put off by the idea that there are unextended thinking substances. One philosopher ridiculed this as the doctrine of the "the ghost in the machine."[19] He suggested that it is an unintelligible set of doctrines generated by a serious misunderstanding of some common figures of speech. Of course, that isn't an argument against dualism. It's just a claim about what has led some philosophers into accepting it.

However, there are plenty of arguments against Cartesian dualism.

The Problem of Other Minds

One of the most interesting objections to this view is based upon some alleged epistemological consequences of dualism. To appreciate these, let us suppose that someone has carefully designed a robot that can mimic every sort of human behavior. Suppose this robot can walk, talk, eat, sleep, etc. Suppose it can even shed a tear when we expose it to a sad movie, and it can giggle when we expose it to a good joke. Most importantly, however, we must suppose that there is no soul in this robot. It is just a machine designed to behave outwardly in all the ways humans normally behave.

It is important to recognize that there can be no direct, observational method by which we can determine whether or not there is a soul in a person. Even the most sophisticated CAT scanner would not reveal the presence of the soul (assuming, of course, that there is one in there.) The reason is simple. Although the CAT scanner makes it possible for us to "see" even very tiny tissues inside of our bodies, it cannot enable us to "see" unextended, nonphysical substances. The mind is alleged to be such a substance. It leaves no x-ray shadow. Thus, if we are to determine that a soul is present in some object, we will have to do so indirectly—presumably by observation of the effects of the soul on the outward behavior of the object.

So, let us suppose that we have both the robot and a real, live human being before us. We challenge the person to do something that will show that he, unlike the robot, has a soul. What can he do? Perhaps the person will speak to us. Maybe he will say, "I am thinking. I have a soul. I am conscious." That might give us some reason to suppose that he in fact does have a soul. But, of course, the robot will be able to say exactly the same things—and, if it is a well-made robot, it will be able to say them with the same intonation and "feeling." Since the robot has no mind, and it can speak as well as the person, we must conclude that the ability to speak is no guarantee of the presence of a mind.

We might suppose that one important difference between the person and the robot would concern spontaneity. Perhaps it will seem that the person can engage in a sort of spontaneous movement that is impossible for the robot. For example, the person might sit very quietly for several moments, and then, with no apparent prodding, he might get up and walk away. The robot, on the other hand, might

---

[19] Gilbert Ryle, *The Concept of Mind,* New York: Barnes and Noble, 1949.

remain motionless until someone presses a button, or flips a switch. So whereas the soulless robot cannot engage in spontaneous motion, the besouled person can.

It should be obvious that this proposal doesn't work. It would be easy enough to build a robot that would sit quietly for a long time, and then suddenly burst into action. A small timer, rigged to go off at some randomly selected time in the future, could be placed in the robot. The timer could then be connected to the motors that drive the robot, so that when the timer goes off, the robot starts to move. If this were done imaginatively, it might be practically impossible to predict when the robot would begin to move. Nevertheless, there is no soul in the robot. Therefore, the fact that the person can engage in spontaneous action does not show that he has a soul.

Let us assume, then, that there is no way to tell for sure that there is a soul in something. There is no direct, observational method, and there is no indirect method based upon the consequences of having a soul. So, when confronted by an object, you just can't tell for sure whether it has a soul or not. The impact of this assumption is remarkable.

Recall that according to Cartesian dualism, something is a person only if it does have a soul. A human body lacking a soul would not be person, on that theory. Thus, if there is some problem about telling whether or not there is a soul in a body, then (assuming that dualism is true) there is a problem about telling whether it is a person. Since there apparently is a problem about telling whether anything has a soul, there is a problem, assuming dualism is true, about telling whether any of the walking, talking human bodies we see are the bodies of persons. For all I know, they are thoughtless robot-like corpses!

The upshot is that, if Cartesian dualism were true, I would have no way of determining whether or not there are other people. For me, "solipsism" would be a real possibility. That is, for all I could tell, I might be the only person. This gives us a crucial premise for a strikingly difficult argument against Cartesian dualism. We can call it "The Problem of Other Minds," and it goes like this:

1 If Cartesian dualism were true, then I would have no way of determining whether or not there are other people.
2 I do have ways of determining that there are other people.
3 Therefore, Cartesian dualism is not true.

Descartes seems to have maintained that (1) here is not true. In a few places (unfortunately, not in the *Meditations*) he tried to explain how we can tell when there is a soul in a body.[20] His explanation was based on some linguistic assumptions. He said that he could imagine a soulless machine constructed in such a way that it could utter words when touched, but he could not imagine a mere machine that could respond intelligently to all the different things anyone might say in its presence. It has been suggested that Descartes' point here is that people have the capacity for a special sort of linguistic creativity. With only a finite vocabulary and a relatively modest set of grammatical rules, a person is able to understand any of an

---

[20]The passage appears in Part V of the *Discourse on Method,* HR I, 116.

infinitely large set of sentences. Equally, each of us is able to produce any of an infinitely large set of sentences—including, of course, lots of sentences we have never heard before.[21]

I think that some people do have the sort of ability Descartes may have had in mind. It's not clear to me, however, that it would be impossible for a machine to be constructed in such a way as to duplicate the relevant behavior. That is, I can't see why it is in principle impossible for there to be a soulless machine whose linguistic behavior is just like that of an allegedly besouled human being.

A Cartesian Dualist could also attempt to deal with the argument by rejecting (2). He could insist that solipsism really is a possibility. He could say that we just "go on faith" when we assume that the bodies we see each day are the bodies of people. He could say that he really doesn't know whether, when he talks with his friends, they are conscious. For all he knows, they might be nothing more than mindless corpses. This is obviously an unattractive position. I leave it to the reflective reader to determine whether it can be accepted. Let us turn to another objection to Cartesian dualism

Problems about Causal Interaction

This second, and perhaps more important objection to Cartesian dualism is based on some apparent problems concerning psychophysical causal interaction. In order to understand the problem, let us imagine a sort of scientific experiment.

Suppose we have a tiny jar. In the jar there is a living, disembodied soul. We have access to every sort of laboratory equipment—electrical probes, chemicals of all sorts, various heat sources, lights of all descriptions, mallets, clamps, scalpels, etc. Our task is straightforward: we have to make contact with the soul in the jar.

A moment's reflection should make it clear that we cannot communicate with the soul by speaking to it. Since it has no ears, it will not be able to hear us. Nor will we be able to contact it by shining lights on it. Since it is an unextended, nonphysical object, light cannot strike it. Nor will it be able to see the light, since it has no eyes. Thus, it appears that the normal modes of communication will not be feasible. Each such mode works only if the "receiver" of the communication has some sense organs. Since the soul in the jar has no body, it has no sense organs.

It might be thought that we could affect the soul by passing a minute electric charge through it. Perhaps we could place one wire on one side of the soul, and another wire on the other side of the soul, and then make a tiny spark jump across the gap. Won't that have an impact on the soul? Can't we then teach the soul some sort of code, so that we can communicate by giving it lots of little shocks?

The answer, it seems to me, is that it will be impossible to affect the soul electrically. Since the soul is not made of atoms, and has no physical structure, it is very hard to see how electricity could have any effect on it. Surely it could not be

---

[21] See Noam Chomsky, *Cartesian Linguistics,* New York: Harper and Row, 1966.

shocked. In order to be shocked, something needs to have a nervous system. The soul, if it exists, has none.

Further reflections along these lines will lead to the conclusion that there is no conceivable way in which we can causally affect the soul. We can't heat it up, or burn it with acid, or magnetize it. We can't shake it up, or squash it, or cut it in half. None of these operations can be performed on an object without physical structure. The soul seems to be immune to causal intervention. We can conceive of no way in which we can causally influence what goes on in it. Thus, we cannot communicate with it. The experiment ends in failure.

At this point, we must recall that one of the principal tenets of Cartesian dualism is "interactionism." That is the doctrine that there is two-way causal interaction between mind and body. Mental events, such as decisions and acts of will, are supposed to cause bodily motions. And physical events, such as stimulations of sensory nerves, are supposed to cause mental events, such as sensings. Yet it may now seem that such interaction is at best very hard to imagine. What, exactly, is the nature of the causal connection between a physical event, such as the stimulation of some nerves, and the mental event that it allegedly causes?

Of course, it is pretty easy to imagine the purely physical steps in the process. For example, suppose someone dips his toe into a swimming pool to test the water. The cold water quickly cools the skin on his toe, and changes the temperature of the nerve endings that are "scattered" there. Then some sort of electrical charge flows up the nerve, jumping across various gaps between one nerve and the next. Perhaps there are stages in which the electrical event causes some chemical change, which in turn causes a suitable electrical event in the next nerve. This purely physical chain of events eventually reaches some part of the brain. Here is where the trouble begins. How does it make the last step, the one that gets it from the physical apparatus of the nervous system, and into the mind?

As we have already seen, the last step cannot be electrical in nature. No electrical event can causally influence the mind—it's not a physical object. Nor can the last step be chemical, thermal or mechanical. Each of these requires a physical object. How does the body finally influence the mind? How does all the electrical and chemical activity in the nervous system finally bring about that distinctive feeling of cold that reveals that the water is too chilly for swimming? Many philosophers would say that this alleged causal connection is simply inconceivable.

The causal connection in the other direction is no easier to understand. Suppose you have been thinking about a certain friend. You decide to call her on the telephone. Precisely how does this decision, apparently a mental event, give rise to the first physical event in the causal chain that ultimately leads to the movements of your fingers? Your mind cannot rub against the nearest nerves in your brain, nor can it give off heat, or light, or chemicals, or an electric charge. Only a physical object could do such things. Thus, causal interaction is equally perplexing, whether it is mind-body interaction, or body-mind interaction. And Cartesian dualism cannot be true unless such interaction happens all the time.

Let us now formulate the objection. We can call it "The No Interaction Argument." It goes this way:

1 Causal interaction between mind and body is inconceivable.

2 If causal interaction between mind and body is inconceivable, then it does not occur.

3 If causal interaction between mind and body does not occur, then Cartesian dualism is not true.

4 Therefore, Cartesian dualism is not true.

I think it is fair to say that this argument constitutes the most important objection to Cartesian dualism. If we view the matter historically, we will find, I think, that no other argument crops up more frequently in the antidualistic literature. It is a formidable problem.

Nevertheless, there are still some replies open to Cartesian dualists. One maneuver involves claiming that line (2) is false. There are many things that are very hard to understand, but which apparently happen anyway. For example, most people find it virtually impossible to conceive in any clear way of a black hole, and yet the astronomers insist that there are quite a few of them out there. So, from the fact that we can't conceive of mind-body causal interaction, it does not follow that such interaction is impossible. Maybe it's just one of those mysteries—something beyond human comprehension.

If the Cartesian takes this line, he seriously diminishes the interest of his theory. Cartesian dualism is introduced as an account of the nature of persons. It is supposed to provide an answer to the question, "what is a person?" The answer we have imagined surely leaves a lot to be desired. For, according to this answer, the Cartesian tells us that a person is a compound of mind and body, related in some incomprehensible way. That hardly offers enlightenment!

ALTERNATIVES TO CARTESIAN DUALISM

It is important to recognize that the no interaction argument is really directed against just one component of Cartesian dualism—the interactionist thesis. The argument has no direct bearing on the other components of the view. Thus, it constitutes no objection at all to the idea that a person is a compound substance composed of a mind and a body, and it constitutes no objection to the Cartesian conception of the mind as essentially thoughtful and unextended. So, we can remain dualists even if we think interactionism is unacceptable. We just have to be sure to provide some alternative account of the connection between mind and body—it can't be causal interaction.

Parallelism

One possibility here would be "parallelism"—the view that the mind and body are causally independent of each other, but nevertheless behave as if they were causally connected. The parallelist account of the mind-body relation is just like the interactionist account, except at this one crucial point. Where the interactionist sees causal connections, the parallelist sees none. So, for example, suppose a person dips his toe into some cold water. Both parallelist and interactionist will agree about the early stages of the event. Each will say that nerves in the affected area are stimulated, and each will say that the stimulation causally affects transmitter nerves in the spine, neck, and brain. The interactionist, as we have seen, will go on to say that there is a causal connection between some final event in the brain and the feeling of cold "as if it were in the toe." The parallelist will disagree. He will say that there is no such causal connection. The mental event—the feeling of cold—occurs just when the final brain event occurs, but there is no causal connection between them. The mental event stands in causal relations only to other mental events, and the brain event stands in causal relations only to other physical events. The two causal sequences, though causally unrelated, are nevertheless "parallel."

It should be obvious that parallelism is an unattractive view. Instead of explaining the puzzling connection between mind and body, it asserts that there is no connection. It posits an inexplicable noncausal linkage between mental and physical events.

Occasionalism

Some of Descartes' contemporaries thought that the best way to explain the connection requires an appeal to God. They maintained that God miraculously sees to it that mental events and physical events occur in exactly the right order. So, for example, when a person puts his toe in cold water, and the nervous signal reaches his brain, God intervenes and affects the person's mind with the feeling of cold. Similarly, when the person decides to pick up the telephone, God intervenes and sees to it that the nerves leading out from the brain are appropriately stimulated. Then, as a result of a sequence of purely causal connections, the muscles are provoked into the necessary actions, and the person lifts the telephone. This view has been called "occasionalism," since, according to it, the appropriate mental events provide the occasion for God to intervene so as to induce the appropriate physical events, and vice versa.

In a marvelous passage in an essay entitled "New System of the Nature and Communication of Substances, as Well as of the Union Existing Between the Soul and the Body," Leibniz presented some objections to interactionism and occasionalism. In order to make his objections more striking, Leibniz first presented an analogy. He wrote:

> Imagine two clocks or watches which are in perfect agreement. Now this agreement may come about *in three ways. The first* consists in a natural influence.... *The second method* of achieving the constant agreement of two clocks, albeit imperfect ones, would be to have them continually supervised by a skilful craftsman who should be constantly setting them right. *The third method* is to construct the two clocks so skilfully and accurately at the outset that one could be certain of their subsequent agreement.[22]

Leibniz went on to assert that the "agreement" of mind and body might be explained in three similar ways. The Cartesian sees it as a matter of "natural influence" or causal interaction. But this is impossible. The occasionalist sees it as a

---

[22] Parkinson, 130–131.

matter of constant divine intervention—a miracle every second. But this suggests that God is like a poor craftsman, whose watches need constant readjustment.

> Thus there remains only my hypothesis, that is to say *the way of pre-established harmony*—pre-established, that is, by a Divine anticipatory artifice, which so formed these substances from the beginning, that in merely following its own laws, which it received with its being, it is yet in accord with the other, just as if they mutually influenced each other, or as if, over and above his general concourse, God were for ever putting in his hand to set them right.[23]

The Pre-established Harmony

So Leibniz' view, the pre-established harmony, is that the mind and the body were constructed at the outset by God in such a way that there is no need for causal influence, or for divine tinkering. Each is made in such a way that it will be behaving properly at the right moment. Thus, to return to our example of the person who puts his toe into cold water, Leibniz would say that the mind of this man was so constructed that, without any causal influence ever impinging upon it, it would inevitably be feeling cold at a certain time in the future. Furthermore, the body of this man was also so constructed that, even though nothing would ever causally affect it, it would be testing the water in a swimming pool at that same moment in the future.

Leibniz maintained that his own view is best because, according to it, God behaves in "the finest way and the worthiest of him." In other words, since it is better to have constructed things in such a way that they wouldn't need readjustment, that must be how God did it.

Obviously, neither occasionalism nor the pre-established harmony will be acceptable to someone who does not believe in God. And even for someone who does believe in God, neither of these views is nowadays terribly attractive. According to each of them, the mind-body connection is miraculous. On one view, there are indefinitely many miracles. On the other view, there is just one huge miracle at the outset. If you prefer to view human beings in less supernatural terms, you will have to reject both views. But that seems to mean going back to something like Cartesian dualism—and we've already seen that there's serious trouble there, too. In light of these difficulties, many contemporary philosophers have rejected dualism altogether.

[23] Parkinson, 131.

CHAPTER 11

CONCLUSIONS

KNOWLEDGE OF THE EXTERNAL WORLD[1]

By the beginning of the *Sixth Meditation*, Descartes thinks he has gained justification for reinstating a significant number of his earlier beliefs. He thinks he has become metaphysically certain of his own existence, and of God's existence. So he can believe in these things. Furthermore, he thinks he is metaphysically certain of all of his own "directly accessible" current mental states, and so these things are now worthy of belief, too.

Since he thinks he has established that God is no deceiver, Descartes is also convinced that all of his clear and distinct perceptions are true. This enables him to have metaphysical certainty with respect to a variety of propositions in mathematics, geometry, and abstract metaphysics. Thus, he feels entitled to believe such things as that $2 + 3 = 5$; that the angles of a triangle add up to 180 degrees; and that nothing can both have and lack a given property at the same time.

We have also seen that Descartes thinks he has established a variety of beliefs concerning himself. He thinks he has proven that he is not a physical object. He is absolutely certain that his mind is an unextended thinking substance. Its essence is thoughtfulness, and its accidents, or inessential properties, are the various thoughts that he entertains from time to time. In addition to this, the mind has several "faculties." These are best thought of as properties, such as the property of being able to calculate, and the property of being able to entertain propositions. If he is a genuine person, then he also has a body, which is an extended thoughtless substance. As a person, he would be a compound substance composed of these two substantial parts in intimate conjunction.

---

[1] Reading Assignment: The *Sixth Meditation*, Cress, 45–56.

All this is quite impressive, but a vast array of beliefs remains less than metaphysically certain. Among these, the most important are all those beliefs concerning the "external world." Thus, at this stage, Descartes is not entirely certain that there is an earth and a sun; that there are tables and chairs; that he has a body; that there are other people. If he sticks to his epistemic principle, Descartes will not be able to regain these beliefs unless he can make them metaphysically certain. He will have to continue to suspend judgment with respect to every one of them until such time as they are entirely beyond doubt.

In the *Sixth Meditation*, Descartes attempts to make some of these propositions metaphysically certain. Thus, we can view his project here as the attempt to reconstruct his knowledge of the external world.

It is important to remember that Descartes is not attempting to achieve *practical* knowledge of the external world. As we saw above in Chapter 2, Descartes was not very interested in the question whether he has practical knowledge. He wanted to achieve maximal epistemic purification. He wanted to have the most extensive *metaphysical* knowledge that it would be possible for him to have. So when I speak of "reconstructing his knowledge of the external world," I mean to indicate a rather special task. Descartes is trying to gain metaphysical knowledge concerning the external world. In order to have metaphysical knowledge, he must have metaphysical certainty. In accordance with his epistemic principle, he has decided that if he doesn't have metaphysical certainty about the external world, then he will continue to suspend judgment.

The Argument from Sensing

After a somewhat confusing start, Descartes produces an argument for the conclusion that there is indeed a world of corporeal substances, or physical objects. The argument is rather long and complex, and so it may be best to split it into several parts, and to consider them separately. The first part of the argument is contained in this passage:

> But now there surely is in me a passive faculty of sensing, that is, of receiving and knowing the ideas of sensible things; but I cannot use it unless there also exists, either in me or in something else, a certain active faculty of producing or bringing about these ideas.[2]

I think it must be admitted that the argument presented here is somewhat less than fully satisfactory. Descartes really hasn't given us very much to go on, but perhaps we are justified in assuming that what he meant to say can be formulated in this way:

The Argument from Sensing—Part I

1 I sometimes use my passive faculty of receiving ideas of sensible things.
2 If I sometimes use my passive faculty of receiving ideas of sensible things, then some substance has the active faculty of producing ideas of sensible things.

[2]Cress, 49.

3 Therefore, some substance has the active faculty of producing ideas of sensible things.

Although a modern reader might be somewhat put off by the rather old-fashioned terminology Descartes has used, the main point here seems to be quite reasonable. As I see it, that point is just that since Descartes has ideas of sensible things, something must be causing him to have those ideas. Unless the principle of universal causation is in doubt, this must be granted.

Descartes then goes on to point out that this "faculty of producing ideas" must reside either (*a*) in Descartes himself, or (*b*) in God, or (*c*) in some other substance. Descartes first attempts to rule out the first possibility. He claims that he himself cannot be the cause of his ideas of corporeal substances.

not from self

> This faculty surely cannot be in me, since it clearly presupposes no intellection, and these ideas are produced without my cooperation and often against my will.[3]

In this passage, Descartes has suggested two reasons for thinking that he himself does not have the faculty of causing his ideas of corporeal objects. The first reason is based on the notion that all of his faculties "presuppose intellection." I take this to mean that each faculty that Descartes has is one that entails thinking. For example, he has the faculties of calculating, of believing, of denying, of imagining, etc. Each of these entails thinking. But the faculty of *producing* ideas does not entail thinking. Even a nonthinking corporeal substance could have that power. Hence, Descartes does not have that faculty.

His second reason for thinking that he himself is not the cause of his own ideas of corporeal substances is that these ideas are produced "without my cooperation and often against my will."

I think it must be admitted that neither of these reasons is conclusive. The first argument seems to me to be quite weak. Why can't Descartes have some faculties that entail thinking, and some that don't? If it should turn out (as he thinks it will) that he is a compound substance with both a body and a mind, then it would be perfectly natural for him to have faculties of both sorts. The second argument is no better. Surely, we have plenty of "faculties" that operate without our "cooperation." Consider the "faculty" of dreaming, or the "faculty" of hallucinating.

not from God

In any case, Descartes goes on to argue that the faculty of producing these ideas cannot reside in God:

> But, since God is not a deceiver, it is absolutely clear that he sends me these ideas neither directly and immediately—nor even through the mediation of any creature, in which the objective reality of these ideas is contained not formally but only eminently. Since he plainly gave me no faculty for making this discrimination—rather, he gave me a great inclination to believe that these ideas proceeded from things—I fail to see why God cannot be understood to be a deceiver, if they proceeded from a source other than corporeal things. For this reason, corporeal things exist.[4]

The fundamental point here is obvious: Descartes has a "great inclination" to believe that his ideas of corporeal things are in fact caused by corporeal things. If

[3]Cress, 49.
[4]Cress, 50.

God were actually the cause of these ideas, then God would be a deceiver. Since God isn't a deceiver, the faculty of producing these ideas must not reside in God. In addition to this, Descartes seems to be claiming that God cannot be sending these ideas "indirectly." As I see it, Descartes means to rule out the suggestion that the ideas of corporeal things are sent to him from God, via other minds. If God did such a thing, Descartes seems to be saying, he would be a deceiver. Hence, he doesn't.

This part of the argument strikes me as being particularly unpersuasive. Surely, if God had some sufficiently important reason for doing so, he might cause Descartes to have ideas of corporeal objects, even though there are no such things. Is there some absolutely conclusive proof that God has no good reason to do this?

In any case, the second part of the argument may be formulated as follows:

The Argument from Sensing—Part II

1 Some substance has the active power of producing ideas of corporeal substances.

2 If some substance has the active power of producing ideas of corporeal substances, then it is either (*a*) Descartes himself, or (*b*) God, or (*c*) corporeal substances.

3 Descartes does not have this power.

4 God does not have this power.

5 Therefore, corporeal substances have the active power to produce ideas of corporeal substances.

It goes without saying that if this power resides in corporeal substances, then there must actually be some corporeal substances. A power cannot reside in a thing unless that thing actually exists.

I think that Descartes realized that this is a rather weak argument. Indeed, in the passage immediately following, he almost seems to admit that the argument fails. He suggests that he really doesn't know that corporeal substances exist. He says:

> Be that as it may, perhaps not all bodies exist exactly as I grasp them by sense, because this grasp by the senses is in many cases very obscure and confused. But at least everything is in these bodies that I clearly and distinctly understand—that is, everything, considered in a general sense, that is encompassed in the object of pure mathematics.[5]

The unwary reader could easily be misled here. Descartes seems to be saying that his knowledge of bodies is limited to their mathematical features. Perhaps he means to suggest that, if he measures it very carefully, he can gain metaphysical knowledge of the fact that his desk is exactly 31 inches high, and that its top has a surface area of just 800 square inches. I do not think that this accurately represents Descartes' view. I think his view was that, strictly speaking, he could not have metaphysical knowledge of anything that entailed the existence of his desk. Thus, he could not metaphysically know that his desk was 31 inches high, or that it had a top at all.

In order to understand his view properly, we must notice that he suggests that his knowledge of corporeal bodies is severely restricted. The only things he can know with metaphysical certainty about them are things that he can clearly and distinctly

[5]Cress, 50.

perceive—things "considered in a general sense, that are encompassed in the object of pure mathematics." I take this to mean that he can have metaphysical knowledge of such things as these: if there is a desk, and it has a perfectly rectangular top, and it is 20 inches wide and 40 inches long, then the surface area of that desktop is 800 square inches. This bit of knowledge is suitably general, and it is encompassed in (relatively) pure mathematics. It is extremely important to recognize that this knowledge is not based upon sense experience, and does not imply that there actually is a desk. It is hardly to be considered knowledge "of the external world."

Another Route to Knowledge of the External World

In the final paragraphs of the *Sixth Meditation*, Descartes outlines another way in which one can come to have knowledge of the external world. This route is sometimes known as "the method of concurrence." It is summarized in the final paragraph when Descartes says:

> Nor ought I to have even a little doubt regarding the truth of these things, if, having mustered all the senses, memory, and intellect in order to examine them, nothing is announced to me by one of these sources that conflicts with the others. For from the fact that God is no deceiver, it follows that I am in no way deceived in these matters.[6]

To see how this works, consider the case of a man who thinks there is a chocolate cake before him. If this man looks toward the spot where he thinks the chocolate cake is located, he will have the visual experiences one would have if one were seeing a chocolate cake. Suppose he does this. Suppose he also reaches out and touches the chocolate cake, and has the tactual experiences one would expect if one were touching a chocolate cake. Furthermore, suppose he leans over and sniffs, and it seems to him that he is smelling a chocolate cake. Going still further, he takes a small bite out of the chocolate cake, and it even tastes like a chocolate cake! (You may have noticed that I have not mentioned hearing. That's because I have no idea what a chocolate cake sounds like.)

Suppose, in addition to all this, the man's memory also concurs. He seems to remember that he had baked a chocolate cake just the night before, and he has no recollection of eating it, or giving it away, or otherwise getting rid of it. His memory tells him he should still have the cake.

Even all of this is not quite sufficient. In order to know that there is really a cake there, the man must also examine the matter with his intellect. He must consider whether there is anything inconsistent or unlikely about the notion that there is a chocolate cake there. He must reflect carefully, to see that the evidence of each sense fully concurs with the evidence of each other sense and with memory. He must rule out the possibility that he is dreaming, or hallucinating. Let's suppose he does all this and finds that all the evidence points in the same direction—there is a cake.

In this sort of case, all the man's senses and his memory and his intellect concur. They all agree in the judgment that there is a chocolate cake there. In that case, according to the method of concurrence, the man is fully justified in believing that

[6]Cress, 56.

there really is a cake there. For if God allowed us to be mistaken, after having done all this, then we would be justified in saying that he is a deceiver. In this way, then, we allegedly can achieve metaphysical knowledge of particular facts about the external world.

I am afraid that I cannot fully endorse this line of reasoning either. It seems to me that the method of concurrence faces certain objections, too. For one thing, it seems to me that a person might dream that he had satisfied all the requirements of the method when in fact he hadn't. For another, it is hard of understand exactly why God couldn't have good reason to deceive us in this way. Furthermore, if the arguments for the existence and veracity of God are judged to be unsuccessful, then the appeal to God here must be judged to be equally unsuccessful.

So it appears that, in the end, Descartes has not been able to show how we can have metaphysically certain knowledge of particular contingent facts about the external world. Perhaps he meant to acknowledge this unfortunate skeptical conclusion when he said, in the final sentence of the *Meditations*, that "...the life of man is vulnerable to errors regarding particular things, and we must acknowledge the infirmity of our nature."[7]

It is important to appreciate the nature of this skeptical conclusion. I am not suggesting that, in the end, Descartes is forced into *practical* skepticism concerning the external world. Rather, my point is that he seems to be committed to the view that we don't have any *metaphysical* knowledge of particular contingent facts about the external world. In itself, this is not a terribly shocking conclusion. Of course, if Descartes continues to suspend judgment with respect to everything that's less than perfectly certain, he will have to suspend judgment with respect to all particular contingent facts about the external world. Clearly enough, that could make life rather difficult.

AN EVALUATION OF DESCARTES' ACHIEVEMENT

We have now concluded our examination of the main arguments and doctrines of the *Meditations*. It would be natural to expect, by way of conclusion, some sort of assessment of Descartes' achievement. However, it seems to me that it would be silly, in this case, to consider the question whether Descartes is a great philosopher, or the question whether the *Meditations* is an important philosophical work. There is virtually universal agreement that Descartes is one of the very greatest of Western philosophers, and that the *Meditations* is one of the most brilliant philosophical works of all time.

While I think it would be silly to consider the question *whether* the *Meditations* is a great work of philosophy, I do not think it is silly to ask *why* it is a great work of philosophy.

It might be suggested that Descartes' book earned its place in the philosophical hall of fame because it contains so much truth. Correspondingly, it might be claimed that Descartes is a great philosopher because he discovered so many important philosophical truths.

[7]Cress, 56.

In my view, this cannot be the correct answer to our question. I am inclined to reject this answer, I suppose, largely because I think it rests on a couple of faulty assumptions. For one thing, it does not seem to me that there's all that much truth in the *Meditations*. I am not convinced that there is a God, and I am not convinced that people are compound substances of the sort that Descartes described. Thus, even though I think Descartes produced a magnificent book, I am skeptical about the truth of several of its most central doctrines.

Furthermore, it seems to me that a philosophy book might contain lots of truths, and still be a pretty worthless book. This could happen, for example, if the argument in the book were all so weak that no one could come to know the truth of the conclusions by reading the book. It could also happen if the various truths were unconnected, so that even a careful reader could not see how they fit together. Thus, even if every major doctrine of the *Meditations* were true, that would not explain why it is a great work of philosophy.

It might be suggested that the greatness of the *Meditations* is due to the strength of the arguments to be found there. This proposal is no more plausible than the first. Many of Descartes' arguments are not very successful. Hardly anyone nowadays is persuaded by Descartes' cosmological argument for the existence of God, and the ontological argument is almost universally viewed as being based on some sort of trick. The arguments for dualism are puzzling, but serious materialists are rarely upset by them. They can be rebutted fairly easily. The epistemological arguments of the *Sixth Meditation* are, as we have just seen, pretty weak. Thus, the importance of Descartes' work cannot be explained by appeal to the alleged power of his argument.

I think there are several important facts that together help to explain the greatness of the *Meditations*. The first of these is that, in this book, Descartes gave a clear and persuasive presentation of a conception of the structure of human knowledge that was to dominate Western philosophy for centuries to come. According to this conception, each person is directly acquainted with the present contents of his or her own mind. In addition to this, of course, Descartes recognized that each of us knows, in a similarly direct way, that he or she exists. We may think of this sort of knowledge as providing a foundation upon which all the rest of our knowledge is constructed.

If we assume that an individual's knowledge does have this sort of structure, then we face a number of profoundly difficult questions. First of all, we have to give a clear account of the nature of the items included in the foundation. Just what can we know "directly" and "immediately," and what is it about these facts that makes it possible for them to be known without further evidence? Furthermore, we have to face up to the question concerning the place of the most fundamental metaphysical and logical principles. Do they belong in the foundations, as Descartes sometimes suggests? Or are they somehow justified by appeal to the foundations? Having answered these questions, we must next explain how the "upper stories" rests upon the foundation. That is, we have to give an account of the way in which our knowledge of the past, the future, the external world, and other minds is justified by our knowledge of the present contents of our own minds.

Descartes suggested answers to these questions, but not many of those answers are widely accepted today. So I'm not claiming that Descartes' greatness is to be explained by appeal to the truth of his answers to these questions about the structure of knowledge. Rather, my point is that Descartes raised the question in a clear, straightforward, and captivating way. Although other philosophers had surely toyed with closely connected questions before him, he succeeded in making this question the central focus of modern philosophy.

Another great virtue of the *Meditations* is a fact about its style. Descartes had an extraordinary ability to isolate the most fundamental questions. He then was able to meditate upon them in an almost painfully direct and focused way. He rarely digressed, or lost the track of his reasoning, or introduced cute irrelevancies. His reflections proceed with utter singlemindedness. This philosophical purity is rarely matched, and never surpassed. I think it is one of the great stylistic virtues of the *Meditations*, and it goes a long way toward explaining why this work is so timeless, and why it is just as engrossing today as it was when it was first written.

Commentators often praise Descartes for his clarity. I think there are some respects in which Descartes' writing is not very clear at all. I think, for example, that it is very hard to understand just what is going on in the Cogito. Similarly, it is hard to understand how Descartes proposed to deal with the problem of the Cartesian circle. Some important doctrines, such as the theory of psychophysical causal interaction, remain extremely obscure. So there is a respect in which Descartes' style lacks clarity.

However, if we view the matter from another perspective, I think we will see that the *Meditations* does have a sort of clarity. As I see it, Descartes did a magnificent job of making the questions clear. When, at the beginning of the *Second Meditation*, Descartes asks what he can know with certainty, the reader knows precisely what question he means to ask. A careful reader will also know just how that question arises, and why it must arise just where it does. Sometimes, when reading the works of other great philosophers, I am puzzled. I have to turn back the pages, trying to figure out why the author is discussing the question he is discussing. Sometimes, especially when the terminology is turgid or idiosyncratic, or the argument is contorted, I have to admit that I really don't know what question he is discussing. This rarely happens with Descartes. A patient reader will always know what's at issue, and why.

Although others may disagree with me, I think the *Meditations* is a remarkably beautiful book, too. Descartes had a marvelous talent for selecting familiar and strikingly apt images. His discussion of the piece of wax, for example, seems to me to be especially noteworthy. It is easy to imagine the philosopher, alone in his study, intently observing the little piece of sealing wax on his desk. He notices that it still retains a little of the smell of flowers, and the taste of honey. Descartes uses this humble example to illustrate an important point about knowledge by perception— even in this "best case" example, what we know about the external world by perception is not as certain as our knowledge of our own minds.

It should also be recognized that the book is organized with great care and subtlety. The argument progresses in an orderly and systematic way, with very few digressions or false starts.

There are several places in the *Meditations* where Descartes suggests that he is weak, or ignorant, or otherwise incapable of carrying out his project. In spite of this,

I think that another remarkable feature of this work is its boldness and self-confidence. Descartes undertakes the project entirely on his own. He does not appeal to God for assistance until he has established, to his own satisfaction, that God exists, and is no deceiver. He never appeals to the work of other philosophers. When, at the beginning of the *Second Meditation*, Descartes draws a comparison between himself and Archimedes, we all recognize that the comparison is apt. Archimedes was bold enough to say that, if given a long enough pole, and a suitable place to rest it, he could move the earth. Descartes seems to be suggesting that, entirely on his own, he will seek the "immovable point" of epistemology—a bit of knowledge so certain that nothing casts doubt upon it. Just as Archimedes' task would be a solitary one, so would Descartes'. Entirely on his own, he would attempt to reconstruct all of his knowledge.

Of all these virtues, the one that impresses me the most is philosophical purity. Descartes focusses intently upon the most profound of philosophical questions, and he refuses to be diverted from his path. All of his intellectual energy is in this way directed to the crucial questions: what am I? what can I know? is there a God? Although we may not accept his answers, we surely must respect his integrity in asking the questions.

A FINAL WORD

In the first chapter of this book, I described several conceptions of philosophy. I said that some people think of philosophy as the queen of the sciences, and others think of it as a pure conceptual analysis. Still others think of philosophy as a method for thinking clearly. Traditionally, it has been said that philosophy is the love of wisdom.

I claimed in Chapter 1 that every one of these conceptions of philosophy is a misconception. I tried to explain why it is wrong to think of philosophy in any of these ways. I then attempted to give some sense of the nature of philosophy by describing some of its main fields. I had to admit, however, that my descriptions were pretty inadequate. I urged patience, and I suggested that if you were to read Descartes' *Meditations* with suitable care, you would come to have a clearer conception of philosophy.

If you have studied Descartes' *Meditations*, and you have read this book, by now you have a much clearer conception of metaphysics, epistemology, philosophical theology, and philosophical anthropology. You are familiar with a variety of important doctrines and puzzles in each of these fields. Thus, you also know something of the history of philosophy. In addition to this, you have gained a number of important philosophical skills. You have a pretty clear idea of what makes for a good philosophical argument, and you have some sense of how to go about criticizing such an argument. You understand the use of technical terms, and may be able to formulate suitable definitions, if they are needed. You can appreciate a carefully drawn distinction, and you understand why we need to formulate our philosophical doctrines precisely. Furthermore, I think that by now you are capable of going on to read other classic philosophical texts on your own.

I do not claim to have explained, in this little book, all there is to know about philosophy. My goal here was far more modest. I merely wanted to assist Descartes in providing an *introduction* to philosophy. I am bold enough to think that, if you now have a clearer conception of metaphysics, and of epistemology, and of the other areas I mentioned, and if you have begun to develop the ability to formulate an argument, and to evaluate one, and if you now can see more clearly what's relevant to a philosophical doctrine, and what's not, then this book has been a success.

INDEX

INDEX